More Praise for *Learning* for the Long Run

"Don't miss this opportunity to hear from one of the foremost learning experts how to benefit from, build, or lead the kind of sustainable learning culture that engages talent, sparks innovation, and optimizes performance and productivity. Packed with practical strategies, proven daily practices, assessment tools, and more, *Learning for the Long Run* is a trusted resource that you will turn to again and again."

—*Amy Dufrane*
CEO, HR Certification Institute

"*Learning for the Long Run* makes a compelling, thought-provoking case that the key for leading a sustainable organization for the long run is for it to be a resilient learning organization. Holly Burkett's seven practices will transform organizational professional development thinking and behaviors like Covey's seven habits of highly effective people did for personal professional development."

—*Timothy R. Brock*
Founder and CEO, The Institute 4 Worthy Performance

"*Learning for the Long Run* is so full of ideas and examples that it can be your blueprint for learning success. Holly is the rare writer who understands the importance of both business and learning needs."

—*Howard Prager*
President, Advance Learning Group

"Holly Burkett has done a magnificent job of outlining and expressing how learning professionals and executives can work together to deliver innovative, flexible learning experiences amidst rapid change in the workplace. Hands down this book provides the tools to create sustainable learning solutions. Bravo and a job well done!"

—*Tammé Shinshuri*
Founder and CEO, Shinshuri Foundation

"This book presents an energized, highly developed formula for creating sustainable talent development and workplace performance. Holly Burkett provides an abundance of well-organized, comprehensive examples, diagrams, and assessment tools. It's a must-have for learning and performance improvement professionals."

—*Darlene M. Van Tiem*
Associate Professor Emeritus, University of Michigan, Dearborn

Learning
for the
Long Run

7 Practices for Sustaining a Resilient
Learning Organization

HOLLY BURKETT

ATD Press is an internationally renowned source of insightful and practical information on talent development, workplace learning, and professional development.

ATD Press
1640 King Street
Alexandria, VA 22314 USA

Ordering information: Books published by ATD Press can be purchased by visiting ATD's website at www.td.org/books or by calling 800.628.2783 or 703.683.8100.

Library of Congress Control Number: 2016953175
ISBN-10: 1-56286-994-9
ISBN-13: 978-1-56286-994-6
e-ISBN: 978-1-56286-108-7

ATD Press Editorial Staff
Director: Kristine Luecker
Manager: Christian Green
Community of Practice Manager, Human Capital: Ann Parker
Developmental Editor: Jack Harlow
Associate Editor: Caroline Coppel
Cover Design: Kara Davison, Faceout Studio
Text Design: Iris Sanchez and Maggie Hyde
Printed by Versa Press, Inc., East Peoria, IL

To my father, who inspired me to learn more about myself and the world every day. To my grandfather, whose love of books introduced me to worlds of infinite possibilities. You both showed me what it means to be a true learning leader. Your examples and teachings deepened my commitment to learning as a noble calling, one worth sustaining over the long run.

Contents

Foreword

A FEW YEARS AGO, ROI INSTITUTE served as expert advisers for a benchmarking project with the American Productivity and Quality Center. The project focused on measuring the impact of a corporate university and was organized at a time when traditional learning functions were being converted to corporate universities with new titles and functions. The project involved about 25 well-known and respected organizations, all very interested in learning more about how to measure the success of their corporate university.

Over the two to three months of the project, much to our surprise, two of the organizations in the study dropped out because their companies disbanded their learning function. This was particularly disturbing because these organizations were considered to be very progressive and wanted to know more about how to measure the value of their learning function. As one of the departing learning executives told us, "Unfortunately, our executives just don't seem to value having a centralized corporate learning university." At the same time, we noticed that new corporate universities were created at a couple of other respected companies. The announcements were high profile, with press releases stating how these learning functions would help grow the organization and make it successful.

This experience brought into focus the need for sustainable learning organizations. Sustaining the value of the learning function is ultimately the key to a successful learning organization.

Ongoing Dilemmas

Learning leaders today face several dilemmas, making it a challenge to add and drive value—and to be consistent. The first dilemma is the perception of learning as the number-one solution when an organization has a problem.

Executives and managers who request learning programs often see any problem as being caused by someone not knowing what to do. As a result, they assume learning is the solution. Yet at the same time, when budgets get tight and times get tough, these same executives and managers will be the first to cut the learning function. This perception must change.

A second dilemma is the great amount of wasted learning. Learning and development professionals often discuss "scrap learning," the portion of learning that is not used on the job, although you wanted it to be applied. Depending on which study you examine, this waste can range from 50 to 80 percent or more of learning. So say your learning and development budget is $10 million. The waste could be $5 million, and that's if you take the low estimate. Whether learning is transferred is a constant and perplexing problem that needs to be corrected. And with a reasonable amount of effort, it can.

A third dilemma is the need and desire to have training "just in time," "just for me," and "just in the right amount." This ultimate customization often means bite-size learning, which is difficult to achieve logistically unless formatted into technology-based learning. Some technology-based learning, particularly online and e-learning, is not as effective as facilitator-led learning when measured at the application and impact levels. While it is convenient, accessible, and low cost, learning often breaks down at these higher levels of evaluation. The concern is making technology-based learning work, using the creative spirit of designers and developers and the business-minded focus of administrators.

Finally, a fourth dilemma is the definition of success for learning. This is perplexing to many learning leaders. Years ago, success was principally measured by the number of learners involved, the time involved, and the cost of the involvement. Measures of learner satisfaction were added. This evolved to measuring the success of learning based on what people have learned. Now this has moved to application and impact: Learning should be defined as successful not only when participants use what they have learned, but also when that learning has had an impact. This changes everything for some learning centers because, under this definition, without impact, the learning center is not successful.

More Challenges

These dilemmas create not only challenges but also opportunities for the learning leader. Complicating these dilemmas are the changing complexity of the workplace, the competition with other functions for resources, and the desire to learn from all types of employees, among other trends. For some employees, access to learning is a part of the decision to stay with the organization. Added to this is the speed of change in organizations, which makes it difficult to rely on traditional ways to design, develop, and deliver learning. All of this makes sustainability harder to reach.

And yet, sustainability is needed for the longevity of the learning function. The learning function needs to remain stable, adding value for long periods of time, not going through up and down cycles of budget cuts and additions. The budgets need to be appropriately funded so that highs and lows are avoided to the extent possible. For example, during a recession, executives need to realize that it may be better to increase the learning budget, not reduce it.

The turnover rate of chief learning officers (CLOs) is quite high, probably the highest of the C-suite jobs in most organizations. This, too, makes sustainability more difficult. We need steady growth, ample budgets, credible results, and a constant focus on making the organization more innovative, profitable, and yes, sustainable.

What This Book Will Do

Learning for the Long Run addresses these dilemmas and challenges with an innovative approach. Holly Burkett begins by defining sustainability and discussing the challenges facing learning, some of which I've highlighted here. In the meat of the book, she delves into the seven fundamental practices of sustainable, resilient, highly effective learning organizations. She has packed this book full of tips, tools, action items, and case studies. *Learning for the Long Run* will spark the needed change for you to bring a sense of long-term value, worth, and overall sustainability to this important function in your organization.

Holly has the perfect background to write this book; four sets of experiences come together to make her the ideal author. First, she has worked as a learning practitioner for several decades inside one of the world's most respected organizations. Second, she has spent the last 20 years as a consultant, helping learning functions show, add, and sustain value. Third, she has taught a variety of university programs, teaching others how to do what she has learned to do so well. And fourth, she has conducted a tremendous amount of research on sustainability, including her PhD dissertation. Holly masterfully blends experience, consulting, teaching, and research into this truly well-thought-out book.

Please enjoy and use *Learning for the Long Run* to make sustainability work in your organization.

Jack J. Phillips
Chairman, ROI Institute
Author of 75 books, including *Show Me the Money*

Preface

In the long run, the only sustainable competitive advantage is your organization's ability to learn faster than the competition.
—Peter Senge

I GREW UP AS A MILITARY BRAT, moving from state to state, school to school, and neighborhood to neighborhood throughout my childhood and late teens. Like most kids who experienced that kind of nomadic lifestyle, I developed a certain level of resiliency in facing the unknown, along with an innate curiosity about how new people, places, and things worked. As a member of the military community of dependents, we were all driven—by both necessity and design—to "depend" upon our ability to learn quickly. We had to learn how to gauge the lay of the land, decipher cultural cues, pinpoint leaders and followers, and figure out where to get the information we needed to adapt. We needed to learn whom to trust and how to behave in unfamiliar terrain. We needed to learn what to do to not only get along but also get ahead. How to not just survive, but to thrive in each new setting.

The capacity to learn quickly and to bounce—not only back, but forward—are key survival skills that benefit us all, no matter how old we are, how we were raised, or where we live or work. As individuals, a strong capacity to learn makes us better equipped to gather information about the world around us, which is especially critical because the conditions are increasingly more volatile and complex. A strong capacity to learn helps us make better, more informed decisions about how to seize opportunities for using our talents and strengths to create better teams, organizations, and communities. A strong sense of resiliency helps us adapt in a world that is full of complexity, uncertainty, and ambiguity. In short, learning and resilience matters more today than ever before. This is especially true for the modern learning leader and the modern learning organization.

Much has been written about the importance of the learning organization and the role of learning as a key source of competitive advantage. Successful organizations have found learning to be a critical asset used to:

- Attract, retain, and engage talent.
- Fuel the breakthrough ideas needed to spark innovation.
- Build the critical capabilities needed for a strong leadership pipeline.
- Grow change responsiveness and adaptability.
- Enhance performance and productivity.

Organizations that consistently produce the best business results demonstrate a strong commitment to learning and have robust learning organizations that foster a learning culture. While there are obvious benefits to a stable learning organization with an established, well-integrated learning culture, studies show that a high proportion of organizations have well-developed cultures of learning. In an increasingly complex and volatile landscape, it becomes more difficult to not only build, but also sustain a high-performing learning organization. Yet there is an even more critical need. Organizations must learn faster, and adapt faster, to meet the demands of globalization, the increased competition for talent, and advancing technology, or they won't survive. Some experts have predicted that within the next 10 years, only true learning organizations will be left standing. In a true learning organization, learning is not seen as a separate activity or event, but instead as an intrinsic way of operating and being productive on a day-to-day basis. In a true learning organization, the value of learning is embedded and embodied by corporate culture, leaders, managers, teams, and all employees. Learning processes are nimble, customized, and available at the time of need. Employees are responsible for their own development and learning leaders serve as facilitators rather than gatekeepers of learning. Learning leaders who create the most short- and long-term value are those who focus on effectively teaching organizations how to learn and transfer that learning into performance capabilities that propel organizational growth. Here, the focus is on collective capability building across the whole organization.

Of course, elevating and sustaining the strategic role of learning is easier said than done. Many learning leaders, performance improvement specialists, and talent managers continue to struggle with the strategic partnership roles required for effective integration, alignment, and adaptability of the learning function, which has increasingly fallen under the umbrella of talent management. In today's VUCA business environment, change happens faster than learning strategies can be devised, strategic priorities become moving targets, learning sponsors and advocates may come and go, skills and knowledge depreciate more quickly, and pressures for showing the learning function's contribution to the business intensify as competition for talent and resources increase. In this climate of shifting sands, it's tough for any business function, including a learning enterprise, to stay grounded, relevant, and intact, making it more challenging for a learning culture to take hold and fulfill its promise of making a real difference.

Who Will Find This Book Useful

This book is for all of you who, at various learning, performance improvement, HR, organization development (OD), higher education, grants management, or consulting meetings, conferences, or coffee breaks over the years, have shared your joys and frustrations in trying to make learning cultures "stick" in your respective settings. Some of you have had little formal training as a learning leader and are struggling to keep up with the pace of change in the business world and the world of learning and development. Many of you worry about increased demands to do more, prove more, and be more, not only as a practitioner but as a business partner. Many of you have successfully stepped up to meet these challenges, only to see your hard work and supporting foundations torn down in the wake of organizational downsizing, rightsizing, or capsizing. Others of you have been recognized as best-in-class, exemplary learning champions and talent builders, who have made steady progress in developing a stable, value-added learning culture, despite periodic speed bumps and disruptions along the way.

Whether you're a new or seasoned professional involved in learning and development, talent management, performance improvement, human resource development, OD, or higher education, you'll find practical tips, tools, and lessons learned from others who are actively transforming their learning organization to ensure its long-term strategic value in the midst of changing conditions and competing pressures. If you're an executive, director, or manager, you'll find valuable guidelines, assessment tools, and best-practice examples showing how you can leverage your learning organization as a key driver for talent development, improved engagement, high performance, and increased innovation. You'll find compelling testimonials and anecdotes from other executives and sponsors who have found a culture of continuous learning to be a key source of competitive advantage and sustained value, and who actively champion learning by serving as leader-teachers in their organizations. If you're a consultant, you'll find insights from other consultants who have helped shape learning organizations from the outside in, and who have successfully forged the partnerships needed to help others build and sustain a learning organization. You'll find strategies and tools that will help you with clients who want to optimize their processes and maximize their value. Educators and students will find this book to be an important supplement to other learning, HR, performance improvement, or OD textbooks because it provides the extra dimensions of real-world case studies, diagnostic assessments, and job aids.

Regardless of your title or role, learning is likely to be an important element of any strategy or solution you recommend or implement. Understanding how learning works and how mature learning organizations enable improved work performance and engagement will enhance your effectiveness as a strategic adviser and decision maker.

Origins of This Book

First, *Learning for the Long Run* draws upon several years of perspiration and inspiration from firsthand experiences as a learning leader in a wide range of public- and private-sector organizations. On a personal level, my "good, bad, and ugly" experiences positioning learning as a mission-critical enterprise have given me a deep sense of admiration and respect for learning leaders who are facing similar challenges. As an internal and external consultant, I've had the good fortune of learning with and from diverse, talented experts from around the world on topics related to learning and performance, culture change, leadership, human capital development, and sustainability. Many of those insights and conversational highlights are shared here. Second, as an active global citizen and passionate learning champion, I care deeply about developing relevant strategies and solutions that achieve their intended social and economic impact. That passion spurred my doctoral pursuit, which led to extensive research about the relationship between change resilience and a sustainable culture. In my dissertation, hundreds of learning leaders shared their culture building and organizational change experiences through a combination of survey participation and structured interviews. Many of the lessons learned, comments, and findings gained from that mixed-methods research are provided here. Some examples have been adapted for clarity and anonymity.

The topic of creating sustainable value as a learning leader seemed to strike a chord. Many individuals I originally interviewed during 2009-2010 encouraged me to write a book describing how important a sustainability focus is in helping learning leaders deliver on their promise to add value and on their desire to make a meaningful difference. So began the process of telling those stories and gathering more. Nearly two dozen learning leaders who are actively attempting to jump-start or sustain a value-added learning organization have been interviewed for this book. Examples were drawn from both internal and external learning professionals; those with performance improvement, learning, or HR roles and titles; and public and private sector organizations of varying sizes and geographic locations. The case examples are taken directly from transcripts of those recorded interviews and have been approved by those involved. The Voices From the Field sections include highlights from conversations held with learning leaders during workshops, conferences, networking meetings, or professional association events.

All and all, this book is designed to provide practical strategies, practices, assessment tools, job aids, and real-world examples that will help your learning organization sustain its relevance over time.

How This Book Is Organized

The introduction sets the stage and builds the business case for a well-developed, sustainable learning organization. The value proposition of a sustainability focus is explored from the perspective of a learning leader.

Chapter 1 provides clarity on what a mature, sustainable learning organization is, why it's important, and why it's so difficult to achieve. Seven proven practices for driving sustainable value are introduced.

Chapter 2 dives deeper into the notion of an integrated, sustainable learning organization, and provides a framework for viewing sustainability as an evolutionary growth cycle with progressive value propositions. The chapter describes four distinct stages of the evolutionary process, key tasks within each stage that will facilitate forward movement, and provides examples of how those tasks have been applied by progressive learning leaders to create more momentum and traction for their learning organizations. Ten characteristics of a mature learning organization are also presented, along with a self-assessment tool, allowing you to assess the level of process maturity within your own learning organization.

Chapters 3 through 9 detail each one of the seven practices, and will provide a case example showing how each practice has been applied. You'll see how each case mirrors the sustainability growth cycle. You'll also see how each case stacks up to the 10 characteristics of a sustainable learning organization, based upon common use of the seven practices and unique enabling strategies highlighted by each learning leader. In essence, sustaining a mature learning enterprise is about how you work the practices to meet the unique needs, strengths, and capability challenges within your own environment.

Chapter 10 provides a recap along with closing tips, tools, and a call to action encouraging you to put key lessons learned into practice so you can achieve higher levels of process and practice maturity with your learning organization. Guidelines and recommendations for how to use each of the assessment tools, job aids, and case scenarios are also included.

Appendix 1 includes an overview of the case studies and enabling strategies. Appendix 2 reviews the characteristics of a sustainable learning organization and provides a tool for assessing your learning organization's maturity level. Appendix 3 reviews the plan, do, check, and act actions from chapters 3-9 and has a tool for you to assess your learning organization's pattern of practice with each.

Final Thoughts

Whether to become a mature learning organization is no longer the question. Learning matters and continuous learning is the path to adding a sustainable, competitive advantage. Now the question is how to keep continuous learning processes in place given volatile change conditions and shifting business demands. Unfortunately, there is no simple, one-and-done solution for meeting modern day sustainability challenges. However, there's a lot to be learned from those who are successfully navigating the maturity continuum so that their learning organization remains credible, flexible, and adaptive over time, despite these challenges. A common piece of advice is to treat the growth process like a marathon, not a sprint. How to train for that marathon and prepare for the long run is the essence of this book. I hope these stories, practices, and tools guide you in making the impact and difference you seek with your learning organization and mobilize your efforts to shape a meaningful legacy as a learning leader.

Holly Burkett
November 2016

Introduction

"Someone is sitting in the shade today because someone planted
a tree a long time ago."
—Warren Buffett

CONSIDER THE FOLLOWING SCENARIOS.

Scenario 1

Ann is a performance consultant at a global healthcare company with commercial operations in more than 100 countries, along with a strong network of manufacturing sites and international research centers. When she first started, executive support and advocacy for a learning and performance focus was minimal. She could not get support from senior management or establish any traction for integrating performance-based learning into existing business or HR processes. Then, about five months after she assumed the role, a middle manager asked her to help measure the effectiveness of a corporate university program on sales training. His main purpose was to prove that the program didn't have any value and that its training dollars needed to be cut.

The person in charge of the training program didn't want its performance evaluated for fear of how the results would be used. "It took months to convince the learning team to get surveys out, to get feedback electronically instead of by paper," Ann said.

Despite the naysayers, the evaluation found that the sales training program had a positive return on investment of 168 percent, with a clear connection to increased sales revenues. "When those results came out it was like opening a floodgate. Everybody wanted to use our services; managers wanted to measure results on everything to 'fix holes' in their departments," Ann said. "Employees wanted to learn how to use results as a personal and professional improvement tool so they get promoted more easily and stand out from the crowd. The culture was one where people needed data to justify career paths and performance rewards. The VP of sales became one of our biggest advocates."

With executive and management support, the learning and performance team was able to build a solid foundation for a performance-based learning organization, including supporting policies, processes, and standards. The team members established and strengthened business partnerships with managers across all organizational levels. They educated and engaged business units to promote shared responsibility for learning and performance results. And they regularly monitored and measured the impact of learning investments to ensure that programs and services were contributing to important job performance and business measures.

"Then about two years later, the company went through a reorganization and started . . . downsizing," Ann said. "We got a new VP of sales training and he came from the school of 'as long as I train, people benefit from it.' He frankly said, 'You're doing great stuff here, but we can't afford to have such a specialized position when we're eliminating so many positions.'" As a result, the company eliminated more than 5,000 jobs and most learning and performance measurement processes, including Level 1 satisfaction surveys.

With her position eliminated, Ann opted for early retirement. However, she was recently hired back as a contractor to facilitate other corporate training programs on the consumer product side of the company. "We're in the process of reintroducing some of the performance and results-based approaches to learning that we put in place when I first started," Ann said. "Metrics around getting products launched faster are a big source of interest. So it's come full circle and we'll see what happens with that."

Scenario 2

Bill is an analytics consultant for a global financial institution with more than 5,000 locations and more than $1 trillion in assets. When he first joined the company, he was a member of a commercial training team, managing projects as an assistant vice president. At that time, the company was investing heavily in training and development efforts associated with re-engineering and decided to hire a training manager, Sue, to lead training and development, including the commercial and wholesale banking colleges. Sue was a 20-year veteran on the commercial banking side of the business, but she was brand new to the learning and HR side. Soon after Sue started, the company completed the re-engineering training for some 100,000 employees across all locations. According to Bill, Sue was the first one who wanted to find out what the company really got from spending such large sums of money. She started asking questions like, "Are people really doing anything any differently, or have they just gone back to their old habits? Is anyone checking to see what difference all this training has made?"

Those questions became the catalyst for the training team to develop more discipline, more-standardized processes, and more-consistent goals around evidence-based practice. "My role was to work with other learning leaders to drive the development and implementation of the learning and measurement strategy," Bill said. "Our team consulted, coached, and mentored others along the way 'to catch them if they fell' so to speak. We also worked to get the supporting technology we needed. I had two people working with and for me and about 40 employees throughout the learning community who were also reporting to me."

To help establish more discipline and accountability, the training team partnered with ROI Institute to evaluate a high-profile curriculum that was part of the original expenditures around re-engineering and culture change. The team dedicated itself to learning more about how to add value and make learning programs and services more effective.

"We spent a lot of time developing capability in the company around doing measurement and ROI work as well," Bill said. "We hired consultants like [Dana Gaines Robinson and James C. Robinson] to show us how to ask better questions up front and how to be better business partners and performance consultants. We helped senior leaders and managers understand that adopting a broad measurement framework and a performance improvement perspective was more than just conducting a thorough needs analysis or an isolated impact study."

Over the course of five-plus years, the training team's efforts ultimately led to an enterprise-wide practice around performance improvement as well as measurement and evaluation that expanded beyond the learning community to other lines of business, including HR. Part of that evolution was the creation of a workforce analytics division within the HR group that Bill ended up leading. The analytics division grew into a consultative, project-based function that helped assess and evaluate the value of various HR initiatives—such as compensation, benefits, and recruiting—so that senior leaders would have the information they needed to make evidence-based decisions.

"We were solid, an ingrained part of the business, with a regular 'seat at the proverbial table,'" Bill said. "We spoke regularly at conferences and were viewed as experts in the field, inside and out of the organization. Then the company was acquired by another financial services institution and everything changed."

Due to the acquisition, a large number of learning and performance positions were eliminated or reconfigured. With the exception of a small enterprise-level group focused on managing technology, the learning organization became decentralized and consolidated with the state government line of business. Some of the measurement work done previously in the learning community carried forward, but on a very limited basis.

The current enterprise learning team now focuses on exploring what people need to know and do from training and what measures need to be in place, much like discussions between the learning and senior leadership team more than five years earlier. "As senior and executive leaders from the old organization have grown their influence and authority on the new side," Bill said, "there's been more word of mouth about the value of our legacy work in learning and performance at the old institution."

Driving this interest from the training and development side are real concerns over readiness: Are employees in various parts of the business ready for the various integration efforts that are and will keep unfolding? To that end, the current learning enterprise is "starting from scratch to build a learning organization," says Bill, with all the integrated business processes needed to drive results.

"Instead of making either the assessment component or the measurement component an add-on piece of learning, they want to make it a systemic part of what they're doing with the end in mind of being more credible as true strategic partners," Bill said. "They're still figuring out what that looks like in this new culture. Some of the old-guard learning members from our former organization are helping the new guard get to where we were as a learning organization before the organizations merged. But they're essentially starting all over and reinventing the wheel, which is tough to see."

Outside the learning community, the analytics division remained intact during the reorganization, although the focus is more on HR and business analytics than learning and development (L&D) or performance consulting. But the company seems to be coming around to the true value that the division—and the learning community—can have during turbulent times. "The leaders of the business unit that I'm working with now are more in tune to the accomplishments we made before," Bill said. "They don't know much about it but they are very interested in it. So we've developed some good analytics around operational measures, but there is a lot more maturity needed there. I'm thankful for the support and accomplishments that we've made as a group in this new environment, and we do feel like we've accomplished something and developed some credibility, but we haven't 'arrived.' It is an evolution . . . and my knowledge continues to evolve."

❀　❀　❀

What do each of these scenarios have in common? Both learning leaders planted seeds for improved organizational, team, and employee effectiveness that grew into a mature, fruitful enterprise over time. Both developed modern strategies and business models to increase alignment with organizational objectives and propel capabilities forward. Both created and integrated standardized, systemic measurement approaches to ensure that learning and performance improvement efforts closed critical skills gaps and met relevant business needs. Both established credibility as value-added business partners, coaches, and consultants. Both acted as responsible stewards of time, money, and resources so they could provide shelter and shade (as in Warren Buffet's opening quote) for future learners and learning leaders. Yet despite all their hard-won success, both had their deeply planted foundations uprooted—unable to sustain the momentum of their learning organization amid major organizational changes, leadership transitions, and culture shifts.

How Does Learning Take Root?

What does it mean for a learning organization to take root and remain intact, despite the perpetual disruptions of the modern business world that threaten to derail the momentum of even the highest-performing learning functions? Patrick Taggart, managing director of Odissy LTD, a business improvement consultancy in the United Kingdom, describes it as the process of moving from stony ground to fertile soil: "We tell our clients that they need a fertile organizational climate for learning and performance to take hold, that casting seeds on stone is a wasted exercise."

All learning organizations are susceptible to shaky climate conditions. For example, French winemakers use the term *terroir*, from *terre* (land), to describe how the characteristics of a certain geography, geology, and climate interact with plant genetics. At its core is the assumption that the land from which the grapes are grown will impart a quality specific to that growing site to the agricultural products (such as wine) produced there. Terroir, very loosely translated as "a sense of place," embodies the sum of the effects that the local environment has on the production of the product. In much the same way, the environment in which learning strategies, processes, and practices reside has a direct impact on the quality, integrity, and long-term value of a learning enterprise and its products. An organizational environment represents its culture, vision, values, and patterns of behavior.

While there are many perspectives on this, for our purposes, a learning organization takes root when the whole learning and performance infrastructure or ecosystem—its content, practices, processes, strategies, technologies, and tools—is fully embedded, with a firm "sense of place," into an organization's cultural DNA.

The What and Why of a Learning Organization

Learning continues to gain traction as a source of strategic advantage. Organizations that learn better and faster can adapt more quickly to increased demands for capable knowledge workers in a technologically advanced, rapidly changing global economy. Learning is a chief asset and a necessary resource for driving innovation, higher profit margins, and improved levels of service. According to author Harrison Owen, an organization that does not continuously adapt to the environment through speedy, effective learning runs the risk of extinction. "There was a time when the prime business of business was to make a profit and a product. There is now a prior, prime business, which is to become an effective learning organization. Not that profit and product are no longer important, but without continual learning, profits and products will no longer be possible" (Owen 1991).

Learning organizations are places "where people continually expand their capacity to create the results they truly desire, where new and expansive patterns of thinking are nurtured, where collective aspiration is set free, and where people are continually learning how to learn together," according to Peter Senge, who popularized the term in his 1990 book *The Fifth Discipline*. The notion of organization-wide learning can be traced back to research from the 1940s, when companies began to realize its potential for increasing organizational performance and competitive advantage. In the 1980s, Shell Oil started relating organizational learning to strategic planning and, after experimenting heavily with teamwork and group communications, concluded that organizational learning provided a competitive edge for corporate success. Companies such as General Electric, Nokia, Pacific Bell, Honda, and Johnsonville Foods helped further pioneer the learning organization concept (Marquardt 2011).

The *learning organization* concept represents the "what" of learning: the systems, principles, and characteristics of organizations that learn. The *organizational learning* concept represents the "how": the skills and processes used to build and use knowledge. Most experts view organizational learning as a process that unfolds over time and agree that while all organizations learn, not all organizations can be considered learning organizations. For example, an effective learning organization has developed the capacity to support and maximize learning at all three institutional levels of an organization: individual, team or group, and organizational. Here, learning is not a separate, isolated activity reserved for certain groups or individuals, but rather a higher form of learning capability in which structures and systems support the continuous acquisition, creation, and transfer of knowledge across boundaries. Peter Senge (1990) proposed the use of five "component technologies" to achieve these ends: systems thinking, personal mastery, mental models, shared vision, and team learning. Together, these integrated components shape an organization's overall capability to harness learning for its continuous growth and revitalization.

To fully grasp how learning organizations put these components into practice, it helps to examine what high-performing learning organizations do in comparison with others. Over the last decade, the Human Capital Institute and Bersin by Deloitte, among other groups, have conducted research on the characteristics of learning organizations and how successful ones have linked learning to high performance. Figure I-1 shows the hallmarks of high-performing learning organizations based on collective research findings.

Figure I-1. Hallmarks of a High-Performing Learning Organization

From This	To This
Learning focused on isolated, episodic events for individual audiences	Continuous, collective, and daily learning across all organization levels
Learning focused on facilitating interaction and engagement among training groups	Learning focused on facilitating connection and engagement across boundaries
Learning leaders function as facilitators and gatekeepers	Learning leaders function as strategic business advisers
Learning driven by the learning organization	Learning self-directed and driven by employees and managers on their own
Learning leaders assess individuals' learning progress or skill gains and provide feedback	Learners, managers, and peers constantly involved in feedback loops about one another's learning progress or skill gains
Learning leaders unable to demonstrate their contribution to the business	Learning leaders provide qualitative and quantitative measures of business impact
Learning as a stand-alone function	Learning as an integrator of strategy, talent, and knowledge
Learning leaders isolated and vulnerable to environmental influences	Learning leaders continuously interacting with and influencing their environment

Driving organization-wide capabilities means focusing less on training and more on creating an organizational culture of learning through supporting strategies, structures, staffing levels, program design, and governance practices that add and create value. A high-performing learning enterprise is one that excels at building organization-wide capabilities that drive business growth (O'Leonard 2014). For example, findings from a survey on high-performance organizations show that high-performing learning organizations typically outperform low-performing groups in revenue growth, market share, profitability, and customer satisfaction (AMA and i4cp 2007). Other research reports that high-performance learning organizations are eight times more likely to be viewed as strategically valuable by executives and are three times more likely to align learning and development initiatives with overarching corporate goals (O'Leonard 2014). In short:

- **Capability development is a high priority for most organizations.** A capability can be anything an organization does well that drives meaningful business results. Building organizational capabilities, such as lean operations or project or talent management, is a top priority for most companies. While companies are increasing their skill development focus, few executives report that their efforts are effective in driving desired results. Executives say that learning and HR functions need to adopt more formalized approaches, tools, and metrics for maintaining and improving capabilities so that skill development is better aligned with evolving business needs (Benson-Armer et al. 2015).

- **Learning is a core capability and a key source of competitive advantage in today's modern workplace.** Learning is the catalyst for broadening and deepening the organizational capabilities needed to thrive in complex, turbulent times. Talent is the energy that drives competitive advantage, and learning is the fuel that attracts, develops, and retains talent.

- **Learning is simply the means; performance is the end.** Learning and development can do a great deal to enhance and produce capability at both the individual and organizational level. But learning is not enough in and of itself. Only when new capabilities are acquired and then transformed into new behaviors is the potential for improved performance realized. A learning organization without the means to assess, define, develop, inspire, and measure performance will not add sustainable value.

What Is a Learning Leader?

The definition, strategic role, and reach of learning leaders has continued to expand since the founding of Motorola University in 1981 and the naming of the first chief learning officer (CLO) at General Electric in the mid-1990s. This is partly due to demands from a growing knowledge economy, where learning and performance continue to shape the capabilities needed for organizations to keep a competitive edge. For example, Figure I-2 offers a snapshot of a high-performing, strategic learning leader, adapted from early research with CLOs conducted by the Association for Talent Development and the University of Pennsylvania in 2006.

Figure I-2. Profile of a Learning Leader as Business Partner

What They Do	Common Challenges	Top Skills Necessary for Success	Criteria for Evaluation
Strategy Development and Planning	Alignment and Integration	Strategic Planning	Alignment With Business Strategy
Communications With Executives	Communicating and Measuring Value	Articulating Value	Value Contribution to Business
Management of Learning Staff	Resource Constraints	Leadership	Efficiency of Learning Function
Communication With Lines of Business	Responding to Change	Business Acumen	Budget Management
Performance Improvement	Learning Governance	Knowledge of Company and Industry	Employee Performance

Adapted from ASTD and the University of Pennsylvania (2006).

Regardless of title or functional area, today's learning leader, talent manager, or CLO generally has key responsibilities focused on managing talent, developing and coaching leaders, leading organization development and culture change, and addressing strategic business challenges. Learning leaders are most successful in fulfilling these roles when they have credibility as a business partner who can provide sustainable value.

The What and Why of Sustainability

Sustainability can mean different things to different people and is often a source of much debate. However, in general, sustainability seeks to meet "the needs of the present without compromising the ability of future generations to meet their own needs" (World Commission on Environment and Development 1987). This concept reflects the idea of sustainability as the capacity to endure, evolve, and adapt, even when confronted with such setbacks as political challenges, mergers and acquisitions, resource constraints, or increased competition. The capacity to remain durable, flexible, and credible, while simultaneously adapting to continuously changing business and client needs over time, is especially challenging for learning leaders as times become more ambiguous, fast-paced, and complex. The two opening scenarios highlight those challenges.

Business practices that promote aspects of sustainability—whether through environmental stewardship, community relations, labor practices, or corporate social responsibility—are on the rise, but they're not really new. For example, DuPont's sustainability philosophy dates back to the firm's history as an explosives manufacturer, more than 200 years ago. The underlying social principle was simple and well suited to the times: "Don't blow up workers and mind the town well." It took another 200 years for DuPont and society at large to develop comparable concerns for the environment.

Today, many companies are dealing with sustainability as a business imperative, with measurable and reportable goals connected to the triple bottom line: people, planet, and profits. Walmart is one example. Its social responsibility policy encompasses three goals: Be fully supplied by renewable energy, create zero waste, and sell products that sustain people and the environment (Knowledge@Wharton 2012). When companies like Walmart strive to be more environmentally, socially, and economically responsible, they are more likely to:

- Influence the speed with which they enter or grow within a market.
- Drive innovation in products and services.
- Benefit from the rise in socially responsible investing.
- Attract talent, because good people want to align with a company that cares about its employees and the broader community.

To sum up, interest in socially responsible, sustainable business practices continues to boom, with both the C-suite and frontline employees emerging as key players in these efforts.

Implications for Learning Leaders

So how does a focus on social responsibility and sustainability relate to learning and performance? How can best practices in corporate sustainability influence the process of building a durable, high-performing learning organization? First, a commitment to sustainability, on any level, requires an ongoing pattern of practice with future-focused perspectives, which include many aspects.

Sustainability Is Part of Our Core Mission

Creating a sustainable learning organization is part of a learning leader's core mission, because growing and nurturing the talent of future leaders and knowledge workers is critical to an organization's immediate and long-term success. For instance, Millennials now make up more than half of today's workforce, so there are higher expectations for meaningful work and constant learning and development opportunities. At the same time, skills are depreciating faster than they were a decade ago because of technological advancements, lower graduation rates, and changing skill needs (De Grip and van Loo 2002). Increasingly organizations are focusing on building and sustaining workplace cultures that provide continuous, accessible, and innovative learning experiences that accelerate capability development, engagement, and innovation.

Sustainability Is Part of Our Value Proposition

Adopting and cultivating learning practices that promote aspects of sustainability is essential to learning functions that want to be proactive, future-focused, and oriented toward solutions that add and create value beyond the success of one-shot initiatives for isolated user groups. Many professional associations for learning, human resource, coaching, and performance improvement emphasize aspects of adding sustainable value in their vision, mission, or ethics statements (Figure I-3). Here, the concept of sustainability is associated with a global mindset and the idea of global citizenship and social responsibility. Learning leaders establish their credibility, brand, and sustainable value by being sensitive to the needs of the learning communities they serve and by being an active community citizen, both in and out of the organization. This means focusing on meeting customer, investor, and other external expectations to strategically plan for the long term and helping executives to do the same. Leaders in high-performing organizations rate external relationships with government officials, partners, resellers, and customers as integral to their business success in global settings and their competitive advantage as a conscientious global citizen (AMA and i4cp 2015). One learning leader in a financial institution describes his sustainability focus this way: "It's about doing the right thing for our policyholders, for our employees, for the markets, for the industry, and for the global community we're in."

Figure I-3. Associations' Value Propositions

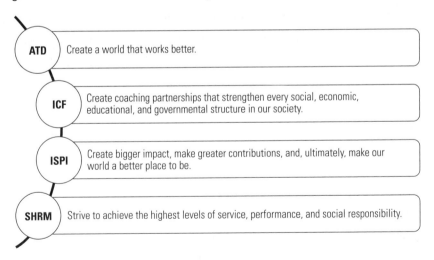

ATD Create a world that works better.

ICF Create coaching partnerships that strengthen every social, economic, educational, and governmental structure in our society.

ISPI Create bigger impact, make greater contributions, and, ultimately, make our world a better place to be.

SHRM Strive to achieve the highest levels of service, performance, and social responsibility.

Associations: ATD (Association for Talent Development), ICF (International Coaching Foundation), ISPI (International Society for Performance Improvement), and SHRM (Society for Human Resource Management)

Sustainability Is a Responsible Business Process

A common mainstream approach to sustainability centers on the idea of lean thinking, which emphasizes business as a process, where all activities surrounding the life cycle of products or services are examined for ways to improve the efficiency of the value chain. Lean thinking processes, much like learning and development processes, seek to:

- Understand the real value and benefits associated with each product or service.
- Engage consumers and customers in defining value that is driven by actual versus arbitrary needs.
- Minimize waste and resource depletion by eliminating activities that don't add value.
- Continually examine and re-examine value during each phase of improvement.

Learning leaders can adapt lean thinking principles to examine how well their L&D processes are integrated and viewed as a sustainable business process, beyond the life cycle of individual projects or initiatives, to add more value.

Sustainability Is a Responsible Business Practice

A sustainable business practice behaves in a responsible way with its human, financial, and material resources so that balanced attention can be given to the social (people), environmental (organizational, contextual), and economic (productivity, profit) needs of multiple stakeholders. Balance implies that the pursuit of a profitable impact is seamlessly blended with pursuit of the common good through the spirit of servant leadership and stewardship. In simple terms, the core principles of stewardship are shown in Figure I-4. These principles involve seeing your learning function as the vehicle for adding sustainable value to an organization and your organization as a vehicle for adding sustainable value to a shared society. Following these stewardship principles can be considered another form of value management, which is a primary goal of most learning organizations—and an organizational priority for many HR practitioners.

Sustainability Is Essential to Organizational Learning

Organizational learning is not a static business objective or a singular event, but rather a never-ending process of building the critical, collective capabilities needed to propel and create business growth for both the short and long term. Developing needed capabilities for future growth is about ensuring the continuous improvement of skills amid changing needs, which can only be accomplished with a mature, stable, and sustainable learning enterprise. For instance, Cognizant, a global technology solutions company, supports evolving growth needs with an adaptive learning strategy focused on developing business-aligned capabilities across all organization levels. This represents the new work of L&D, in which learning strategies and models are continually improved, transformed, and adapted to align with changing objectives and emerging business needs.

Figure I-4. Stewardship Principles

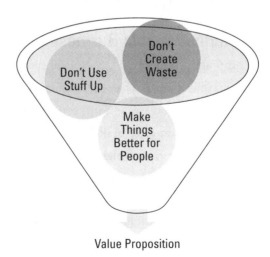

Value Proposition

In general, then, a sustainable learning organization adds and creates organizational value by being more:

- proactive and future-focused
- aligned to immediate and long-term challenges related to engagement, retention, and capability development
- focused on organizational, collective capabilities to drive high performance and business growth
- accountable for delivering strategic value and optimizing results
- efficient, effective, and innovative in managing its resources
- systemic, collaborative, and socially responsible in its approach to learning and performance
- adept at creating adaptive learning models that will continuously expand organizational capabilities
- attuned to business practices that actively contribute to the greater good.

Today's Learning Landscape

Learning organizations today must navigate a new world of work where dramatic changes in strategies, processes, and practices are needed to help organizations increase their readiness to lead, manage, develop, and inspire people. Critical challenges include greater emphasis on the larger organizational culture as a lever for improved engagement and retention, especially among Millennials, who are expected to make up 50 percent of the workforce by 2020 (PwC 2011). When it comes to engagement, there are also unique talent challenges associated with both the "overwhelmed employee," who struggles to manage a flood of information amid perpetual and volatile conditions, and a growing part-time and contingent workforce. Challenges associated with leadership development have become more paramount as organizations face heightened pressure to fill critical skills gaps, including a short supply of leaders. Many companies consider it a priority to develop leaders so they're equipped to drive culture change. Yet many organizations are not developing leaders fast enough to keep up with the pace of change and the demands of business (Figure I-5).

Figure I-5. Fast Facts

70%	19%	17%
More than 70 percent of organizations cite capability gaps as one of their top five challenges.	Only 19 percent of high-performing organizations say they can effectively manage predicted talent shortages.	The percentage of executives confident their organizations have the right leadership in place to deliver on their strategic priorities.

Sources: O'Leonard (2014); AMA and i4cp (2015); Korn Ferry Institute (2015).

Associated with leadership development challenges are rising demands for new technologies and innovative, consumer-like learning models that offer end-to-end learning experiences versus learning events. In short, learning leaders face increased expectations from executives to drive engagement, manage talent shortages, and close gaps related to bench building and leadership development. Business executives consistently rate learning and development and talent management as crucial elements of organizational growth and competitive advantage. While most learning leaders clearly understand their role in developing a high-performing, engaging workplace, many remain unprepared to meet the challenge. Consider the following:

- A high percentage of CLOs say that they lack "structured processes for creating a learning strategy linked to business objectives" (Anderson 2014).
- Only 34 percent of top companies indicate that they are effective at developing leaders; in fact, they are getting worse at it (ic4p 2014).
- More than half of learning professionals describe their learning and development function as slow to respond to the changing requirements of their business during economic turbulence.
- Less than 8 percent of HR leaders expressed confidence in their teams' ability to execute strategies and drive business impact (Benko et al. 2014).
- A high proportion of CEOs and board-level executives continue to see training as the least strategic function of the business.

Despite the rise in high-performing, sustainable learning cultures, many of today's learning organizations are in trouble and need to significantly transform their own business orientation and business acumen. Since van Adelsberg and Trolley (1999) made the case for evolving the learning function by "running training like a business," updated research shows that the rate of adoption among most learning organizations remains low. Most training is ad hoc, fragmented, and tactical, and most learning investments are poorly managed. All of which raises important questions:

- How can a learning organization position learning as a key driver of business strategy if it lacks credibility as a strategic business partner?
- How can a learning organization develop and engage talent if critical capabilities are lacking within its own talent pool?
- How can a learning organization help leaders anticipate and react to the challenges of constant change without adaptive learning models and demonstrated change capability?
- How can learning leaders build a relevant, resilient, and sustainable learning organization if even the most basic foundations of its learning function are in need of repair?

Consider the capability gaps that impede the relevance and resilience of your own learning organization. What roadblocks get in your way when trying to frame learning as a credible, durable driver of business strategy?

Going Forward

As sweeping demographic, technological, and global changes continue to influence the business landscape, learning leaders face increased demands to shape the future, engage talent, and make performance happen in an increasingly complex environment. To survive and thrive, learning leaders must focus less on static, individual training, and more on adaptive, organization-wide capability development that balances immediate business needs with the needs of the future. This means being more deliberate in understanding which capabilities truly affect business performance and aligning programs and services accordingly. It also means adopting a proactive lens toward organizational learning strategies that will add sustainable value, beyond the value gained from one-shot solutions. Consider how well your learning organization meets these criteria for adding sustainable value.

Chapter 1 will highlight common roadblocks related to building and sustaining a relevant and resilient learning organization and will introduce seven proven practices for managing them. The remaining chapters show how progressive learning leaders have used these practices to transform the credibility, maturity, and sustained value of their own learning organization.

Managing the Learn Amid the Churn

"The loftier the building, the deeper must the foundation be laid."
—Thomas à Kempis
13th-Century Dutch Priest and Author

What's in This Chapter

- common challenges to building and sustaining a high-performing learning organization
- seven practices for building and sustaining a high-performing learning organization.

FACED WITH GAPS IN TALENT AND SKILLS, most CEOs report a pressing need to create performance-driven cultures that can build bench strength, drive execution and results, and move quickly to innovate products and services. Executives know that sustainable performance and results depend on committed and capable talent. It's not surprising, then, that capability building was cited as a top three priority by half of all business leaders (Benson-Armer et al. 2015). As the competition for talent tightens and the business climate becomes more complex, the spotlight has intensified on learning and development as a strategic lever for addressing capability challenges. Organizations that are most effective at capability building are much more likely than others to focus on sustaining capabilities over time and linking learning to critical performance goals. A mature, resilient learning organization has the greatest potential for building sustaining capabilities.

Building a high-performing learning organization with all the necessary foundations and infrastructures is never easy. Sustaining one is much harder, even under the best circumstances. The two scenarios in the introduction attest to that fact. Making it more difficult is the new normal of a volatile, ambiguous world, in which one in four organizations is experiencing major change every eight weeks or more (ASTD and i4cp 2014a).

Simply put, learning leaders today have to manage the learn amid the churn. They have to continually keep core functions intact while shoring up, reimagining, and reinventing learning strategies as needs shift and conditions change. Most learning leaders clearly understand the need to be future-focused, results-based, and agile in their approach to talent management and capability development. Yet many remain unprepared and ill-equipped to inspire the trust and confidence from senior leaders needed to keep learning strategies front and center. For example, a large proportion of executives say that their learning organizations lack effective approaches for assessing current capabilities and identifying skills gaps, which are integral parts of successful capability-building efforts (Benson-Armer et al. 2015).

So, while the capabilities that companies need most have evolved, the methods of building those skills have not. What gets in the way?

Common Detours and Roadblocks

When it comes to developing learning and performance strategies for sustaining capabilities, the most successful learning organizations not only support the business, but also are run like a business. Yet many learning leaders struggle in business partner roles because they lack the business savvy needed to establish the credibility and alignment of the learning function. To that end, common detours and roadblocks to sustainability include faulty strategic focus, faulty alignment, faulty execution, faulty measurement, failure to adapt to the speed of change, and failure to innovate.

Faulty Strategic Focus

Many CEOs report that the learning function within their organizations is stuck in a business as usual mindset, in which learning strategy is not linked to performance and performance is not linked to results. Without these links, the learning function will suffer from a weak strategic focus and a poor line of sight to critical performance needs. This is evident in the fact that higher-performing organizations are much more likely than their lower-performing counterparts to have clear strategies that are well matched with performance measures. In fact, the single largest gap between high and low performers relates to how well organization-wide performance measures link to organizational strategy (ATD 2015a).

For instance, ConAgra's learning strategies are continually renewed to ensure alignment with top business priorities around staff retention, development, and innovation. To help learning leaders increase their credibility as a strategic partner, Jennie Reid, ConAgra's senior director of human resources, advises them to adopt a "business-first, function-second" mindset by speaking advanced "business" and demonstrating business acumen (Dearborn 2015). This includes shifting learning's strategic focus from creating individual, course-centric development strategies to building collective learning capabilities, in which learning is embedded into everyday roles.

Faulty Alignment

Andre Martin, former CLO of Mars Corporation, has said that alignment occurs when learning is "relevant to our business leaders" (ATD 2015a). An aligned learning strategy helps define relevant performance requirements and guide the design, delivery, and evaluation of learning and performance results. Organizations with high levels of alignment perform better than those with lesser degrees of alignment.

While learning leaders seem to understand the importance of alignment, few learning organizations link targeted performance competencies to overall business success or routinely measure how well learning initiatives are aligned to business impact (ATD 2015a). In addition, full-scale, systemic integration between learning and other talent management systems is still relatively rare (Oakes and Galagan 2011).

Effective alignment of learning and business strategies is further complicated by today's fast-paced climate, where strategy has become more of a moving target. In addition, many learning organizations continue to struggle with how to integrate and use data from their learning management system, weakening the alignment of learning tools and technologies with cultural fit, function, and organizational relevance (Ramani 2012). In short, poor alignment is one of the most common reasons learning organizations fail to add immediate or long-term value. Aligning learning strategies, tools, and processes with business priorities is central to the job of a learning leader and is at the heart of a mature, sustainable learning organization.

Faulty Execution

Proper alignment does not necessarily lead to proper execution. Even when learning and business strategies are aligned, translating strategy into execution is often an exercise characterized by stalled initiatives, politically charged turf battles, lost opportunities, and important work that remains undone. Up to two-thirds of large organizations have trouble implementing their strategies, with one of the biggest obstacles being failure to coordinate across units (Sull, Homkes, and Sull 2015).

For example, most companies lack clear processes or structures for managing horizontal performance commitments across silos, including cross-functional committees and centralized project management offices. Even among those companies with disciplined and formal coordinating systems, few managers believe those processes work well all or most of the time. This lack of discipline and accountability in execution makes it more difficult for learning leaders to achieve commitment and buy-in when implementing learning strategies, which ultimately thwarts performance results.

Lack of agility is another major obstacle to effective execution. Learning organizations that fail to adapt to changing circumstances will struggle to exist in the coming years. Even those functions that are now successful at adapting to changing business demands foresee problems in being too slow to seize opportunities or mitigate emerging threats in the future.

No matter how well aligned its learning strategy may be, a learning organization needs to be able to coordinate execution activities, manage performance commitments, and remain agile in the face of shifting needs to be sustainable.

Faulty Measurement

In 2014, organizations spent $1,229 per employee on learning (ATD 2015c). However, only a small portion of that investment produces any real value in terms of contributing to critical work measures such as productivity, costs, quality, and time. According to the 2015 Towards Maturity Benchmark Study, only three out of 10 organizations are achieving improved productivity and engagement from their learning and development initiatives, and only four out of 10 are achieving increased efficiency as a result of their training strategies. While most learning leaders agree that their organizations need strong measurement strategies and practices, many fail to maintain relevance and establish sustainability because they focus more on learning than on the performance that results from learning. In fact, linking learning to performance has been defined as one of the most important topics in talent development today (ATD 2015b). Yet only 21 percent of learning practitioners measure whether learning is used on the job (Filipkowski 2015).

Complicating the issue is the concept of big data, where questions about what to measure and what to do with the results can be overwhelming. Higher expectations for evidence-based success metrics have only heightened the dissatisfaction of both learning leaders and their CEOs with current measurement practices. Mining learning data from a measurement and analytics function is essential for informing overall strategy, yet few learning or HR departments have an analytics function. People analytics has been cited as one of the biggest capability gaps facing learning and HR organizations today (Deloitte 2015).

Impact measures tend to be highly correlated to the effectiveness and durability of a learning organization, the presence of a learning culture, and market performance. Measures and methods for assessing learning and performance impact are critical enablers to a relevant, sustainable learning organization. Even a learning organization with perfectly aligned and flawlessly executed strategies will be unsustainable if it lacks credible processes and practices for communicating the tangible and intangible value of those strategies to key stakeholders and investors.

Failure to Adapt to the Speed of Change

Just as companies need to rapidly adapt to business conditions, learning organizations need to demonstrate change capabilities that allow for a just-in-time response to shifting needs. Without these capabilities, a learning function, like any other business enterprise, is especially vulnerable to threats brought about by organizational change, situational disturbances, or even new opportunities. In fact, the success or failure to adapt to unpredictable change is commonly cited as a key factor separating high- and low-performing organizations (ASTD and i4cp 2014a). While there is no shortage of literature about how to manage change, attending to change issues remains an elusive leadership practice. Few business leaders (17 percent) rate their organizations as highly effective at managing change (ASTD and i4cp 2014a). In the face of explosive change patterns, learning leaders face formidable pressure to help organizations manage change while keeping core learning functions intact.

Quite simply, a learning organization that cannot adapt to change cannot be sustained. Change capability and organizational resilience are key enablers to sustainability.

Failure to Innovate

Innovation drives sustainable value and growth for any business, including a learning enterprise. Almost all high-performing organizations consider innovation "extremely" or "highly" important to their success (ASTD 2011). And "accelerating the pace of innovation" is now one of the most pressing business priorities for executives, which is roughly in line with more traditional priorities such as improving profitability and increasing market share (Korn Ferry Institute 2015). Yet most learning organizations lack strategies or systems that foster innovation for leadership development and business growth. For example, many leadership initiatives fail to integrate real-world innovation challenges and action learning opportunities within their existing curriculums.

In addition, a large proportion of learning organizations are not up to speed with innovative learning approaches—such as microlearning, gamification, and social learning—that have a strong influence on employee engagement and organizational performance. Many rate themselves as ill-equipped to apply modern technologies or prepare for how learning needs will change in the future (ATD 2015a). Despite ever-changing needs, many executives complain that their learning organizations do not use experiential approaches or risk-free environments that foster innovation, and tend to rely on the same methods to deliver learning and build skills as they did four years ago (Benson-Armer et al. 2015). Learning leaders cannot expect to help drive innovation within the business if their own learning practices are out of touch with the needs of the modern learner, workplace, or world. Relevant, resilient learning strategies must focus on the dual goals of optimal performance and continual innovation as key differentiators. In many ways, continual innovation is really just another form of continual learning (Quinn 2014).

Given all these challenges, how do mature learning organizations do what they need to be doing to sustain their value and relevance?

The 7 Practices of Highly Sustainable Learning Organizations

The process of managing threats to a sustainable learning organization is an ongoing one; there are no quick fixes, magic bullets, or shortcuts. Learning leaders who have achieved this level of excellence emphasize that learning and development process maturity takes time, effort, and a dedicated focus on the long term. Process excellence occurs through a future-focused mindset, fluid processes, and the consistent use of fully integrated, disciplined practices that develop into behavior patterns. Like any behavioral change process, meaningful practice is required to grow proficiency. With practice and repetition, however, these patterns of behavior ultimately become the capabilities representing "what the learning organization is known for, what it's good at, and how it prioritizes its activities and services to deliver value" (Ulrich et al. 2009). A learning organization is all about driving and growing capabilities. It cannot do so without a strong foundation of capabilities that become building blocks for adding immediate and long-term value.

To that end, the following seven practices highlight the core capabilities of highly sustainable learning organizations, based upon research and extensive interviews with hundreds of learning leaders who have successfully sustained a mature learning organization for five years or longer (Figure 1-1). The remaining chapters will describe each of the seven practices in more detail and provide examples of how diverse learning leaders have applied them to sustain process excellence in their own learning organizations.

Practice 1: Lead With Culture

In today's global marketplace, a healthy company culture is the only sustainable competitive advantage and the most powerful way to find, build, and keep an engaged, high-performing workforce. Employees want an environment that's conducive to continuous learning and growing; if employees aren't learning, they're leaving. Organizations that consistently produce the best business results in terms of revenue growth, profitability, market share, and customer satisfaction are distinguished by their robust learning cultures. Consider Campbell Soup Company. In 2001, Campbell's was the rock-bottom performer of all the major food companies in the world and its stock was falling steeply. Doug Conant, the former president and CEO, described the company's culture as "very toxic" when he took over. In restoring the company to world-class levels of performance and engagement, Conant led with a culture that celebrated contributions, helped employees make personal connections to strategy and direction, and encouraged "change-friendly" leadership focused on listening and learning (Duncan 2014).

Figure 1-1. Seven Practices

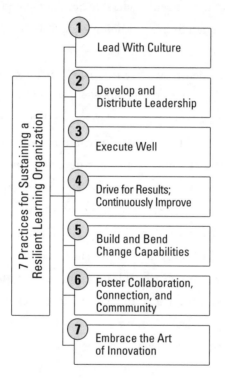

Chapter 3 describes how the Tennessee Department of Human Resources built a sustainable, performance-based learning culture to "future-proof" the workforce and address unique talent challenges in the public sector. With the increased emphasis on building, engaging, and retaining core capabilities for competitive advantage, a business-centric learning culture is perhaps the most important asset a company can have.

Practice 2: Develop and Distribute Leadership

Leadership skills contribute most to a company's winning culture and business performance. While organizations clearly understand that developing leaders is vital to their ability to drive strategy, innovation, and change, few executives are confident that their organizations have the right leadership in place to deliver on their strategic priorities (Korn Ferry Institute 2015). Many CEOs lack confidence in their current leadership development processes and believe that learning professionals are not doing enough to build talent and leadership bench strength. In Deloitte's *Global Human Capital Trends 2015* report, 86 percent of respondents, which included C-suite executives, said they are seriously worried about their leadership pipeline and cite leadership as a "staggering" capability gap. In addition, a high proportion of respondents reported that their overall capability gaps have grown in magnitude over the past year, despite increased investments in leadership development (Deloitte 2015).

The success and long-term value of a learning enterprise is increasingly judged by how well it addresses executive concerns about retaining, developing, and attracting leaders to close skill gaps. Developing and distributing leadership across all levels is more important than ever before because midlevel and frontline supervisors must also be able to coach, develop, and inspire multigenerational, dispersed work teams. In fact, employees' experiences of company culture will be largely dependent on who they have as a manager, so honing managers' leadership style is a key component of business success.

Sustainable learning organizations recognize that leadership development is a perpetual journey of cultivation, not a series of one-time, ad hoc events. As such, learning leaders must also be able to demonstrate credibility as a strategic business partner to cultivate senior leaders' support for development efforts, through good times and bad.

Chapter 4 describes how one exemplary executive developed and distributed leadership skills among his senior management team to build a succession pipeline and a sustainable leadership legacy at Horizon House in Seattle.

Practice 3: Execute Well

Sustainable learning organizations close the gap between strategy and execution by making exceptional execution part of everyday work. Jack Welch rates the "talent to execute" as one of the essential traits of effective leaders (Welch 2016). In practice, the talent to execute is not only about having the right people in place to get the right things done. It's also about knowing how to get things done in the right way. It's about being able to seize opportunities that align with strategy while coordinating with other parts of the organization on an ongoing basis. Effective execution is often the missing link between learning alignment and results. Poor execution diminishes the potential of a learning organization to add immediate or future value.

Factors that contribute to sound execution include:

- the consistent use of disciplined, data-driven approaches
- communication planning around a shared vision
- role clarity and accountability
- skill development and performance support
- clear measurement targets
- defined governance processes.

Chapter 5 describes how the learning director of a large home improvement organization uses governance processes to enhance execution results and improve accountabilities with corporate learning strategies. A case study is also provided to show how a disciplined performance improvement approach was used to enable execution of a comprehensive change strategy in the public sector.

Practice 4: Drive for Results; Continuously Improve

Sustainable, high-performing learning organizations not only plan and prioritize around important business measures, but also relentlessly monitor the impact of learning to determine whether initiatives are hitting their mark and adding value. For example, the multiple-award-winning learning team at Defense Acquisition University (DAU), the education arm of the U.S. Department of Defense's acquisition workforce, regularly measures the success of its performance-based learning strategies. The team tracks metrics such as organizational capacity, customer satisfaction, speed to market, and individual productivity through a web-based, real-time performance measurement system. Results are used to identify improvement opportunities and to make sure that learning—both formal and informal—is fully integrated with leadership priorities (Prokopeak 2013).

Consistent, disciplined use of metrics is a prerequisite for building capabilities in a sustainable way. Solid measurement practices also reinforce the strategic alignment of learning initiatives, help position the learning organization as a value-added partner, and enable learning leaders to speak the same business language as senior management. At the same time, metrics are a growing concern of executives, who cite a lack of credible metrics as one of their companies' biggest challenges in building capabilities (Benson-Armer et al. 2015).

Chapter 6 describes how learning leaders at FlightSafety International applied comprehensive measurement practices to assess the impact of a mission-critical learning strategy and inform executive decision making about the value of learning assets in building needed capabilities.

Practice 5: Build and Bend Change Capabilities

Today's turbulent business landscape, combined with the amount of knowledge needed to sustain high performance amid growing complexity, requires sophisticated learning capabilities and evolving change capacity from organizations, leaders, and talent management professionals. In any endeavor, the ability to recover quickly separates winners from losers. If organizations and employees don't learn to bend and recover quickly from changing conditions, they'll break. These realities led 79 percent of CEOs who responded to a PricewaterhouseCoopers survey to say they intend to increase focus and investment on how to manage people through change (PwC Saratoga 2010).

Change is at the center of every learning and performance improvement strategy, talent development efforts are designed to drive organizational change, and today's learning leader plays a vital role as a change agent. As the speed of change increases and the market for high-skill talent tightens, learning organizations can add sustainable value by continuously improving the way that change capabilities are grown, recognized, and rewarded. Developing a network of change-ready employees across the entire organization will not only meet capability challenges, but also accelerate business performance. Finally, building change capabilities is not just about becoming more flexible or agile. It's also about shaping the future and helping organizations create the change they want to see.

Chapter 7 describes how learning leaders at the U.S. Army served as change agents to create a network of agile, change-ready warrant officers through a learning organization founded upon principles and practices of institutional resiliency.

Practice 6: Foster Collaboration, Connection, and Community

In today's knowledge economy, in which the half-life of knowledge progressively shrinks each day, organizations need solid networks to enable fast and free information flow across boundaries. Jobs today require more collaboration among people from different units and supervisory levels. Leadership, in general, is becoming increasingly more horizontal, shared, and collective, with growing democratization of work.

If executed properly, learning strategies that emphasize collaboration, connection, and social learning can lead to more innovation and better engagement. Consider Workday, which is consistently named the number 1 Top Workplace in the Bay Area for large companies. A supportive and collaborative environment is key to its success. Employees, scattered across the United States and the globe, use technology like WebEx, Skype, Google Docs, and Slack to connect and share insights about projects and goals (Coffin 2016). Providing meaningful connections for easy knowledge sharing drives the relevance and sustained value of the learning organization. Individuals are far more motivated and engaged when they are connected to a shared purpose and feel like contributing members of their team, workplace, community, and society. This is especially true when you consider that learning in the modern workplace is less about taking in new information than it is about connecting with people who can help put new information into context and suggest new ways of understanding it. Technology has its place, but the social component will always be a major factor in the success of any sustainable learning culture.

Chapter 8 describes how collective actions, a sense of community, and a shared purpose enabled the growth of a mature learning organization at the University of Southern Mississippi.

Practice 7: Embrace the Art of Innovation

Innovation is needed at every turn in a world of constant disruption, and high-performing organizations consider it very important to their success. Executives are pushing for more innovation, not only among leaders but across all organizational levels, and are turning to learning as a catalyst for forward-thinking approaches that will propel growth. To boost innovation and reward creativity, high-performing organizations promote a culture in which employees feel safe to take risks, generate new ideas, and learn from failure.

Learning leaders play a key role in helping to drive innovation across an organization. Traditional learning approaches and organizational structures are no longer enough to remain competitive. What sets sustainable learning organizations apart is their commitment to continual innovation, their ability to renew or even reinvent themselves and their organizations in significant ways as the need arises. Sustainable learning organizations approach innovation as a key competency and have formal strategies and systems in place that proactively look toward the future to identify trends and capitalize on opportunities.

Chapter 9 illustrates how learning leaders at Blue Shield of California took risks and learned from failures to embrace innovative learning models and methods in support of increased organizational performance.

How the 7 Practices Work

Consistent, integrated use of these seven practices can help learning organizations gain traction as a business-centric, future-focused pocket of process excellence. While each of these practices has stand-alone merit, it's the collective, continuous application of these practices that then become the capabilities needed to propel value creation for the long run (Figure 1-2). Here, the immediate value added by each capability produces a multiplier effect when practiced in tandem with other capabilities.

Figure 1-2. Seven Practices Value Chain

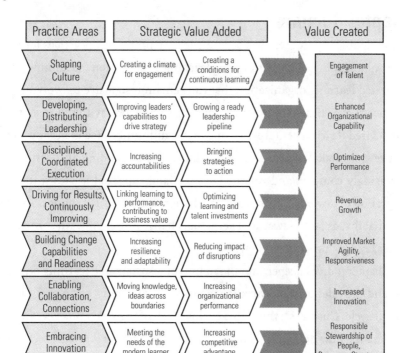

For example, an organization may have sophisticated technologies in social and blended learning that enable collaboration and connection, but lack measurement processes to show how those technologies have contributed to knowledge sharing and innovation. A lack of measurement would likely lead to some questions or issues around continued resource allocations for tech-based learning solutions. Or an organization may have robust and progressive leadership processes, but lack capabilities in effectively executing them throughout the organization. A limited ability to execute cripples the capabilities of an organization and diminishes the role of the learning organization as a partner in driving business results.

In essence, sustaining a mature learning enterprise is about how you use the practices to meet the unique needs, strengths, and capability challenges within your own environment.

Chapter Summary

While significant progress has been made in defining best practices for building a value-adding, high-performing learning organization, sustaining a fully integrated learning organization that can remain responsive to evolving business needs over time still presents challenges. Experts say that a sustainable, "hard-wired" learning enterprise—one that is fully embedded in organizational culture—may take several years to achieve. Compounding this issue is an increasingly complex and volatile business landscape that makes sustainable integration of any business process much more difficult and tenuous. As such, sustainability is best viewed as a perpetual change process toward consistently higher levels of process excellence.

Chapter 2 dives deeper into the notion of a sustainable learning organization and provides a framework for viewing sustainability as an evolutionary growth cycle. Chapters 3 through 9 explore each of the seven practices in detail and describe how diverse learning leaders in the public and private sector have applied them to facilitate movement along the sustainability continuum. You'll learn from stories of those who share your passion for learning and gain insights from the experience of those whose passion and commitment have been vigorously supported by executives and stakeholders. Self-assessments for each of the seven practices are provided in appendix 2, so that you and your team can compare current efforts with recommended best practices. Finally, chapter 10 provides a recap of the book and a review of tips, tools, and job aids, and closes with a call to action encouraging you to put what you learned into practice.

Chapter Highlights

Learning is the catalyst for sustaining capabilities.

As the modern learner and workplace continue to undergo perpetual, volatile change, learning has emerged as a strategic lever for closing skills gaps, building leadership pipelines, and driving employee engagement. The essential mission of any learning organization is capability building. Most CEOs describe an urgent need to grow organizational capabilities by leveraging well-aligned, business-critical learning strategies focused upon talent, innovation, and performance. For learning leaders, this means being more deliberate in understanding which capabilities truly affect business performance and aligning programs and services accordingly.

Sustainable value implies the capacity to remain credible, flexible, and responsive to changing business needs, and the changing needs of multiple users.

While the capabilities that companies need most have continued to evolve, studies suggest that the methods of building those skills have not. Learning organizations cannot lead the way forward without first repairing and transforming the structures or practices that derail their influence and credibility as a future-focused, proactive business partner. Adopting sustainable practices draws upon learning leaders' ability to adjust and reinvent, perspectives, processes, and practices to enable continuous learning across the whole enterprise.

Building a value-adding, high-performing learning organization is not easy. Sustaining one is even harder.

Increasingly organizations are focusing on building and sustaining workplace cultures that provide continuous, accessible, and innovative learning experiences that accelerate capability development, engagement, and innovation. To survive and thrive, learning leaders must focus less on individual training and more on adaptive, organization-wide capability development. By developing the right capabilities, perspectives, and practices, learning leaders can be more relevant and resilient, and can add more sustainable value in the face of chaotic times. For the sustainable learning organization, the journey from individual to organizational learning is the destination, and continual change, innovation, and transformation are key elements in the journey.

Transformation is an inside-out process.

Focusing transformation efforts on processes, practices, and new efficiencies is not enough. Learning and development will never experience true transformation until practitioners are also willing to transform themselves. One place learning leaders can start is by recognizing the value of running learning like a business. This means continually growing the business-savvy capabilities and mindsets needed to be credible as a talent builder, change enabler, and strategic adviser.

The Sustainability Cycle for Learning Organizations

"Great things are done by a series of small
things brought together."
—Vincent van Gogh

What's in This Chapter

- stages in the sustainability cycle and maturity continuum
- how sustainability represents a change and transformation process
- how to recognize and assess your learning organization's level
  of maturity
- how to facilitate movement from one maturity level to the next
- characteristics of a sustainable learning organization.

HOW DOES YOUR LEARNING ORGANIZATION COMPARE?

Whenever USAA, a financial services group, launches a product or service
or redesigns an organizational work flow, its talent development function is
always involved. At USAA, talent development is viewed as a critical partner
in helping the company develop its business strategy and achieve its objectives.

Every training initiative from Hilton Worldwide University is a sustained
program that measures the link between training and performance. A third-
party analytics system provides access to best-in-class data reflecting measures
of learning effectiveness, business results, and return on investment. Learning

and development (L&D) scorecards are integrated with an enterprise-wide HR dashboard from each center of excellence.

At Wipro, a global information technology consulting firm in India, the CEO and the head of learning and development work together to set the direction for talent development. Competency teams reside in six business units and four service lines, with competency directors reporting to the head of learning and development. To align business and learning strategies in a constantly changing IT market, talent development initiatives set the stage for "continual resilience" and "constant reskilling," as well as unlearning and relearning, to prepare the workforce to be more agile and more successful in their execution of more than 2,500 customer projects across diverse technologies.

What do these award-winning learning organizations have in common? Each reflects learning and talent development practices that link learning with performance. Each reflects levels of continuity and process maturity that can only be gained by learning leaders who consistently seize opportunities to serve as both talent enablers and business enablers in dynamic environments (ATD Staff 2015a).

The end goal of most learning leaders is to be in a position like the ones above, where they too can help set strategic direction, link learning and performance, and create a culture of continuous learning, consistently, over time. After all, it's one thing to achieve performance goals in the short term. It's quite another to ensure that the commitment and momentum for dynamic learning is deeply embedded into an organization's DNA, beyond the fanfare of a single program or initiative. Achieving that level of continuity and consistency does not happen overnight. Those that have succeeded say that it involves perpetual growth, where small, evolutionary stages, rather than revolutionary ones, form the basis for transformation and continuous improvement. Continuous improvement is essential to the learning organization because:

- Learning strategies, products, and services become stale or obsolete in shorter periods of time.

- Employees' skills and knowledge are depreciating faster than ever.
- Learning leaders no longer "own" the learning experience; employees are increasingly responsible for their own development and can access information in multiple ways outside a traditional learning environment.
- Learning strategies can be disrupted or derailed more easily in the face of increased business disruption.
- Improvement measures, or lack thereof, need to be collected, integrated, and used to inform decisions, make necessary adjustments, and facilitate action planning.
- Learning cannot retain its competitive edge as a driver of business strategy and performance without continuous improvement and innovation.

Subsequently, the people, products, services, and processes associated with a learning organization need to be regularly renewed and transformed to remain relevant amid shifting business conditions.

Transformation and the Sustainability Cycle

CEOs know that strong learning and talent management practices are needed to grow an engaged, high-performing workforce and maintain a competitive edge. Yet despite investments of up to $50 billion in developing leaders worldwide (Kellerman 2012), a high proportion of executives say they are dissatisfied with the quality and nature of their organization's development offerings—dissatisfied with their learning organization's efforts to grow future bench strength, enhance frontline leadership skills, or ensure that leadership selection and succession management systems are driving leadership quality (Sinar et al. 2015). Perceived gaps between the capabilities needed and delivered by today's learning leaders have caused many executives to call for a radical transformation of their learning organizations. Even esteemed learning gurus such as Clark Quinn and Jane Hart have called for a learning "revolution" due to the mismatch between what's needed in today's learning landscape and what's being provided by learning and development in its traditional state.

For learning leaders, this kind of transformation may involve:

- re-engineering of the learning and development function
- restructuring workplace training and talent development strategies
- changing old habits of conceiving, designing, delivering, and evaluating learning and development or performance improvement projects
- reconfiguring roles and responsibilities to be more business- or results-focused
- actively engaging executives, managers, and employees as learning champions
- integrating technology for more blended and social learning solutions
- functioning more as an enabler of learning than as a learning gatekeeper
- incorporating advanced measures of learning effectiveness, including the use of analytics.

It's important to note that these kinds of changes represent a transformation process that goes beyond including more efficiencies or tracking more effectiveness measures. True transformation is about building and sustaining a more innovative, adaptive, and resilient learning organization and then expanding it to reach more people in more effective ways. Transformation has more to do with how the learning organization adds sustainable value outside the boundaries of its own function than with how it manages its own internal operations. Yet expanding too quickly, without an adequate foundation and supporting infrastructure, can cause the learning function to implode or flounder. Much like the stories of a building, the stronger the foundation is at the lower levels, the more stable the higher levels will be.

Building a foundation for high levels of stability, relevance, and sustainable value generally represents a procession of small, evolutionary stages. These evolutionary stages are often likened to maturity levels, where development processes are transformed from ad hoc, undisciplined states to disciplined processes or practices capable of predictable, sustainable results. These processes build on the infrastructure established at earlier maturity levels and, subsequently, become the foundation for more sustainable, sophisticated processes at the next level. As a learning organization moves between stages, its business alignment, business impact, learning and performance capabilities, and overall efficiencies improve. Evolving learning practices and processes to achieve more sustainable, relevant impact requires progressive changes from the learning function as well as from the business. The focus for learning leaders in each evolutionary change period is to find a new set of organizational processes that will become the basis for managing the next period of growth.

Establishing a fully integrated, sustainable learning organization is ultimately about cultural change: the act of moving from an old state of activity-based learning to a new state of results-based, sustainable learning that is unequivocally part of an organization's DNA. In keeping with the idea of sustainability as a holistic change process, each stage in the cycle reflects specific elements of both organizational change and learning and development process maturity. The focus here is on the capability and maturity of the whole learning organization, rather than specific initiatives (good results are possible even with low levels of maturity). "Achieving high levels of development process maturity is not about creating a single system that does one thing really well; it is about creating a flexible system that can be used to support a range of development needs that shift over time" (Hunt 2014). For our purposes, then, sustainability is like a wide-angle lens through which you're examining the long-term endurance and business value of the whole learning organization (or ecosystem)—its strategies, services, processes, practices, programs, personnel, and results—instead of the outcomes or strategic value achieved by a single project, program, or initiative.

As shown in Figure 2-1, there are predictable stages of development in this change process. While the degree of complexity and duration of each stage will vary from organization to organization, the Sustainability Cycle has proven true across all types and sizes of learning organizations and across all industries. Based on research and interviews with hundreds of learning leaders, Figure 2-2 illustrates the defining features of each stage in terms of the learning organization's process, people, and structures.

Figure 2-1. The Sustainability Cycle for Learning Organizations

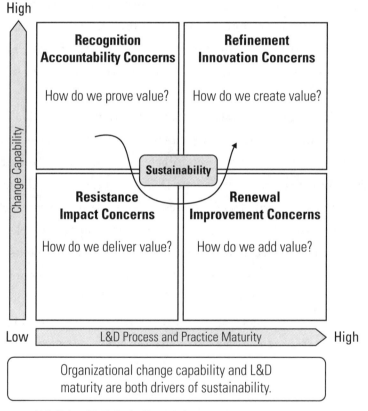

Holly Burkett (2016). Used with permission.

Figure 2-2. Sustainability Stages and Their Features

	Initial (Recognition)	Managed (Resistance)	Defined (Renewal)	Optimized (Refinement)
Process	Ad hoc or reactive	Inconsistent ability to meet emerging needs	Learning used to support business needs	Learning part of strategic business development
Process	Inability to define learning's contribution	Inconsistent measures of learning effectiveness	Quantitative and qualitative measures of effectiveness	Performance and impact data drive business decisions
Process	No operating standards, processes, or practices	Limited to moderate quality control	Quality control processes in place	Embedded quality control and governance processes
Process	Predominantly classroom	Mostly classroom, some e-learning	Blended or social learning tools and resources	Continuous, on-demand learning embedded in work
People	Learning leader as solution provider	Learning leader as problem solver	Learning leader as business partner	Learning leader as strategic adviser
People	Learners minimally involved in defining needs	Learners involved as subject matter experts	Learners support learning, use of learning on the job	Learners are collaborative and self-directed
People	Minimal executive and stakeholder support	Some pockets of executive and stakeholder support	Executives, stakeholders involved in learning	Executives and stakeholders champion and model learning
Structure	No system integration or business alignment	Minimal system integration and business alignment	Moderate system integration, business alignment	Full-system integration and business alignment
Structure	Highly vulnerable to changing conditions	Some resiliency and ability to buffer change and disruption	Moderately resilient, adaptable, agile	Highly resilient, adaptable, and self-renewing
Key Theme	How do we prove value?	How do we deliver value?	How do we add value?	How do we create value?

Finally, Figure 2-3 shows how each stage represents progressively mature levels of L&D capability and business value. In other words, the more capable the L&D organization is at optimizing services, processes, and programs to close strategic gaps, the more value is added, created, and multiplied.

Figure 2-3. Sustainability Maturity Cycle

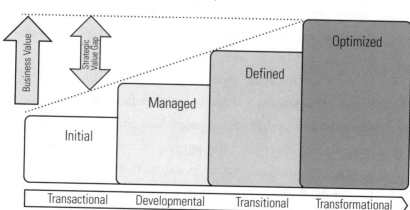

25

A Few Words About Maturity Models

The notion of process maturity levels has its roots in Total Quality Management. For example, in 1979, Phillip Crosby suggested that small, evolutionary steps, rather than revolutionary ones, are the basis for continuous process improvement. He defined five evolutionary stages for adopting quality practices in an organization based upon a maturity grid. Since then, other researchers have refined the concept of maturity, leading to the emergence of several models and frameworks around process and project maturity. Prevalent maturity models include the following:

- **Capability Maturity Model (CMM).** Developed in the early 1980s, the CMM is a methodology used to develop and refine an organization's software development process. It provides a framework for continuous process improvement that describes a five-level evolutionary path of development processes. Each maturity level is characterized by the implementation of several clusters of practices (or process areas) that contribute to the development capability of that level and to the overall transformation of the culture through the evolutionary improvement of its development processes (Paulk, Weber, and Chrissis 1999).

- **People Capability Maturity Model (PCMM).** Developed by the Software Engineering Institute of Carnegie Mellon, PCMM complements the CMM by incorporating people management capabilities that can be used alone or with existing process appraisal systems. PCMM guides organizations in selecting a five-level progression of workforce practices—compensation, competency development, training and development, performance management, organizational capability management, and continuous capability improvement—that continually improve the maturity and capability of an organization's human resources (Curtis, Hefley, and Miller 2001).

- **Center for Business Practices in Project Management.** This model emphasizes that an organization's performance is directly related to its level of project maturity based on nine measures: schedule performance, budget performance, customer satisfaction, resource allocation, optimization, strategic alignment, estimating quality, employee satisfaction, and portfolio optimization. In general, the higher the level of project maturity, the better the performance in all areas measured, with the biggest improvements showing up in risk management (Anderson and Jessen 2003).

Common Threads

Ultimately, all maturity models emphasize the concept of process and practice maturity as a contributing factor to optimal performance on an individual and organizational level. Maturity models have proven to be helpful road maps for quality-improvement practitioners, software developers, HR professionals, and project managers seeking to build organizational capabilities. Using a maturity framework to assess and steadily improve existing practices and capabilities has helped organizations achieve tangible gains in such areas as operational excellence, customer satisfaction, and market performance.

In much the same manner, distinctive practices and capabilities form the building blocks of a mature, high-performing learning organization. The Sustainability Cycle is meant to help learning leaders assess and enhance process and practice areas of the learning function that contribute to optimal performance and capability. The future of learning and talent development rests not only on its short-term ability to optimize capabilities, but also on its ability to sustain capabilities over time. To that end, recognition of the following stages can help learning leaders know where to best target learning resources and prioritize efforts.

Stages in the Sustainability Cycle

Now that we've explored how sustainability represents a transformation process, let's delve into the four stages of the Sustainability Cycle: recognition, resistance, renewal, and refinement. Each stage has its own key indicators and specific tasks that can help facilitate movement along the maturity continuum. Chapters 3 through 9 will offer case examples showing how various learning leaders have experienced these stages of development and applied key tasks to move from one stage to the next in their journey of transformation.

Voices From the Field

We believed [it] was critical to evolve into strategic business partners, to be really focused on the business from a performance consulting perspective . . . which would ultimately make us better business leaders, not just learning or HR leaders.

—Deb, Vice President, Learning and Organizational Effectiveness,
Global Electronics Company

When we started transforming the learning enterprise, the organization was undergoing a lot of change. A new senior-level operations director had been hired to drive re-engineering efforts. When he first met with me, he said, "You know, I am . . . looking at all the money that we have spent and I am wondering what did we get for all this money—are people really doing anything any differently than they would have if we hadn't spent all this money in learning and development?" I knew then that our department had to do something to prove our value.

—Melissa, Director, Learning and Development
Midsize Retail Organization

Stage One: Recognition

During the last two decades, there's been increased recognition of the role learning plays in the war for talent. Investments in learning organizations have continued to rise as businesses seek to close skills gaps, attract and retain talent, streamline processes, and improve efficiencies. In fact, learning and development issues have risen to the third most pressing talent challenge (Deloitte University Press 2015). In addition, as learning leaders seek to enhance their role as strategic business partners, there's been increased recognition that transforming traditional processes and practices is a vital part of the transition to a high-performing, sustainable learning organization.

Key Indicators

As shown by the Voices From the Field, the energy and motivation to transition from a traditional, transactional-based learning function to a more transformational, performance-based one can come from a proactive or reactive desire to prove value.

Here are some common signs that a learning organization has entered the recognition stage:

- Learning expenditures are identified as questionable or significant.
- The learning organization is exploring how to be a more strategic partner.
- The larger organization is undergoing significant change.
- There is a history of more than one program failure.
- The learning organization has a low investment in measurement and evaluation.

Key Tasks

In early stages of growth, these actions have been shown to create a strong foundation of processes and practices that will enable a learning function to successfully move from one stage to the next on the maturity continuum.

Align learning and business strategies. In broad terms, a learning strategy identifies what a learning organization is trying accomplish, how it will add overall business value, and how it will achieve its goals. Most high-performing organizations now periodically assess their learning strategies to ensure that they remain tightly aligned to central business objectives and specific business metrics. At Comcast Cable, the chief learning officer, with support from the chief operating officer, developed a centralized learning model with a top-level executive advisory council to ensure ongoing alignment of learning to strategic business objectives. Council members meet quarterly and include the presidents of the company's three divisions and executive vice presidents of products and functions, among others. The talent management function was also integrated into L&D team's domain in 2012. Having the entire life cycle of talent development from assessment to development to career movement "under one umbrella" enables its corporate university to better drive alignment and impact (Harris 2015).

Well-aligned strategies are important because they help learning organizations stay relevant and build a stronger business case for learning. The specific attributes of a learning organization's strategy will vary depending upon its values, mission, and business imperatives. However, a 2012 Towards Maturity benchmark study identified common characteristics of a well-aligned learning and development organization:

- the active involvement of business leaders in learning decisions
- the use of strategic business objectives to determine learning priorities
- a focus on end results and outcomes
- integration with HR and talent strategies
- demonstrated business value
- clarity among staff around their contribution
- proactive management commitment.

It's important to remember that a strategic focus doesn't end with strategy formulation. For sustained relevance and value, learning organizations must continually ensure that strategy execution is properly linked, monitored, and measured to map to key objectives and desired results. Chapter 5 talks more about how to ensure successful strategy execution.

Engage leadership support. While learning leaders need to develop the vision and mission of a mature learning organization, senior leadership must champion and embody the message that continuous learning is an important workplace value for sustainability to take hold. For instance, Richard Wyckoff, CEO of Georgia-based U.S. Security Associates, considers company investments in learning and talent development to be a key driver of enterprise value because they lead to improved workforce skills and expertise, which trickles down to better service for clients (ATD Staff 2015a). Senior leaders at Marriott International actively champion learning by sponsoring a talent network team (live or virtual) that works on a business challenge specific to its line of expertise or business (ATD 2016a). Then there's the classic example of Jack Welch teaching half-day management classes for new GE managers every two weeks and never missing a class. He demonstrated a visible, profound passion for learning-driven talent processes. Likewise, at PepsiCo, former CEO Wayne Calloway would spend weeks with key managers reviewing strategy, often mentoring their development. McKinsey's "The War for Talent" established that a leader's talent mindset is the primary distinguishing factor between successful and less successful organizations within industry cohorts (Chambers et al. 1998).

Sustainable learning organizations are more likely to have leaders who serve as teachers and are accountable for demonstrating the importance of a learning culture through compatible mindset and behaviors. Chapter 3 looks more closely at the importance of a distinguishing learning culture, while Chapter 4 examines how to engage senior leaders' support in building and sustaining a learning culture.

Link learning to performance. As discussed in chapter 1, many learning organizations fail to maintain organizational relevance and establish sustainability because they focus more on learning than on the performance that results from learning. In fact, research shows that about 60 to 90 percent of learning is not used on the job (Phillips 2015). So while the organization's employees are going through learning initiatives, the learning is not having an impact on performance. In a true learning organization, learning is viewed as the catalyst for providing critical skills, knowledge, and perspectives for improved job performance and effectiveness.

Learning is rarely the end, but rather the means to performance improvement. Because many performance problems cannot be solved with quick-fix learning solutions, learning and performance must go hand in hand. Best-in-class learning organizations have shifted their training or learning focus to a performance consulting role, in which a variety of learning and nonlearning solutions are explored to improve performance. In fact, research from a 2016 Towards Maturity report found that 54 percent of L&D professionals have now shifted to a performance consultancy role to add more value (Overton 2016). *Performance consulting* means coaching and guiding a client through a process of decisions and actions to meet a goal or objective. It means helping managers make constructive decisions through involvement in gathering and analyzing data, considering options, establishing goals, developing action plans, evaluating outcomes, and sharing responsibility for outcomes. Table 2-1 highlights common terms and definitions associated with a performance focus.

Table 2-1. Common Terms Associated With a Performance Focus

Term	Definitions
Human performance improvement roles (HPI)	• Analyst (performance and cause analysis) • Solution specialist • Change manager (implementation, change management) • Evaluator
Human performance system	• A complex system of variables, such as outputs, inputs, resources, consequences, feedback, and the performer, that influences individual job performance. Emphasizes that most performance problems are due to problems in the system rather than problems with the performer; advocates a systemic view.

Human performance technology (HPT)	• The means used to improve individual, group, and organizational performance. The methodology used requires a systematic approach to:
	  ◦ Assess a need or opportunity.
	  ◦ Identify causes or factors that limit performance.
	  ◦ Design solutions.
	  ◦ Develop solutions.
	  ◦ Implement the solutions.
	  ◦ Evaluate the results.

Human resource development	• The integrated use of career development, training and development, and organization development to improve individual performance.
Factors that support performance	• Clear performance specifications • Necessary resources and support • Appropriate consequences • Timely and relevant feedback • Individual capability • Necessary skills and knowledge
Gap analysis	• The process of determining the current state of performance and comparing it with the desired state. The difference between the two is the gap.

Cause analysis	• The process of determining why the gap exists. Involves root cause analysis, typically at three levels:
	  ◦ organizational level (policies, strategies)
	  ◦ work process level (insufficient work flow, outdated methods)
	  ◦ job or performer level (problem related to the six aforementioned factors that support performance)

Term	Definitions

Change-of-state analysis	• Focuses on four possible ways that performance must be changed to close gaps:
	  □ Extinguish performance.
	  □ Maintain performance.
	  □ Establish performance.
	  □ Improve performance.

Performance	• A combination of behaviors by performers and the results or accomplishments that they produce.

RSVP	• Principles of performance improvement focusing upon successful alignment of the work, the worker, and the workplace to facilitate desired results:
	  □ R: Focus on results
	  □ S: Take a systems viewpoint
	  □ V: Add value to the organization
	  □ P: Establish partnerships

Systems thinking	• Acknowledges that organizations are complex systems. If one part of the system is changed, the entire system will be affected.

Of course, Table 2-1 lists just a few of the key terms of a performance-based focus. References for further reading are provided at the end of this book. In addition, Chapter 5 has a case example showing how a systemic performance improvement framework was used to enable successful alignment and execution of a mission-critical learning and business strategy.

Establish a measurement framework for defining the value of learning. Learning organizations exist to drive business outcomes that add strategic value. Administrative excellence does not equal strategic value. While various organizations may use different techniques for measuring that contribution, learning leaders need a common framework to guide the practice and process of collecting, analyzing, and reporting qualitative and quantitative data about key performance measures. Most measurement efforts target various levels of results, as introduced by Donald Kirkpatrick more than 50 years ago and adapted by Jack Phillips in the 1980s. The Kirkpatrick and Phillips frameworks account for 80 to 90 percent of models used today globally (Phillips and Phillips 2009). These levels and their measurement focus include:

- Level 1: reaction and planned action (satisfaction, relevance, intent to use)

- Level 2: learning (skills, knowledge, confidence in using what was learned)
- Level 3: application and implementation (use of content and materials on the job)
- Level 4: business impact (productivity, quality, revenue, time, customer satisfaction)
- Level 5: return on investment (monetary benefits of a program compare to program costs).

While a results-based measurement framework is typically used to assess the value of an individual program or a series of programs, keeping a credible, robust measurement system in place beyond the life cycle of a single program is a challenge that will be further reviewed in chapter 8. Suffice it to say that formal measurement and metrics should be an overall part of any learning strategy. Measures of impact and business contribution help establish a learning organization's brand and define its value chain in the organization. Demonstrating the value of learning expenditures also means knowing what learning costs and properly managing the learning budget.

Now that we've looked at typical factors associated with the early initiation of a learning organization, let's explore common barriers that may arise as learning processes and practices begin to gather more visibility and create more expectations for managers' and learners' participation.

Stage Two: Resistance

Change is a central element of any major transformation process and any learning solution designed to improve performance. Transforming a learning organization from an activity-based, transactional enterprise to a results-based, strategically aligned business function is a change process with predictable speed bumps. No matter how well endorsed, well designed, or well executed the transformation plan may be, there are bound to be barriers along the way. In this stage of the Sustainability Cycle, it's not uncommon to find that initial or existing support and goodwill for learning and performance focus has waned. It's also not unusual for the organization to either abandon its learning and performance commitment entirely or significantly scale back resources.

Key Indicators

As the learning organization moves from recognition to resistance, the organization's change threshold and the learning and performance process maturity are both low. There may even be clear signs that the learning function is having trouble achieving its intended objectives. For instance, the learning organization may face:

- new business demands that compete for time and resources
- new business leaders with new agendas and priorities
- complaints about the time or cost of learning activities
- limited communication about the process
- a lack of participation and involvement of the management team
- constant shuffling of people involved in measurement projects
- poor organizational readiness (unstable or ill-equipped infrastructure)
- false assumptions, myths, or fears about a growing reliance on performance data and how they will be used.

Key Tasks

During the resistance stage, the following actions have been shown to create a strong foundation of processes and practices that will help learning leaders navigate roadblocks and maintain momentum for continued growth.

Educate and advocate. Education, across all organizational levels, is one of the best ways to overcome resistance or misconceptions about an increased results-based or performance focus with learning and development. This can include presentations at executive meetings, management briefings, or success stories shared across social media about how learning solutions have helped solve performance problems. Education is especially critical for illuminating the role of managers in supporting a learning and performance culture. The following illustrates one approach to educating managers and engaging them as learning advocates. Other examples are included in the case studies through-out the remaining chapters.

Voices From the Field

I'm an HR director at a food distribution company in Miami. I joined the company eight months ago, and one of my tasks has been to develop more of a learning culture in the organization. It's been challenging to get commitment and buy-in from the management team for more standardized and recurring learning. For one thing, they're really busy and it's hard to take them away from the job for formal training. Another challenge comes from the old-guard mindset that "we don't really need it" or "we're doing fine without it," with sales or operational deliveries or what have you. We're a small, family-owned company and a lot of managers have been with us for as long as 30 years. A lot of them don't want to change or they don't want somebody telling them how to do things differently. So, I'm starting small, building relationships, and finding out about managers' pain points so that they can be involved in designing and implementing solutions.

As an example, I had one manager who complained about candidates who came to job interviews ill-prepared, wearing inappropriate attire or even cursing. So I worked with our marketing team to create a small training video focused on a simulation of what to do when a candidate comes to the interview ill-prepared. The manager played the role of a manager in the scenario, and she illustrated how to address this problem using HR's recommended solution: stopping the interview and walking the person out of the building. The video addressed an immediate, real-world issue; the manager had a wonderful experience putting the video together, and now she's actively promoting learning solutions with other managers. Her buy-in and advocacy has given us more leverage in implementing standardized training and performance management solutions. It's also created a win-win for managers because it's a simple solution that keeps their time focused on selecting the best talent and it saves them time from attending a full training session."

—Javiel Lopez, SPHR, Director of Human Resources, Quirch Foods

Build capabilities. Capabilities consist of the collective knowledge, skills, abilities, tools, information, processes, training, support, and so on that employees need to do their job. In many situations, resistance to learning new skills may be largely due to employees' fears and anxiety about meeting additional performance expectations, especially as jobs become more compli-cated by rapid change, new technologies, or competing pressures. Building needed capabilities improves employees' confidence and competence, which drives engagement and reduces resistance. Building these capabilities is essen-tial to adding and sustaining value given CEOs' priorities around closing lead-ership skills gaps through effective leadership development. There is a constant need to develop leadership capabilities, not only for existing lines of business, but also for business opportunities not yet imagined.

In addition, more and more learning and teaching responsibilities are being distributed to leaders across dispersed business units or core teams of subject matter experts. Building capabilities across dispersed units and teams means that a sustainable learning organization has to make it easy for employees to connect and share information across boundaries. Many organizations, such as Banner Health and the Tennessee Department of Human Resources (chapter 3), have developed certification processes that teach a set of standard competen-cies for facilitators or "leader-teachers" who are accountable for growing skills within their own business unit.

Finally, learning leaders must also continue growing their own capabilities to make sure learning strategies, services, and products keep up with chang-ing user needs. As your flight attendant would say: Put on your own oxygen mask before helping others. After all, learning organizations cannot expect to influence and grow organizational capabilities without continually assessing whether they have the right people in the right role with the right capabilities to deliver on the promise of learning's value. As the landscape of learning and performance evolves, the roles, responsibilities, and skill sets of learning lead-ers need to evolve with it to avoid extinction.

Deploy well. Regardless of how mature the learning organization may be, aligning learning strategies with effective execution is often a source of resistance. For example, effective coordination across boundaries and busi-ness units is a key to effective strategy execution. Yet, as organizational struc-tures become more matrixed and networked, effective systems for sharing information, coordinating efforts, and holding employees accountable are more challenging to create. Learning leaders can meet these challenges by ensuring that learning and performance expectations are clear, manageable, flexible, and appropriately aligned with business needs. Adopting disciplined, but agile, project management approaches also helps ensure that learning and performance strategies stay relevant and resilient in the face of resistance. Chapter 5 will explore the role of effective execution and risk management, for both individual project planning and business continuity purposes, and will provide examples of successful learning execution in action.

Develop partnerships. Learning leaders cannot affect performance by themselves. Even if learning has a strong sponsor within the organization, the consistent cooperation and commitment of individuals and groups across all organizational levels is needed to influence performance growth, especially in times of diminishing or scarce resources. One seasoned L&D professional describes his partnership activity in terms of "shuttle diplomacy": an influencing process used to filter noise, counter barriers, and negotiate ongoing support from critical stakeholders. Leveraging partnerships is an important way to mobilize the efforts of others when working to prevent change fatigue, apathy, or inertia. Because the key to achieving process and practice maturity is a progressive movement, collaborations and connections are critical for ensuring that traction for building and sustaining a learning culture doesn't get blocked in certain parts of the organization.

Promoting partnerships across all organizational levels also helps learning leaders improve their knowledge of the business and identify areas where learning and performance improvement can help solve problems in real time. Management and stakeholder partnerships are also critical for ensuring that learning leaders can properly identify the:

- best solution to meet needs (not all problems require a learning or training solution)
- context in which learning solutions will be used

- extent of environmental support available to reinforce learning transfer and application of knowledge and skills on the job
- specific performance and impact measures for assessing the success of learning and performance improvement solutions.

Show how learning and performance solutions solve real problems. One of the best ways to create sustainable value and relevance is to consistently demonstrate how the learning organization solves issues that are important to business leaders. Consider Resource Residential, a real estate mortgage company. To overcome performance discrepancies in selling interactions across the enterprise, the company's L&D team partnered with senior executives and field leadership partners to develop a proprietary selling model that was more aligned with key behavioral requirements. This led to a standardized learning experience for leasing associates and community managers that closed performance gaps and allowed for quicker, more effective customer interactions (ATD Staff 2015a).

The reality is that most executives and line managers recognize that they need the help of skill developers to meet pressing performance challenges. Yet many business leaders hesitate to engage the L&D organization because learning professionals often don't take the time to understand the business so that learning solutions or processes can be linked to key business objectives. Despite significant advances in growing the business acumen of L&D, there's still a tendency by many learning leaders to view the world through a learning lens versus a business lens. Staying relevant over time requires thinking and acting like a business person first and a learning leader second. This includes managing the learning function as a business service center where quality, cost, speed of execution, and service determine its value.

Stage Three: Renewal

Renewal is the stage where an organization moves past organizational barriers, begins to recover lost momentum, and explores how to renew its initial commitment to results-based learning focus. In addition, standardized learning and performance processes start to get increased visibility and attention from internal stakeholders, including senior management.

Key Indicators

Common signs that a learning organization has entered this stage include:

- increased focus on linking learning and performance to strategic directions
- increased focus on developing learning experiences rather than learning events
- increased energy and coordination around identifying where and how to support internal business units
- increased investments in growing learning capabilities across the organization
- improved mechanisms for enabling learning connections across boundaries and reducing reliance on siloed structures and hierarchies
- improved operating policies, procedures, and standards for governing learning and performance improvement
- increased use of learning and performance scorecards to communicate how the learning organization is contributing to the business in terms of efficiency and effectiveness measures.

Key Tasks

During the renewal stage of process maturity, the following actions have been shown to help firm up previous foundations and enable further movement toward a mature, sustainable learning culture.

Communicate, communicate, communicate. While communication is critical at every stage of development, some learning organizations tend to get complacent or lax about the need for ongoing messaging about learning's role in business success. Consistent, focused communication is vital to keeping learning strategies up front and visible. One seasoned learning professional says she continually "pushes success stories" in the form of learning and performance results, testimonials, project reports, or impact studies out to the organization to keep a constant line of sight on the value of learning to the business. Communicating about the role of learning in meeting critical needs around talent management, skill development, customer service, increased revenue, or improved productivity is necessary for generating ongoing investment and resource support for learning.

Stabilize links and infrastructure. Building stable links involves integrating learning and performance business models, practices, and processes with organizational and operational business processes. These include recruiting, hiring, onboarding, performance management, leadership development, rewards and recognition, succession planning, and workforce planning processes. For example, the talent development framework at EY (formerly Ernst and Young) is managed with stable, integrated links. New hires are assigned a counselor who is responsible for providing one-on-one guidance on goal setting, development planning, and performance management. The talent function, including talent development, is embedded in service lines and geographic operational areas, and talent leaders have dual reporting relationships to the heads of business they serve and to leaders in the talent function (ATD Staff 2016). Stabilizing infrastructures also means making sure that data collection and reporting systems, including learning management systems, can support dynamic needs. Progressive learning organizations shore up links by decluttering cumbersome, overly complex processes to reduce workload, improve engagement, increase productivity, and simplify how learning gets integrated in daily operations.

Strengthen alliances. The sustained effectiveness of a learning enterprise depends on learning leaders' ability to cultivate cross-functional partnerships with stakeholders who own the business need, have the authority to put learning on the agenda, and make decisions about how learning resources will be allocated. For example, Western Union's learning and talent management team has shifted to a "customer-centric mindset" to support executives' global business model and help managers drive performance priorities focused upon accelerating cross-border business growth, simplifying processes, and demonstrating operational excellence (ATD Staff 2015a). By integrating a customer-focused mindset and strengthening leader-as-teacher alliances, the L&D team has helped accelerate organizational performance and create sustainable value for its learning organization.

Taking the time to establish enduring working relationships founded on mutual trust, rapport, and credibility is essential to a sustainable learning enterprise (Robinson et al. 2015). Solid partnerships and shared commitments help integrate continuous learning as part of the business and help learning organizations recover more quickly from adverse events. In a 2016 ATD conference session, Tamar Elkeles, 2010 CLO of the Year, said that gaining trust and credibility as a business partner was critical to her success in building an award-winning learning organization at Qualcomm. She also emphasized that effective business partnerships evolve over time and require ongoing communications held with a spirit of openness and transparency.

Measure what matters. Every learning organization needs to apply some standardized level of measurement and analysis to its goal setting and strategic decision making if it expects to enable organizational growth and remain relevant amid perpetual change. For instance, top-tier learning organizations are twice as likely to identify key performance measures that are important to the business and to have clear working partnerships with the line of business, compared to the average (Towards Maturity 2015).

This means moving beyond tactical, activity-based metrics such as courses, participants, and hours of training and moving toward actual, predictive measures of learning impact. CEOs are demanding more use of analytical data to support increased investments in learning and development and identify how capability gaps are being closed. It's important to not only report on results achieved, but also be ready to present findings about poor outcomes to identify problems and present lessons learned for continuous improvement purposes. Chapter 6 will talk more about the important role of measurement in building a sustainable learning culture.

Incorporate continuous improvement mechanisms. As learning and performance processes become more standardized and visible, and as the competition for resources becomes more intense, continuous improvement mechanisms are needed to ensure that processes and practices are keeping up with evolving needs and still adding value. Chapters 5 and 6 profile examples of mechanisms, such as governance systems, scorecards, and dashboards, that have worked well in tracking learning effectiveness for a single program, a series of programs, or the entire learning enterprise.

Now that we've looked at how to better define stable, value-added learning processes and practices, let's explore how to move into refinement, the optimal stage of process maturity.

Stage Four: Refinement

Refinement is the stage where the learning organization has successfully transformed itself into an integrated, business-centric function. On a functional level, refinement is where sustaining strategies and learning and performance infrastructure are firmly embedded into organizational business planning and day-to-day operations, and a learning culture is universally and mutually supported by all involved. In this stage of maturity, continuous learning is viewed as a core capability and a strategic priority. Here, the key driver for every learning strategy is value creation. Enabling mechanisms are in place to support collaborative knowledge sharing and networked communities of practice across all levels of the organization. Learning leaders are credible catalysts for mobilizing organizational change and fostering innovation. Learning and performance services, processes, and practices are regularly reviewed against defined measures of effectiveness, and learning and performance results are routinely used for enhanced decision making and continuous improvement purposes.

Key Indicators

In this stage, the organization's change threshold and the learning organization's process maturity are both high, and there are clear signs that a fully integrated, performance-based learning culture has taken hold. Common signs that a learning organization has entered this stage include:

- The learning organization is a key player in strategic initiatives.
- There is a spirit of continuous improvement, innovation, and out-of-the-box thinking around learning, performance improvement, and talent management.
- The learning and development budget is growing or stable.
- Learning leaders are viewed as strategic partners, talent builders, and change enablers.
- Collaboration between learning and other key business units are routine; there is a strong link between L&D and talent management processes and other HR processes.
- Stakeholders across the organization regularly request learning and performance data for decision-making purposes.
- Learning processes and systems are stable, flexible, and adaptive in the face of changing needs or business disruptions.
- Measurable targets for learning and e-learning are regularly reviewed and used for improvement and action-planning purposes.
- The work environment supports a culture of learning anyplace, anytime, with open access to information.
- Learning and talent management professionals perform at best-in-class levels.

Key Tasks

During periods of high performance and production, avoid complacency and develop and maintain avenues for continued innovation and growth. What sets sustainable learning organizations apart is their ability to renew, transform, or even reinvent themselves and their organizations in historically significant ways. To achieve refinement, consider the following actions to help sustain a solid foundation of relevant, resilient learning processes and practices that not only add business value but also create it.

Foster change resilience and agility. Failure to adapt to change is one of the biggest barriers to the overall sustainability of any learning organization, across all industries and sizes. To thrive in today's dynamic business climate, learning organizations have to maintain their core function, while still offering flexible, rapid, value-added solutions, in the face of continuous change, situational disturbances, threats, or even new opportunities. Sustainable learning organizations have the capability to adapt to changing circumstances quickly. To be seen as credible learning champions and change agents, learning leaders must leverage the proper skills, tools, and change management techniques, as well as demonstrate the proper mindset about change. More about that in chapter 7.

Embrace innovation. Best-in-class learning leaders help organizations leverage progressive learning technologies and talent development processes to drive innovation. A learning organization cannot drive innovation at the organizational level with stagnant, out-of-date practices at the functional level. Consider IBM. Globalization and skills gap challenges have led IBM to pursue innovation in its talent development, sales training, and new manager and executive training. The company sees innovative learning design as a tool for adapting to a more competitive landscape and ever-changing market conditions. To that end, IBM's reinvigorated sales training includes simulated sales situations, integrated sales management tools, seller teams competing to win high-stakes proposal challenges, and successful sales advisers who coach trainees on practice sales meetings that are videotaped. Social media tools help employees connect and collaborate across boundaries. A learning app is available so employees on the go can stay current with strategic initiatives, focus on learning goals, and improve job skills (ATD Staff 2015a).

An innovative, continuous learning culture has been shown to spark the ideas and forward thinking that enable organizations to differentiate themselves in a global marketplace. Innovation is also needed to cater to the learning needs of Millennials, the largest demographic in the workplace. This means transitioning from traditional learning perspectives and practices to a modern workplace learning perspective. Advocated by Jane Hart (2015), founder of the Centre for Learning & Performance Technologies, the modern workplace learning perspective is one in which learning leaders:

- Embrace short, flexible, modern resources that can be accessed when needed.
- Encourage social (or employee-generated) content.
- Support teams in their use of enterprise social platforms to improve team learning.
- Embrace a performance-driven world.

Modern workplace learning practices include:

- making the best use of assessment tools for determining needs and simulating work environments in learning design and development
- leveraging a mixture of formal and informal media and social collaboration tools in learning design, development, and delivery
- providing learning infrastructure that delivers easily accessible learning content at the time of need
- ensuring that learners have more choice and personal responsibility for their own development
- regularly experimenting with deviations from a one-size-fits-all learning and development approach.

Chapter 9 offers more examples from learning leaders who have promoted, modeled, and leveraged innovative learning perspectives and practices for improved sustainability.

Continually reflect, review, and refine. A sustainable learning organization takes time to determine what it stands for, what it wants to build, and what it wants to sustain. Its learning leaders continually measure and monitor its progress and pay attention to the internal and external signals that tell how well its mission, vision, and values are being integrated throughout the organization. Some call this process the "Santayana review" in recognition of the philosopher George Santayana, who coined the phrase, "Those who cannot remember the past are condemned to repeat it." Learning leaders can also add sustainable value here by continually benchmarking to uncover and adopt best practices in learning, performance improvement, and talent development. The greatest benefits come from reflecting upon practices and the way that learning and performance work gets done, as well as from involving line managers in the review process. Incorporate the assessments from this book as part of your annual reflection, review, and refinement process when determining which learning practices to maintain, eliminate, or improve.

About the Stages

It's important to remember that the stages of process maturity may vary not only from one organization to the next, but also from one department to the next or one region or one country to the next in the same organization. This is especially true for multinational companies, in which global standards for learning and performance may be well understood, but practiced at different levels of maturity in local markets by local leaders. In addition, it's not unusual for practices that have reached a state of refinement to periodically swing back to previous stages of recognition or resistance due to new leadership, new business structures, or new change demands. Says Ronnie Ashline, experiential learning advocate at Google Fiber and Xerox: "It's hard to sustain momentum for a learning and performance commitment beyond the early fanfare. It's important until something else becomes more important. I think we've all experienced that. Organizations start something with the best of intentions, and then the reality of what's involved is usually more work than people imagined it to be." The two scenarios from the introduction are prime examples of this phenomenon. For these reasons, experts say that a sustainable learning enterprise—one that is fully embedded in organizational culture—may take several years to achieve and significant time to rebuild if disrupted.

Ultimately, there are no short cuts to building and sustaining a high-performing learning organization. It takes time, effort, and a conviction to make a difference through process excellence. However, Figure 2-4 highlights action steps that can be taken to facilitate movement and transformation along each stage of the Sustainability Cycle. The next chapters outline additional steps that will help you and your learning organization in the journey toward creating sustainable value. You'll also be able to choose which actions steps to replicate when reviewing lessons learned from case scenarios.

Figure 2-4. Key Actions During Each Stage of Transformation

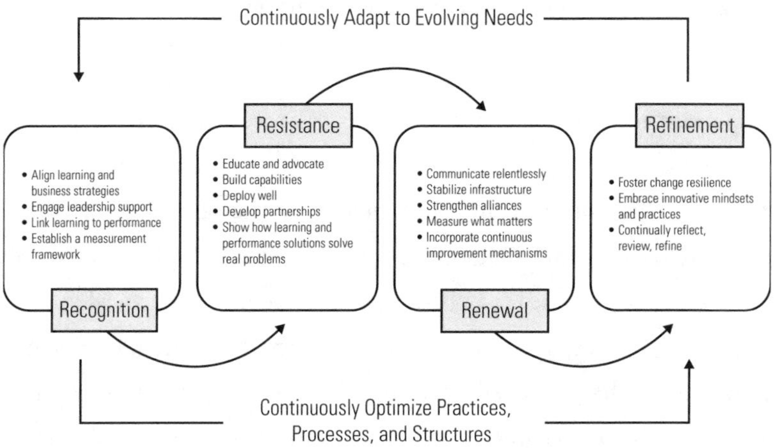

Continuously Adapt to Evolving Needs

Resistance

Refinement

- Align learning and business strategies
- Engage leadership support
- Link learning to performance
- Establish a measurement framework

- Educate and advocate
- Build capabilities
- Deploy well
- Develop partnerships
- Show how learning and performance solutions solve real problems

- Communicate relentlessly
- Stabilize infrastructure
- Strengthen alliances
- Measure what matters
- Incorporate continuous improvement mechanisms

- Foster change resilience
- Embrace innovative mindsets and practices
- Continually reflect, review, refine

Recognition

Renewal

Continuously Optimize Practices, Processes, and Structures

Characteristics of a Sustainable Learning Organization

Now that we've highlighted the stages of maturity in the Sustainability Cycle, let's look at the features of a sustainable learning organization once it reaches an optimal level of functioning. How will you know it when you see it? Figure 2-5 illustrates 10 characteristics of a mature and sustainable learning organization, as defined by those who have successfully sustained a learning organization for five years of longer.

Keep in mind that all characteristics must be present to meet the criteria for learning organization maturity and sustainability. Learning leaders may demonstrate strengths in one or more of these characteristics while falling short in others. For example, as a learning leader, you might have established strong partnerships across the organization, and stakeholders may regularly request learning and talent management data for improved decision making. However, many learning organizations tend to lack proficiency in measuring the effectiveness of learning investments in meeting evolving sponsorship needs.

Figure 2-5. Characteristics of a Sustainable Learning Organization

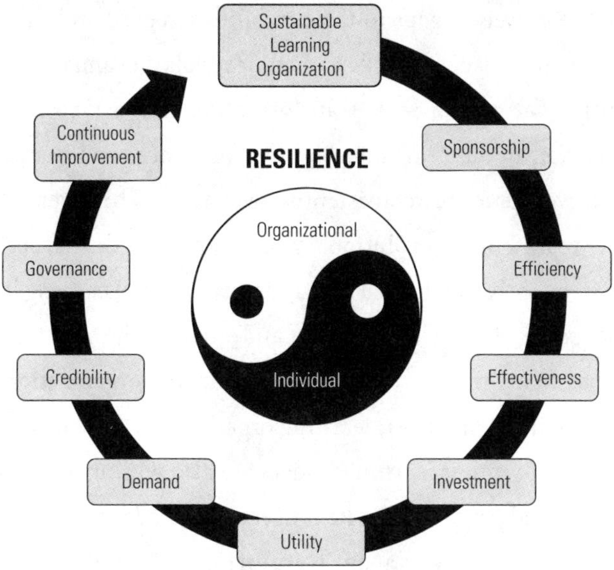

Holly Burkett (2016). Used with permission.

You'll have a chance to see how the case examples in the following chapters stack up against these criteria. For instance, case summaries will profile how each learning organization exemplifies these 10 characteristics and will describe where they may need continual renewal to reach optimal functioning.

In addition, the Characteristics of a Sustainable Learning Organization self-assessment in appendix 2 represents a diagnostic tool you can use to assess how well your current learning organization meets these criteria for sustainability. Ask yourself if members of your L&D team, your sponsors, or your stakeholders would agree with your assessment or have them complete it as well to compare perspectives. Based on this review, identify one to three priority areas for improvement and renewed focus. Make this assessment part of an annual reflection and review process.

Chapter Summary

Many executives, along with many L&D experts, are calling for a radical transformation—and even a revolution—of learning and HR organizations. This is due in part to perceived gaps in the capabilities needed and the capabilities delivered by learning leaders in today's complex, volatile, and rapidly changing business world. The goal of most transformation efforts is to drive a culture that supports continuous learning, high performance, and mature, sustainable, talent-driven practices consistently, over time. The "over time" part of sustainability represents an evolutionary change process that is especially challenging and frequently overlooked and underestimated. Learning leaders need to move past a series of one-shot solutions and embrace the need for continuous change and sustained transformation of the learning organization and all its related components. Remember, learning organizations will never experience true transformation unless learning leaders are also willing to transform antiquated mindsets and practices that no longer serve modern needs.

In short, sustainability is about transforming the learning organization so that it not only survives in difficult times, but also thrives as a relevant, resilient, and value-creating enterprise. Learning leaders can draw upon core capabilities to facilitate movement and progress toward the 10 characteristics of process maturity shown in Figures 2-2 and 2-5. Consistent practice and application of these capabilities, as represented in the seven practices of sustaining highly resilient learning organizations, will serve as levers and change enablers in the transformation process. The remaining chapters will provide details and real-world examples about how to use and grow each of the seven practices for sustained success.

Chapter Highlights

Building a mature, sustainable learning organization is an evolutionary change process.

Sustainability is not a single step or a static business objective, but a process in which small, evolutionary stages, rather than revolutionary ones, form the basis for continuous improvement. These evolutionary stages are often likened to maturity levels, in which development processes are transformed from ad hoc, undisciplined states to disciplined processes or practices capable of predictable, sustainable results. The focus is on the maturity of the whole learning organization, rather than specific initiatives, and its capability to support a range of development needs that shift over time.

There are many ways to build and sustain a learning organization, but leadership support is a key factor.

The demonstrated support of leadership is an essential element of a high-performing, sustainable learning enterprise. It can't exist without committed leaders who shape, and embody, a climate that encourages continuous learning and the open exchange of ideas. Leadership commitment starts with at the top, with the active involvement of CEOs in such roles as leader-teachers, executive advisers, or mentors.

Change resiliency is the glue of a sustainable learning organization.

Transformation of learning processes and practices represents a journey from individual learning and performance to organizational learning and performance, in which change and the need for change resiliency are central elements. Establishing a fully integrated, sustainable learning organization is ultimately about cultural change and change capability on an individual and organizational level.

The future of L&D hinges on sustainable processes and practices.

The future of learning and development rests not only on its ability to grow and leverage capabilities in the short term, but also on its ability to be proactive and future-focused. Continual renewal and transformation of learning processes and practices is needed to keep up with evolving needs and dynamic business conditions. To that end, recognition of the common stages in a learning organization's sustainability cycle can help executives, learning leaders, and talent managers know where to best target renewal resources and efforts for maximum impact.

Practice 1: Lead With Culture

"If you want everyone to be on the same page, put the page in front of them conveniently and often."

—Rosabeth Moss Kanter (2009)

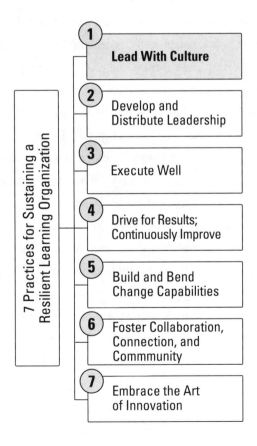

What's in This Chapter

- how a learning culture can drive increased engagement and performance
- why influencing culture change is an "inside-out" process
- how learning leaders can help build better cultures for the good of the business.

IN 2015, THE CHICAGO BLACKHAWKS WON their third Stanley Cup in five years. That's a remarkable feat for a team that, in 2007, was ranked 118 of 122 fan-favorite sports franchises in the United States by *ESPN The Magazine* (Powers 2015).

For the Blackhawks, the progression from loser to champion can be traced to their focus on developing a winning culture through talent acquisition, management, and development. When Stan Bowman was promoted to general manager in July 2009, there was a dedicated focus on building talent; obtaining quality players through the draft, free agency, and trade market; and "trying to build a tradition of winning." Bowman has said that he tried to emulate the culture of the Detroit Red Wings because they won consistently for more than 20 years without the highs and lows other NHL teams typically face (Moore 2015). He wanted to bring stability to the Blackhawks. Bowman was particularly committed to cultivating a mentoring process in which veteran players coached younger players so that each wave of players would help build a stable system of excellence, continuity, and performance consistency. However, as much as the Blackhawks have progressed in the past eight years, Bowman has emphasized that the journey toward a winning culture, while attainable, is still a work in progress.

The Blackhawks have gotten this far by building and sustaining a high-performing culture based on a foundation of talent, coaching, mentoring, constancy of purpose, teamwork, and standards of accountability. This foundation also contributes to a winning culture on the corporate playing field. While culture can mean different things to different people, culture generally reflects the values, beliefs, and behaviors that influence how people interact and perform in an organization every day. Culture manifests through intentional or accidental behaviors that are encouraged with rewards or discouraged with consequences (Ray et al. 2016). As Herb Kelleher, co-founder and chairman of Southwest Airlines, said, "Culture is what happens when people aren't looking."

Formal definitions of culture abound, but the informal elements of a company's culture are equally important. For example, it's not unusual for a company's culture to be defined by its "vibe"—its characteristic sights, sounds, atmosphere, and work environment—as well as its mission and values statement. A company's vibe represents the sense of cohesion and shared identity among employees, a distinguishing characteristic among organizations that thrive through eras of change, whether it be to leaders, employees, or industries (de Geus 2002). We all know it when we feel it. At its essence, a clear organizational culture is the "secret sauce" that keeps everyone pointed in the same direction, provides employees with a shared meaning and purpose about their work, and powers engagement and performance, despite organizational changes (Clow 2015).

The role of culture in driving engagement and high performance continues to evolve and gain visibility. Companies can no longer depend solely on their products and services to distinguish them in the marketplace. Rather, there is growing focus on organizational culture as a key differentiator in the global competition for talent. Companies that create cultures defined by meaningful work, employee engagement, job and organizational fit, and strong leadership, attract top talent and outperform their competition. Here are three companies whose prominent cultures are often emulated:

- **Zappos's** culture espouses 10 core values, and the company hires according to cultural fit. This starts with a cultural fit interview, which carries half the weight of whether a candidate is hired. If new employees decide the job isn't for them once they are hired, Zappos offers them $2,000 to quit after the first week of training. Zappos has a culture book written by employees that details how they feel about the Zappos culture and how they reinforce and develop the culture every day. Zappos believes that when you get the company culture right, great customer service and a great brand will follow (Heathfield 2016).

- **REI's** mission is to equip both customers and employees for the outdoors, have fun, and promote stewardship of the environment. Employees can win equipment through "challenge grants" in which they submit a proposal for an outdoor adventure that would help them develop. Employees can submit questions anonymously at town-hall-style meetings to help management understand issues. REI, a cooperative where profits benefit its member-owners, contends that its employees give "life to their purpose" and its leaders firmly attribute company success to workers. The CEO believes that when employees are completely immersed in the same interests as the company, the culture propels itself forward in its own unique way (Patel 2015).

- **Facebook,** in a highly competitive industry, stands out by offering multiple perks (food, stock options, on-site laundry, outdoor roaming space) and a flat organizational culture where management (including CEO Mark Zuckerberg) works in an open office space alongside other employees. Building and space configurations, along with organizational structures, are all designed to promote a culture of equality and a meritocracy (Patel 2015).

A healthy culture has become the new currency for the modern age. Executives, directors, managers, and employees all believe that a distinct workplace culture is important to business success (Figure 3-1). Global executives consistently cite culture and engagement as a top challenge and "very important" problem in their organization (Deloitte 2015).

Figure 3-1. Fast Facts

84%	60%	51%
Executives who say organizational culture is critical to business success	Executives who say organizational culture is more important than strategy	Executives who say their organizational culture is in need of a major overhaul

Source: Aguirre, von Post, and Alpern (2013).

The more effective a company's culture is, the more engaged the workers, the better the reputation, the greater the company's success, and the stronger the company's ability to attract talent. Research has shown a correlation between employees who say their organization has a clearly communicated and lived culture and those who say they feel "valued" and are "happy at work." (Happiness Research Institute et al. 2015). The cost of disengagement is high, with Gallup (2013) estimating that disengaged workforces cost U.S. companies $450 to $550 billion in lost productivity per year.

Continuous learning and development (L&D) is a common characteristic among cultures known for high engagement. For example, factors that drive high engagement and high performance include growth opportunities, leadership capability, meaningful and collaborative work, and a positive work environment. Most Millennials rank learning and development opportunities as a prospective employers' top benefit, higher than compensation (Elance-oDesk and Millennial Branding 2015). A mature, well-integrated learning organization drives each previously noted engagement factor. In short, we know an engaged workforce creates sustainable value. We also know that an organization needs an enduring, sustainable learning environment, or culture, where employees can grow, flourish, and become engaged. If people aren't learning, they're leaving.

When learning is effectively used to help shape a culture that contributes to commitment, direction, and alignment across the organization, the probability of attaining high performance is quite high (Dinwoodie, Quinn, and McGuire 2014). By some estimates, companies with strong learning cultures are 18 percent more likely to be a market-share leader in one or more of their markets (Vector Learning 2013). Studies show that robust learning cultures add and create value by:

- contributing to high performance and engagement
- developing skills and capabilities needed for future demand
- developing talent capability to meet current and future needs.

Because culture change is the one area in which learning leaders are most likely to partner with executives, there are many opportunities for learning leaders to add value. For example, while most executives believe culture to be a critical source of business success, only 32 percent think that their culture aligns with their strategy (Korn Ferry 2014). Driving alignment between culture and strategy is good place for learning leaders to begin. For learning to support and execute business strategy transformation, the culture and strategy of the learning organization must also be aligned and transformed. Let's look at how sustainable learning organizations have successfully managed this kind of transformation.

Keys to Transformation

Transformation is not a "one and done" event. It's a cumulative process that takes constant effort and a long-term line of sight. But what does it really mean to transform your learning organization, and why does it matter?

Transforming a learning organization means taking it from a business cost to a true business driver, from a tactical nice-to-have to a strategic must-have. It means your learning organization has achieved a level of maturity and sustainability based on the hallmarks of a learning organization described in the introduction and the 10 characteristics described in chapter 2. In practice, it means that every member of the L&D team is clear about the true business of the company, its competitive environment, and its executive strategies. Every member takes an active role in executing business strategy by collaborating and partnering with business units. Every member commits to creating continuous learning environments that enable employees to thrive and manage their own development. Every member focuses on fostering innovation and collaboration instead of focusing narrowly on efficiency or cost-cutting efforts. Every member creates adaptive structures that allow movement in concert with shifting business needs. Every member invests in growing capabilities around talent management, change management, and relationship management, as well as in all areas of business acumen, industry knowledge, social networking tools, and other technologies. And every member collects and reports metrics of success beyond basic output measures.

Why are these areas important? Despite best intentions and efforts, learning organizations struggle to make the grade as companies move away from people administration to a focus on people performance and engagement. Consider these findings from a McKinsey & Company survey (Benson-Armer et al. 2015):

- Few organizations (18 percent of respondents) have an objective, structured process for assessing current capabilities and identifying skills gaps. Instead, most use one-off self-assessments, which can impede effective learning design.
- Fewer than one in five said that business units co-own the learning function. Co-ownership of L&D reinforces alignment of learning objectives with business needs and communicates the importance of employee skill development.
- One in five said their company does not measure the impact of L&D initiatives. Of those that do, most rely on employee or manager feedback rather than quantifiable measures.
- More than 50 percent said that they don't know if their L&D initiatives have achieved quantitative targets in the past three years, or that they have not set targets.

In short, a mature, strategic L&D organization has the power to drive business strategy and boost engagement. Yet studies like this one show that many learning organizations still struggle to gain and sustain cultural influence, which diminishes their potential impact. Many senior leaders still view learning and development programs as cost items rather than strategic investments. Accordingly, executives' involvement and expectations often remain low. How, then, can a learning organization be perceived as a credible partner in driving business transformation without first transforming the values, beliefs, and behaviors that influence how learning is embedded in the organizational culture?

For learning leaders, culture change is first and foremost an *inside-out* process that requires continually upskilling, retooling, refreshing, or reorganizing the function. As Greg Pryor, vice president of leadership and organizational effectiveness at Workday, said in a Work Talk episode, "We don't outsource our culture" (Workday Staff 2016). In short, leading with culture means elevating the role of the learning organization as a cultural catalyst for high performance and engagement. The following actions can help with the transformation process.

Rethink and Renew Your Strategic Focus

A *Harvard Business Review* study found that 70 percent of companies that align learning with business priorities are able to improve company revenue (Shlomo, Jaworski, and Gray 2015). Because the business environment, its strategic priorities, and its workforce are evolving by the minute, it's important to pursue a strategic rather than a tactical approach to L&D. It can be easy to hold onto a learning strategy for too long, so knowing when to adapt, pivot, or reverse course in response to dynamic needs is a critical part of adding sustainable value.

For example, to meet competitive demands, Maersk Line, a Danish container shipping company, has been steadily transforming how it does business, moving from a travel-agent business model to an online service model (Salopek 2015b). To support evolving business models and be seen as an integral part of the culture shift, the head of learning and organizational development had to transform an inefficient learning organization with few projects linked to strategic priorities to one where customer impact drove its strategic mission and purpose. Innovative initiatives that focused on being proactive, building relationships, and sharing ownership helped increase customer service scores and sales volume, ultimately showing the contribution of learning to the business.

Embedding a learning culture into the organizational fabric means learning strategies must focus on business alignment, integration, and continual innovation (see Figure 3-2 for an example of this). Learning organizations that are not well integrated into an existing organizational culture will not be credible as culture change agents and strategic business partners.

Figure 3-2. Learning Sustainability Requires Strategic Alignment

Measure Success With Strategic Objectives

The only way to determine if a learning organization is effectively meeting strategic objectives is to focus on metrics that show how initiatives influence key indicators of business performance. Learning organizations often track a lot of data but have trouble connecting them to business performance through measurement. Sustainable, high-performing learning organizations place considerable stock in the idea of measurement. They use sophisticated techniques to measure, and they focus less on training and more on creating an organization-wide learning culture. While other factors such as how a learning organization is structured, its use of learning technologies, or the presence of a chief learning officer (CLO) may help set the stage, measurement and culture are considered the strongest predictors of success with learning organizations.

Demonstrating the return on people investments is a key factor in sustaining executive support and commitment for the learning organization as a strategic business partner. It's one thing to have learning strategies that are effectively aligned to meaningful business outcomes. It's another to show how execution of those strategies affects performance and adds business value. Chapter 6 describes more about how sustainable learning organizations align strategies to business measures of success.

Review Strategic Priorities

Studies show that increasing or improving leader or manager training is one of the most frequent approaches taken by learning organizations to boost an engagement culture. While having effectively trained leaders is a pressing challenge, simply ramping up new training initiatives won't necessarily improve culture or financial performance. In fact, sustainable, high-performing learning organizations have shifted priorities from individual employee training to a broader focus on building organizational capability, which encompasses training as well as other factors that affect the learning function (as discussed in the introduction). Most executives consider it a strategic priority to maximize talent through collective "capability building." In one example, the learning center at Qualcomm prioritizes mobile learning strategies as the best approach for growing collective capabilities among next-generation learners. Blended learning, curated open source content, and expanded social components provide fresh approaches to learning for project teams and business units faced with the changing world of work, learning, and information (Bell 2015).

Grow Your Cultural Literacy

To facilitate culture change on both an organizational and functional level, it's important to first understand that deeply embedded cultures cannot be replaced with simple upgrades, quick fixes, or even major overhauls. Culture change does not happen overnight. For instance, the University of Mississippi Medical Center (UMMC), one of the largest employers in the state, launched a culture change and rebranding effort that ultimately progressed over 10 years. Dr. David Powe, CEO at telehealthONE in Jackson, helped lead the campaign to make UMMC a more competitive medical center in three mission areas (education, patient care, and research) and improve its "value proposition" as a hospital of choice for employees and the public. Powe described the culture change as having four stages:

- gathering the kindling (starting at the top, focusing your efforts)
- striking the match (educating, communicating, building infrastructure)
- controlling the blaze (measuring progress, strengthening networks)
- maximizing the burn (sustaining progress, staying nimble, continuously improving).

UMMC leaders' commitment to staying the course through these stages was a key factor in achieving such objectives as more grant funding, better talent acquisition, improved research, higher-quality patient care, and a greater number of available medical residencies. Learning leaders need to stress the value of follow-through and commitment during culture change because impatience with the process or conflicting priorities often derail success. More about that in chapter 7.

It's also important for learning leaders to understand what culture is, where it's weak, strong, or inconsistent, and how to best disseminate it through a company. Many organizations use cultural assessments, scans, audits, focus groups, real-time pulse survey tools, or annual engagement surveys to uncover multiple perspectives about what culture is and how it affects employees' motivation, performance, and engagement.

Consider the example of Ericsson, a Swedish communication technology and services provider (Dixon 2016b). To begin the process of creating an employer brand that would help it compete with the world's top companies, Ericsson launched a strategy of "You + Ericsson." The HR and global acquisition team partnered with a recruitment advertising specialist to develop the initial research in 2012. The initial phases included benchmarking and targeted focus groups with the goal of uncovering perceptions about the company as an employer, what attracted employees to the company, and how the company was perceived externally. The brand messages of Ericsson's competitor were also examined. Findings from these efforts defined the direction Ericsson needed to go in terms of building its brand, creating a social media strategy, and designing language around its employer value proposition.

In general, effective culture change needs to draw on positive cultural traits or attributes that are embedded in an organization and minimize negative cultural attributes that might get in the way. Marcia Connor, co-author of *The New Social Learning: Connect. Collaborate. Work.* (2015), also advises learning leaders to conduct periodic cultural audits of their learning organization to identify strengths and improvement opportunities. Similarly, Dave Ulrich, the renowned "father of HR," recommends that talent management and HR professionals conduct regular audits of an organization's underlying "architecture." An organization's architecture determines how it carries out strategy and includes such elements as its culture, competencies, rewards, governance, work processes, and leadership (Ulrich 1998). Here are some factors to consider when developing the architectural foundations of your learning culture.

- **Culture is every day.** Culture is created, sustained, or changed by daily behaviors, interactions, and overall good business practices. Routine emails, meetings, and announcements are all opportunities to communicate and disseminate the message of a desired culture.

- **Culture change doesn't guarantee success.** Having a great learning or workplace culture is no guarantee of sustained excellence or success. It's not something you can impose. Among the biggest barriers to successful culture change are the poor agility and adaptability of the management styles and structures meant to support changes.

- **Culture does not change overnight.** Learning leaders who have successfully grown a strong learning culture admit that it takes time (up to three years or more). Culture doesn't change as much as it evolves.

- **There are always improvement opportunities.** A culture does not have to be toxic to warrant nudges forward. Deckers Outdoor, a leading shoe manufacturer, considers all learning programs to be opportunities for enhancing and driving a corporate culture where people are engaged and inspired to learn (Deloitte 2015).

- **Culture is not one-size-fits-all.** While valuable information can be gained by researching or benchmarking corporate or learning cultures of other companies, it's most important to focus on the values and behaviors that will work best for your business, business unit, or industry.

Chapter Summary

Corporate culture, the shared beliefs and values of organizational employees, is the new currency for growth and competitive advantage. More than ever, executives are turning to learning and talent development functions to transform workplace cultures in pursuit of high engagement and high performance. Culture change and transformation is the one area in which learning leaders are most likely to partner with CEOs. Studies consistently show that organizations with a strong learning culture drive engagement and significantly outperform their peers in terms of time to market, productivity, innovation, and profitability. A mature learning organization has the power to drive business strategy and boost engagement, but only if there is clear alignment between a learning culture and the business strategy. Despite best intentions, most learning leaders fall short in their attempts to create and leverage a mature, credible learning culture, one that can positively move the dial on organizational culture change and engagement.

Use the chapter 3 self-assessment in appendix 2 to identify how your organization patterns its processes and practices to grow a value-added learning culture.

Chapter Highlights

Culture is a key differentiator in the global competition for talent.

Organizations can no longer depend solely on their products and services to distinguish and differentiate them in the marketplace. Organizations that create cultures defined by meaningful work, employee engagement, job, and organizational fit, and strong leadership are better able to attract top talent and outperform their competition.

Learning is a driver for building cultures that promote high engagement and performance.

Factors that drive high engagement and high performance include growth opportunities, leadership capability, meaningful and collaborative work, and a positive work environment, all of which are elements driven by a mature, well-integrated learning organization. These learning and development opportunities are also mechanisms to attract top Millennial workers. If people aren't learning, they're leaving.

Learning leaders must be culturally sensitive and intelligent.

The 21st-century learning leader must be culturally literate and sensitive to facilitate culture change on an organizational and functional level. It's difficult to influence culture change without understanding what culture is and how it affects employees' motivation, performance, and engagement.

Culture takes time to change and evolve.

While many organizations have identified and even begun to implement processes to improve workplace culture, culture doesn't change as much as it evolves. Being able to change an organizational or learning culture requires time, energy, resources, and fundamental shifts in thinking.

Sustainable learning organizations view culture change as an "inside-out" process.

A learning organization cannot be perceived as a credible partner in driving business transformation without first being willing to look at opportunities for transforming, and continually improving, its own strategies, processes and practices. An essential part of "leading with culture" involves elevating the role of the learning organization by continually upskilling, retooling, refreshing, or reorganizing the function.

CASE IN POINT

Background

The Tennessee Department of Human Resources (DOHR) is a cabinet-level department act-ing as the central human resources agency for the state, which is the largest employer in Tennessee. DOHR serves in a strategic support role with overall responsibility for major statewide human resources processes and services for cabinet departments, boards, and commissions in the executive branch, and provides technical and employee development services to the legislative and judicial branches. The department advises the Governor's Office on human resources matters; establishes and maintains statewide human resources policies, guidelines, and rules; provides guidance, consultation, and training to state agen-cies on personnel matters; and directs all professional and leadership development activi-ties for state employees.

DOHR's mission is to provide strategic human resources leadership and partner with cus-tomers for innovative solutions. The department accomplishes the mission and the signifi-cant role of leading human resources throughout state government and providing services to other agencies with 125 employees and an $11.5 million budget. Department leadership has two areas of focus: services provided to customers, mainly within the executive branch, and the management of the department itself, including the continuous improvement of processes and development of employees.

DOHR's role in state government is complex and requires its employees to have solid technical skills and to operate in a constantly changing environment where systems thinking, forward focus, and outstanding customer service are critical. A key component of DOHR's role is to provide a consistent, collaborative platform for the development, implementa-tion, and interpretation of best-practice programs and policies benefiting both employees and state agency leaders. As the state's overarching human resources agency, DOHR views state government as an enterprise and partners with individual agencies in making strate-gic decisions about organization development, employee professional learning, leadership development, and policy implementation.

DOHR has been recognized nationally and internationally for excellence in human re-sources and is the recipient of the 2015 Award for Advancing the HR Profession from the National Association of State Personnel Executives. The Department's commissioner also received the 2009 Eugene H. Rooney Award and the 2014 Honorable Mention Award for Advancing the Profession from the National Association of State Personnel Executives. The department received the 2010 Award of Excellence for a Large Agency from the Interna-tional Public Management Association for Human Resources, the 2012 HR Excellence Facet Awards for Strategy and Learning/Development, and the 2013 Commitment Award from the Tennessee Center for Performance Excellence.

These awards come as a result of programs and processes developed, implemented, and practiced in a continuous learning environment that includes customer feedback and constant process review. The following narrative, based upon interviews with Dr. Trish Holliday, describes how DOHR and the Strategic Learning Solutions (SLS) team became a leader in innovative human resources and learning practices and shaped a high-performing workforce for state government. Elements of the team's five-plus years' journey mirror stages in the Sustainability Cycle.

Recognition Stage

As the assistant commissioner of human resources and chief learning officer for the state of Tennessee, Holliday says her function's key role is to develop the executive branch workforce and provide them with the tools and resources needed to successfully meet talent challenges in state government. The original vision for HR transformation began in 2009, with the alarming recognition that there was insufficient bench strength available to meet the challenge of the impending retirement by talent in critical positions. Other talent challenges at that time included leadership gaps, skill shortages in key roles, heightened competition for talent, loss of experience and knowledge capital, anticipated high attrition of Baby Boomers, and antiquated techniques for employee recruiting or engagement. Given consistent feedback from managers about the negative impact of talent shortages, skill gaps, and outdated employment practices, DOHR and the SLS team committed themselves to the creation of a learning organization as the "true" path to strategic talent development, employee engagement, and continuous improvement. Developing and keeping talent meant shaping a learning culture where people could grow and perform.

From 2009 to 2012, the department made some gradual inroads in refreshing workforce development practices that moved the dial a bit closer toward the vision of a learning organization. However, the enactment of the Tennessee Excellence, Accountability, and Management (T.E.A.M.) Act in 2012 "opened the floodgates" for forward-thinking agencies to start transforming the culture of state government in response to the push for civil service reform. The vision of becoming a more efficient, effective customer-focused government became a call to action for all state agencies and cabinet leaders. Enhancing the government's reputation as a performance-based employer of choice became the top agenda for all state agencies, including Jobs and Economic Development, Education and Workforce Development, Fiscal Strength and Efficient Government, Health and Welfare, and Public Safety. For DOHR, the state's civil service reform brought increased visibility and executive support for replacing and refreshing stagnant hiring and development approaches. With the passing of the T.E.A.M. Act, one indicator of increased support was the elevation of Holliday's CLO role to an executive-level position overseeing L&D for the state's executive branch workforce. DOHR became the proprietor of all professional and leadership development training conducted in government. Tennessee was the first to award a CLO with a seat at the executive table in state government.

Opportunities

To align learning with strategic priorities, Holliday recognized the need to move away from a transactional, activity-based training focus to a more transformational, performance-based one. A renewed purpose, name, and rebranding statement was one of the first steps toward communicating the learning organization's shift from a traditional training role to one focused on learning and performance (Figure 3-3).

Figure 3-3. SLS Purpose

DOHR mission: Providing strategic human resources leadership and partnering with customers for innovative solutions.

DOHR vision: To strategically drive transformation through innovative human resources leadership and practices to shape the best workforce for state government.

SLS purpose: Consulting and partnering with agency leaders to rerate a customized learning strategy that develops and sustains a high-performing workforce.

Source: Holliday (2015).

A continuous improvement perspective was used to create a common language and vision around the transition to a learning organization (Figure 3-4). This helped rally the SLS team around a shared purpose and emphasized the reality that desired changes represented an evolutionary process as opposed to a one-and-done event.

Figure 3-4. Previous and Future States

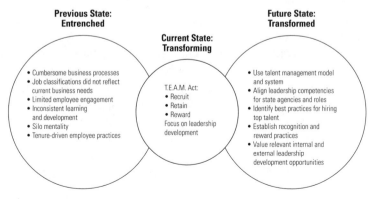

Source: Holliday (2015).

Given the long history of a tenure-based environment, there were many opportunities to refresh or replace antiquated employment practices and "we've always done it that way" mindsets that could block progress, Holliday said.

"We wanted to create more ownership, add more value, and be more collaborative as business partners, not just HR generalists or learning specialists. We saw this culture change as an opportunity to be on the front end of strategic decision making versus just firefighting, reacting, and responding to decisions already made. We had an end goal of supporting our business leaders in hiring, developing, and retaining the talent needed to transform all organizations into a customer-focused, efficient, effective, and sustainable government. The issue of sustainability played into our vision and strategy design from the very beginning" (Figure 3-5).

Figure 3-5. Creating Sustainable Learning Initiatives

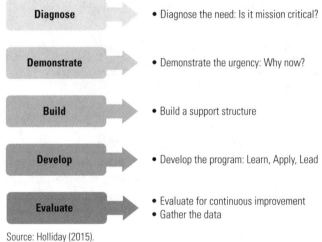

Source: Holliday (2015).

Vision and Alignment

In the process of exploring how to support business needs for standardized learning and development, along with a more customer-centric workforce, SLS team members realized they each held different views about who their "true" customer really was. Differentiating the distinct needs of end users, primary customers, and key stakeholders then became the catalyst for creating a customer-focused learning strategy in which:

- appointing authorities and agency leaders were seen as key stakeholders
- agency training officers and human resource officers were primary customers
- all state employees were seen as end users.

This framework kept "the voice of the customer" paramount in all iterations of learning strategy and solution development. It provided a framework for aligning strategies and solutions with existing business plans, critical talent needs, and established talent management practices. For example, the SLS team of six went from trying to service 43,000 end users to focusing their attention on the learning, performance, and talent management needs of the 41 key stakeholders (the appointing authorities of each agency) overseeing the end user groups.

As illustrated in Figure 3-6, the SLS team developed a Talent Management Wheel to use as their framework for aligning core talent management practices, including:

- Career planning
- Competency management
- High-potential employee development
- Learning and development
- Performance management
- Leadership development
- Succession planning
- Recruitment
- Professional development
- Retention

According to Holliday, all talent management practices are mapped to Lominger Leadership competencies. In addition, SLS team members trained to refine and refresh their own performance consulting competencies to better provide the technical skills and expertise needed to operate in a constantly changing, customer-centric environment. For instance, SLS competencies mapped to the Society of Human Resource Management (SHRM) and International Project Management Association (IPMA) bodies of knowledge with an emphasis on business acumen, systems thinking, forward focus, and customer service.

Learning Solutions and Design

With strategic alignment addressed, the next opportunity became how to tackle and implement change plans for the learning and development function and the organization. The team considered the essential tools, resources, and information each group would need to help them navigate the "massive culture change" from tenure-driven to performance-focused practices. Developing relevant tools and essential learning solutions to fulfill the state's priorities started with focused conversations with agency heads about respective business needs and learning or skill gaps. "We talked with the agency leaders and department heads about how to help them create a high-performing workforce," Holliday says. We moved away from the traditional focus on generic, off-the-shelf training for individual employees to exploring how to drive customized, organizational learning throughout the agency, starting at the executive level." Providing appropriate management support for new performance and coaching processes was key.

Customized Initiatives. Table 3-1 illustrates customized tools and initiatives that grew out of early discussions with stakeholders.

Standardized Facilitation Model. "Elevating the value and responsibility of learning to the executive level was a huge culture shift," Holliday says. Assigning chief proprietorship for learning design and delivery to the CLO and her SLS team led to significant changes felt throughout all levels and departments in the state. The norm had been to have subject matter experts design and provide nontechnical training to their units. Because these experts each had varying skill levels in needs analysis, facilitation, or consultation, there was a lot of inconsistency in what departments were learning and doing to integrate existing initiatives or customer service requirements. Ultimately, this led the SLS team to develop:

- standardized facilitation guidelines
- a Train-the-Trainer certification model for employees, outside of the SLS function, who wanted and were qualified to deliver training.

Figure 3-6. Talent Management Wheel

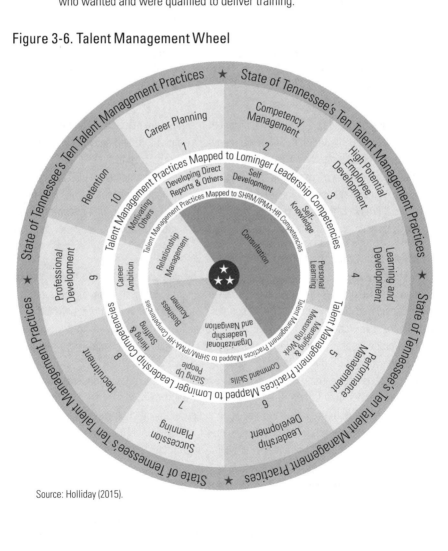

Source: Holliday (2015).

Table 3-1. Customized Learning Initiatives

Professional Development	Tools to Increase Retention
Statewide customer service training	Tennessee Government Leadership (alumni of all state leadership programs)
G.R.E.A.T customer-driven excellence	Tennessee Government Leadership Council
Stat Principles of G.R.E.A.T customer service	Statewide Learning and Development Council
Get S.M.A.R.T. Performance Planning	

Lesson Learned

A key lesson Holliday and her team learned during early-stage strategy and solution development was to stay focused on the mission and the end goal of leveraging a learning culture to foster high performance in the government sector. Specific enabling strategies that helped the team progress through the recognition stage included the following:

Enabling Strategies

1. **Assess where you are.** "To get a bearing on what we were facing—and I thought this was fantastic—commissioners in every state agency (commissioners are like the CEOs of that agency) did a top-to-bottom review. They did a full analysis of all their procedures, practices, policies, workforce, and organizational structures to identify where a customer-focused culture shift would have the greatest impact on the business. That was a really important beginning for us, looking at what messages our policies were sending and what inconsistencies would get in our way."

2. **Define where you want to go.** "The voice of the customer is held throughout everything we do. Having that clarity of direction and clarity of mission has been essential in this change process because we've been able to rally people around it. We also created initiatives and processes that were designed for sustainability from the very beginning."

3. **Follow the rules of engagement.** "We ran culture change like a rebranding campaign and created opportunities to start dialogue and discussion. We started 'listening tours' where agency leaders, directors, and team leaders would reach out to our customers to learn about their needs, challenges, and pain points. These proactive conversations were a nice way to align

people toward a 'customer-centric' workforce because we weren't talking about changing just one branch of government or changing HR; we were trying to change it all. People started wanting to be a part of what we are doing."

4. **Adapt strategies to defined needs.** "We based our learning strategy on the data we gathered from our identified customers and our listening tours. That paid off for us because we were able to not only position ourselves as true partners, but also to catch things before they went wrong."

5. **Engage executive support.** "We changed the conversation from 43,000-plus employees being end users of the training to 'who really should drive learning?' With that, we got away from generic employee training to driving customized learning at the executive level. To me, that was the turning point. Now learning starts with the appointed authorities for every agency, and my primary stakeholder is the head of that agency. I have 41 key stakeholders, in addition to human resources officers and talent management directors. To meet their needs, we sit down and talk about their learning gaps; their talent needs as they create their vision, mission, and strategy; and the most-critical competencies."

Resistance Stage

The path of transformation is rarely trouble-free, regardless of how well designed, supported, or executed the change strategy might be. Following are some of the roadblocks and barriers that the team encountered during its change journey, along with enabling strategies used to move beyond them.

Frontline employees. In the beginning, the SLS team was not well positioned to promote or model aspects of a learning organization with its stakeholders or customers, especially those on the front line. Traditionally, there were few incentives or cultural norms that inspired employees to be lifelong learners. A continuous improvement and growth mindset was not prominent throughout the enterprise. In addition, there was a tendency for employees to be risk averse when confronted with new ways of conducting business or emerging change requirements. This was especially true for those employees who had been conducting training for their department "for years and years" and who were now being asked to standardize learning processes by completing Train-the-Trainer certification requirements if they expected to continue. This issue led to the development of a fundamentals pre-course, meant to provide performance support, increase employee utilization, and improve certification completion rates.

Throughout the change effort, the team prioritized face-to-face meetings with frontline staff when discussing the move from a tenure-driven culture to a performance-based learning culture. "We developed a shared vocabulary for communications and messaging and aligned our change management strategies to help people see where we were going," Holliday says. Ensuring that their primary customers firmly understood the reasons behind the change has been described as "a big part of how we've been able to sustain it. But even now, in this stage of the transformation, it's taken longer than we envisioned. Maybe we could have added more *why* earlier on," she adds.

Training staff. With a training division of six full-time staff, there was some initial concern about meeting new performance demands, combined with a "why fix something if it's not broken?" mentality. Historically, training had been a catalog-driven, generic "check the box" exercise and very employee-centric. Learning and talent development was not well connected to organizational values, mission, and business needs for building and attracting a bench of capable, competent leaders. Upskilling learning and development team members so that they had the proper information and tools to effectively align, design, and deliver performance-based learning (and nonlearning) solutions was key for moving beyond this sticking point. Upskilling focused on growing SLS capabilities (mapped to SHRM/IPMA competencies) in relationship management, business acumen, organizational leadership, and consultation, especially consulting to discern customer needs versus wants. Developing a common language and a consistent performance consulting approach—as in "What business issue are you trying to solve?" versus "What training do you need?"—for working with customers and stakeholders was an important part of building credibility as a strategic business partner.

Middle management. According to Holliday, the largest transitional hurdle during early change efforts was what she called the "forgotten population" in government: the middle managers. From a learning and development perspective, the more than 8,500 supervisors in state government held the key for sending and supporting messages from the executive ranks about how to innovate government. "The middle manager decides who hears what and how it's communicated down throughout the organization. At the same time, middle managers decide which messages from employees to send up the ladder to senior leaders. This is really where the power for change rests. To me, that was the greatest challenge we faced. I think the middle manager is the heart of the organization and where change success lies," Holliday says.

Specific enabling strategies that helped the team progress through these common elements of resistance in the resistance stage included the following:

Enabling Strategies

1. **Link to business objectives.** "With training, we really had to blow up the old ways and change the focus from 'what classes are being offered?' to 'how does learning support the mission and the needs of our leaders so that the workforce is aligned?' And, it might sound trivial, but a significant part of our strategy was to get rid of the word *training* and go to *learning and development.* We took training out of the vocabulary because I wanted to send a message that learning is a process and a continuous journey, not an event."

2. **Use a planned change process.** Top leaders validated and endorsed the holistic change process implemented by the SLS team. "We had to have a starting place with frontline staff. We couldn't just announce the change one day and say, 'mark your calendars, save the date, we're going to become a learning organization!' We focused on what change looks like to go from a tenure-driven culture to a performance-based learning culture. We developed a shared vocabulary for communications and messaging and aligned our change management strategies to help people see where we were going. I brought in some of William Bridges's work on transitions to help employees acknowledge what we were leaving behind and then move to a place where they could see a better future, despite some of the uncertainty and ambiguity that was bound to come. We maintained an active interface with all levels and all groups of customers throughout the entire change process."

3. **Build capability.** "We also knew we had to do more than just talk about change. We had to do something very tangible, something very hands-on with frontline employees to get our message across. We emphasized the role of learning as a critical part of everyone's job responsibility. We trained supervisors on how to write S.M.A.R.T. (specific, measurable, achievable, relevant, time-sensitive) performance plans. We worked to get the subjectivity out of performance reviews so that performance could be evaluated with objective data. We took the time to teach people how to write S.M.A.R.T. goals. Now every single state employee, all the way up to the appointed authority of every agency, has S.M.A.R.T. goals. Another opportunity we

provided was the Fundamentals of Facilitation classes and job aids as precourse support for employees who wanted to be certified facilitators when early passing rates were so low."

4. **Create meaningful experiences.** "With the statewide learning and development council, we solicited their input about what we were trying to do and what tools they needed to be successful in the transition. Then we created an enterprise-wide, across 41 agencies, four-level Leadership Certificate for state supervisors. Level 1 begins with learning modules that provide supervisors with the fundamentals of management. Level 2 focuses on the advanced skills of management. Level 3 focuses on the fundamentals of leadership. Level 4 focuses on the advanced leadership competency. "This created a win-win situation. We were equipping managers and supervisors with learning and core competencies essential for their success. Leaders could now hold supervisors accountable by expecting them to apply the learning. This is what was missing in our old entitlement culture: People didn't have the right knowledge, tools, or competencies to be effective and there was no accountability for employees or managers to grow relevant skills and use them on the job."

Renewal Stage

As noted in chapter 2, renewal occurs when learning transformation efforts have success-fully moved through initial roadblocks and barriers. In this stage of the Sustainability Cycle, the learning organization invigorates its initial commitment to a learning and performance–based culture through increased emphasis on linking learning to strategic directions and ramping up energy and collaboration around identifying where further learning support is needed. Here, Holliday describes how the agency demonstrates a focus on renewal activi-ties, while driving steadily toward full integration of new learning and talent development processes and practices.

Then and Now

In the early stages, the team started with a key group of senior level stakeholders to commu-nicate the vision, develop the strategies around executing it, and work through any areas of resistance among the 43,000-plus people who were affected by the changes, and ultimately responsible for carrying them out. "It wasn't easy and it didn't happen overnight. But we gradually created a whole new performance landscape," says Holliday.

According to Holliday, the department began to see signs of a true learning culture, one that values continuous improvement and feedback. Through a systemic, collaborative approach, they have successfully guided 23 cabinet agencies in their efforts to integrate L&D strategies with performance management, leadership development, talent development, and continuous improvement processes. Most recently, the SLS team refined and customized a performance-coaching curriculum to show supervisors how to coach their employees in the job behaviors needed to meet the changing expectations of work and team performance. "We've designed our own coaching model and taught all supervisors how to coach their employees, with a focus on continually improving their S.M.A.R.T. goals. From linking performance management and coaching, from giving people the information and facilitation tools they need to succeed, we use learning to drive the change toward becoming a more customer-centric organization."

As stated earlier, it is significant that the department's accomplishments have been consistently recognized for excellence in human resources with several awards, including the 2013 Commitment Award from the Tennessee Center for Performance Excellence.

Sustaining Momentum

According to Holliday, sustainability in a public-sector government environment means that change is not driven solely from a political agenda or a single political figure. For instance, every four years in government and, at the most, every eight years (in Tennessee, a governor can serve only two consecutive four-year terms) there will be turnover at the top. "So how do we create and sustain a culture that isn't always feeling flipped, where people feel upside down all the time, and nothing is ever constant? I've had employees tell me, 'Trish, we were here before you got here, and we'll be here after you leave.' That kind of mentality says that things aren't normally introduced in a sustainable way," says Holliday.

Given those conditions, the SLS team deliberately set out to approach this culture change differently. From early stages of development, there was intent to institutionalize changes—to instill a new learning culture that was considered the norm as opposed to a new "flavor of the month." The team worked to create a cultural framework that was agile enough to shift to new leadership, or to allow a new administration to come in and add to it, while ensuring that the true essence of the framework would stay intact.

"We didn't want to build a system that's so tightly closed that it can't adjust to new leaders or new demands," says Holliday. "To be sustainable, it can't be politically charged. Our leadership programs—the Tennessee Government Management Institute, the Tennessee Government Executive Institute, LEAD Tennessee—all of those statewide leadership programs, have already survived administration changes. New leaders have come in and bought into the framework because they could have input and make the programs their own. We intentionally designed them this way."

Integrating the new learning and performance culture with existing Baldrige standards and performance excellence frameworks has been one key to sustaining the value and leadership support of the transformed learning organization throughout its growth. Learning is widely acknowledged as an integral part of any continuous improvement endeavor. Another key contributor to the continuous renewal and sustained success of the learning organization's transformation has been the use of councils such as:

- A Statewide Government Leadership Council composed of alumni from statewide leadership programs led by Commissioner Rebecca Hunter and Assistant Commissioner and CLO Holliday. The council meets monthly and drives five strategic areas.
- A Statewide Learning and Development Council. Led by Commissioner Hunter and Assistant Commissioner and CLO Holliday, the council consists of the one primary individual responsible for learning and development within each state agency. The council meets regularly to ensure a seamless, strategic approach to L&D enterprise-wide. A significant accomplishment by the council has been the development of a universal certification guide for all state certified facilitators.

The councils foster connections, promote a continuous learning community, and engage employees in sharing how they are applying new skills, disciplines, and approaches toward performance excellence goals that have now become ingrained in the organizational culture.

Measures, Metrics, and Continuous Improvement

"Our grounding philosophy is that talent management drives agency results when leaders use the right data to align business and people strategies," says Holliday. Figure 3-7 shows targeted results of the transformation effort, which included increased image or brand power, financial viability, productivity and engagement, andcustomer satisfaction.

Figure 3-7. Desired Results

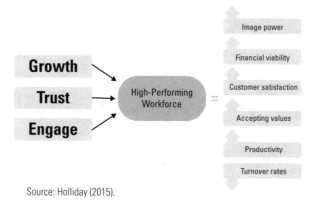

Source: Holliday (2015).

Compiling and collecting individual agency measures of success was originally approached as a hand-off exercise for the 23 cabinet agencies that manage their own continuous improvement processes, including customized milestones for ensuring accountability.

These measures are all submitted to the governor as part of the agency's annual performance plan. A sample dashboard of SLS learning measures is shown in Figure 3-8.

Figure 3-8. Sample Dashboard

Engagement in Statewide Leadership Programs		
Measure Name	Measure Calculation per Quarter	Current Measure
Participation in three statewide leadership programs	Number of agencies, boards, and commissions that participate in statewide leadership programs (LEAD, TGEI, TGMI)	45 out of 45
Participation in the Leadership Black Belt Program	Number of new leadership program alumni participating in the program (target: 25)	88 new members
Participation in TN Government Leadership Conference	Number of participants in the conference (target: 375)	518 attendees
Learning effectiveness: relevance	Percentage of Learning Pyramid Certified Trainers who found the learned skills to be usable in their daily work (target: 90%)	94%
Learning effectiveness: relevance	Percentage of customers in leadership programs who indicate that the learned skills are relevant to their daily work (target: 90%)	91%
Process Measures: Developing Organizations		
Measure Name	Measure Calculation per Quarter	Current Measure
Agency participation	Number of TM Executive Series sessions completed as of 3/31/2016	19
Agency satisfaction	Number of new agencies that rate satisfaction with the TM Executive Series as a 4 or 5 on a 1-5 scale (target: 4)	9
Agency academy participation	Number of leadership academies currently in process as of 3/31/2016 (target: 90%)	6
Quality of SLS-facilitated leadership programs	Percentage of participants surveyed who responded and rate learning programs as a 4 or 5 on a 1-5 scale (target: 90%)	87%
Get S.M.A.R.T.-er	Percentage of managers and supervisors who strongly agree or agree that the learning objectives were accomplished (target: 95%)	92%

Source: Holliday (2015).

According to Holliday, improvement opportunities for metrics and measurement include increased tracking of customer satisfaction at the enterprise-wide level, not just at the department or "miniature business" level. "That's our current target for continuous improvement as a learning organization. We also want to start benchmarking more. Overall though, we've made great strides towards becoming a high-performing, customer-focused learning organization. The journey is ongoing and our vision remains intact. It's amazing to see how people have risen to these new expectations around learning, performance, and accountability."

Specific enabling strategies that have helped the team grow more mature, value-added learning practices during the renewal stage included the following:

Enabling Strategies

1. **Keep it flexible.** "Changes happen all the time in the public sector: changes in priorities, leaders, structures, budgets, and legislation. It's an issue, and organizational leaders have to pay attention to the friction it can cause. We had to create a cultural framework that can be agile enough to shift to new leadership [and] new demands."

2. **Foster connections.** "We still talk about what matters and help people understand how they connect to what matters, how we're learning and growing together, how important it is to treat one other as internal customers. If we didn't take time to build those connections, our desired results likely would not have actually occurred. The Learning Council also helps engage others in being part of an ongoing learning community that's become 'ingrained in our culture.'"

3. **Increase accountabilities.** "We've established milestones of accountability that have helped turn things around. This is what was missing in our old entitlement culture. All of those measures are turned in to the governor on dashboards that are part of an agency's performance plan."

4. **Focus on continuous improvement.** "The voice of the customer is held throughout everything we do. Right now our target for continuous improvement is to track customer satisfaction at the enterprise-wide level."

Figure 3-9. Key Actions

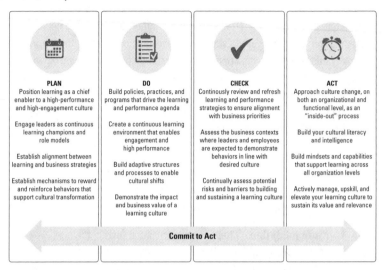

PLAN	DO	CHECK	ACT
Position learning as a chief enabler to a high-performance and high-engagement culture	Build policies, practices, and programs that drive the learning and performance agenda	Continuously review and refresh learning and performance strategies to ensure alignment with business priorities	Approach culture change, on both an organizational and functional level, as an "inside-out" process
Engage leaders as continuous learning champions and role models	Create a continuous learning environment that enables engagement and high performance	Assess the business contexts where leaders and employees are expected to demonstrate behaviors in line with desired culture	Build your cultural literacy and intelligence
Establish alignment between learning and business strategies	Build adaptive structures and processes to enable cultural shifts		Build mindsets and capabilities that support learning across all organization levels
Establish mechanisms to reward and reinforce behaviors that support cultural transformation	Demonstrate the impact and business value of a learning culture	Continually assess potential risks and barriers to building and sustaining a learning culture	Actively manage, upskill, and elevate your learning culture to sustain its value and relevance

Commit to Act

Case Review

This example shows how a pioneering public sector agency transformed the enterprise into a learning organization in response to critical talent management challenges and demands for civil service reform. The drive toward a more accountable, customer-focused government represented a complex, comprehensive culture change for both the organization at large and the learning and development teams as facilitators of the change.

"Leading with culture" was both the means and the end of this large-scale effort. To help employees thrive during the transition from a tenure-based to a performance-based environment, Holliday and her team focused on creating adaptive learning and development structures that allowed movement in concert with shifting business needs. Table 3-2 includes the characteristics of a sustainable learning organization that enabled their success.

Table 3-2. Characteristics of a Sustainable Learning Organization

Characteristic	Examples	
C-Level Engagement	• CLO role elevated to executive level • Demonstrated executive support for learning as a strategic asset • Shared accountability by leaders and managers for championing learning and performance	✓
Efficiency	• Integrated use of nontraining performance solutions associated with quality (Baldrige) or process improvement (LEAN) tools. • Focused alignment of learning solutions with established talent management practices	In Progress
Effectiveness	• Effectiveness of learning solutions mostly measured by qualitative approaches at the business unit level • Measures primarily focused on collecting participation, relevance, and satisfaction data • Measures of customer satisfaction being developed at the enterprise level	In Progress
Utility	• High utilization of performance management support tools, resources by managers and supervisors • Learning utilization measures submitted quarterly for executive review	✓
Investment	• Increased investment in learning and talent management tools, resources to support civil service reform, improvement goals • Increased investments in "up-skilling" DOHR staff to meet changing business needs and new performance requirements	✓
Credibility	• Highly credible, award-winning learning leaders, recognized as best in class internally and externally • Highly credible, award-winning learning organization	✓
Demand	• High demand from stakeholders across all levels for DOHR consulting or coaching services for continuous process improvement purposes, improved decision making, and effective talent management	✓
Governance	• Cross-functional governance councils ensure that learning and continuous improvement processes reflect defined quality standards (Baldrige, LEAN) and are consistently applied across the enterprise	✓
Continuous Improvement	• Learning and talent management processes built upon Baldrige and LEAN foundations of continuous improvement • Learning councils meet regularly to assess improvement opportunities	✓
Resilience	• Flexible, scalable learning and performance framework designed to withstand changes in the political landscape	✓

Since measurement processes and practices are not fully operationalized or optimized, the Tennessee DOHR has not yet reached the refinement stage. Specifically:

- **Effectiveness.** DOHR continues to evolve its measurement and measurement practice. Quarterly dashboard data appear focused on output measures (number of participants) and reaction (Level 1) feedback about learning effectiveness (satisfaction, relevance, utility). Quantitative methods for evaluating organizational impact of the learning organization and its contribution toward customer-focused outcomes have not yet been developed or adopted.

- **Efficiency.** Some monitoring of time, usage, and cost indicators for the learning organization is in place, but more robust efficiency targets and tracking methods are in progress. The team is beginning to explore benchmark data to set standards for efficiency.

Practice 2: Develop and Distribute Leadership

"The more you're engaged in learning, the more successful you are at leading."
—James M. Kouzes and Barry Z. Posner (2016)

"One of the tenets of a good leader is to never stop learning."
—Colin Powell

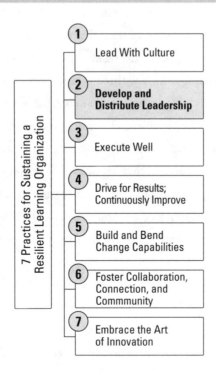

What's in This Chapter

- the role of senior leaders in building and sustaining a learning culture
- how to engage leaders and managers as active business and learning partners
- how solving leadership issues increases executive support for an integrated, sustainable learning organization
- how to leverage learning to develop and distribute leadership across all organizational levels.

IN OCTOBER 2015, KATE RENWICK-ESPINOSA BECAME the first female president of VSP Vision Care, the nation's largest healthcare organization by membership and the largest of VSP Global's five lines of products. Based in Rancho Cordova, California, VSP Vision Care has 75 million members around the world and a network of 32,000 doctors, making it the largest eye care doctor network in the United States. Renwick-Espinosa started working at the company after graduating with a bachelor's degree in economics more than 23 years ago and has moved up through the ranks since then. To prepare for her leadership transition from chief marketing officer to president, Renwick-Espinosa embarked on "a listening-and-learning tour" for three months, meeting with stakeholders from customers to doctors. In an interview with *Sacramento Magazine*, she described learning as a key enabler in her mission to reimagine the vision-care experience and create a better future for Sacramento. "I would describe myself as a learning leader. I believe in making ourselves uncomfortable," she said in the interview. "And by that I mean, to get something you've never had, you have to do something you've never done. And that will likely be an uncomfortable experience. But if you never feel uncomfortable, you probably aren't learning; you probably aren't stretching yourself" (Howard 2015).

A high-performing, sustainable learning culture cannot exist without committed leaders like Renwick-Espinosa who communicate and emulate the value of learning. Leaders shape the culture, structure, and climate that encourage or discourage the movement of ideas through learning and the execution of those ideas through job performance. Leaders play a crucial role in both knowledge distribution and idea creation. They foster the avenues of connection that spark innovation, encourage risk, and inspire creative problem solving. They must be not only advocates of continuous learning, but also active learning consumers, champions, and role models. Put simply, the fastest way for a learning organization to grow and evolve into one that enables high performance and engagement is through the visible commitment and active embodiment of learning by its leaders.

Voices From the Field

Our role as talent development officers is to engage the leaders of our organizations in embedding learning and development and its key innovations into the fabric of our business.

—Rahul Varma, Chief Learning Officer, Accenture (Parker 2016)

Engaging leaders to support and nurture an embedded learning culture is not a one-and-done event, but rather an ongoing development and relationship-building process. Throughout the process, you need to ask yourself two questions: How effective are your leaders at instilling learning into the fabric of your business? And how effective is your learning organization at leveraging learning to engage leaders and build their leadership capability?

The Senior Leader as Learning Champion

GE is a well-known example that illustrates how senior leaders have taken active roles in support of a learning culture. GE's leaders view learning as part of leading. They spend time and energy on regularly developing others' talent. They move employees from one business to another to broaden their perspectives, deepen skills, and provide meaningful challenges that will stretch and build talent. GE also expects its leaders to create and follow an annual plan for their own development so they can keep growing. While GE emphasizes learning through experience, it provides other kinds of stimulation through exposure to thought leaders from inside and outside the organization.

When GE's senior leaders demonstrate a personal commitment, implicit or explicit, to learning and development, it underscores how the organization values learning as a chief enabler of individual and organizational performance. In these situations, senior leaders care about aligning business and learning imperatives, investing in learning and development resources, removing barriers, and empowering leaders across all levels to achieve positive results.

These cases tend to be more the exception than the rule, however. More often, the organization's chief learning officer (CLO) or the HR department has the exclusive responsibility for development, and a very small percentage of leaders consider development to be a critical personal or workplace responsibility. Yet when leaders at the top embrace their role in developing capacity and capability across all levels, it makes a difference.

Laura Hackett, senior director of learning and development at MillerCoors, said that support from senior leadership is a critical part of a business strategy focused on determining the capabilities needed to "set us apart." In a *TD* interview, Hackett described how the North American joint venture of MillerCoors spurred the inception of a robust, blended talent management strategy focused on a continuous learning philosophy in which "leaders teach." According to Hackett, "neither partnering company possessed a learning culture to speak of" and each relied heavily on traditional, off-the-shelf content for development. To stay competitive amid tumultuous shifts in the brewing industry, the CEO of MillerCoors actively partnered with the learning and development team to create a learning culture in which critical in-house capabilities are continually built and maintained (Harris 2015a).

Executive ownership of development begins with what some call a "growth mindset" (*Harvard Business Review* 2014a). Firms with a growth mindset value potential, capacity, and a passion for learning, which in turn makes them more profitable and more likely to attract and retain talent. Sustainable learning cultures have long been associated with high performance, strong financial outcomes, and improved employee engagement. For example, Chico's, a national retailer of women's attire, has placed learning and development at the top of its strategic agenda and has posted 34 consecutive year-over-year quarterly earnings increases. Its executive team believes that enterprise-wide employee development will propel the company to even higher levels of performance and profit.

Voices From the Field

What do executives in sustainable learning organizations do differently? They ask "What can I do to support that?" instead of "What do you need to support that?" It's called ownership.

—Ronnie Ashline, Experiential Learning Advocate, Google Fiber, Xerox

Gaining Executive Commitment

Senior leadership support is critical to the learning leader or CLO position, which rarely exists without the blessing of the CEO. Whether tasked with sustaining results from a single project, momentum for a multiyear change initiative, or support for a fully embedded learning and performance culture, learning leaders need executive support for approval of time, money, expertise, and resources. Approval generally comes from a committed sponsor who has the authority and desire to ensure that learning and performance projects, processes, and practices are implemented as planned. Sustaining sponsors are those stakeholders (staff, managers, clients, board members, labor unions, community members, funders) inside and outside an organization responsible for leading or supporting learning and performance improvement efforts in their functional area of the organization. These groups represent the needs of key business units and are an important source of future talent.

Demonstrated support from both sponsors and sustaining sponsors is needed to build and sustain a learning organization. For example, learning leaders must work hand in hand with both groups to get alignment on development needs and shape the enterprise-wide processes—recruitment and retention, learning and development, succession planning, career development, and change management—that communicate cultural values and drive performance. The best way to engage senior leaders, sponsors, and managers as learning champions is to address the issues that keep them up at night.

Leaders' Top Challenges

According to *The Conference Board CEO Challenge 2015*, human capital is the number-one challenge for CEOs, as it was in 2013 and 2014. To combat this persistent challenge, CEOs and their organizations have invested heavily in talent development, especially leadership development. For example, about $130 billion spent on training annually in the United States goes toward management and leadership training (Bersin 2014). Yet most organizations say that these investments are not working or add little value.

Research also shows that bolstering organizational bench strength to better meet future needs is a major concern for today's executives, with CEOs prioritizing four human capital strategies (Mitchell et al. 2015):

- Enhance the effectiveness of the senior management team.
- Improve leadership development programs.
- Improve the effectiveness of frontline managers.
- Improve performance management.

Learning leaders can influence human capital strategies and elevate their strategic value by contributing solutions to meet key leadership challenges. Let's look at how a learning organization can achieve sustained impact with these four leadership priorities (Figure 4-1).

Enhance the Effectiveness of the Senior Management Team

The most frequent skills gaps identified by senior leaders relate to fundamental business execution skills such as strategic thinking, leading change, motivating people, and making decisions from an enterprise perspective. In a volatile, uncertain, complex, and ambiguous work world, leaders' effectiveness in these areas is key to their ability to plan for and adapt to the future. How do best-practice organizations leverage learning to close these skills gaps and engage senior leaders as partners in building essential capabilities?

Figure 4-1. Addressing Leadership Challenges

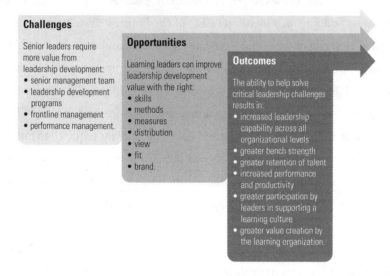

At BNSF Railways, senior leaders take an active role in working with the learning and HR organizations to make talent management and leadership development strategies more effective and visible. For instance, the executive chairman and the CEO participate in monthly executive-level talent management discussions to stay on top of strategy and change issues related to succession planning and looming leadership gaps created by retiring senior leaders. As a result, more than 90 percent of senior leadership openings have been filled internally, allowing BNSF to keep up its bench strength (Salopek 2015c).

Here's another example from Major League Baseball's Chicago Cubs organization. In an article from *Talent Management*, Bryan Robinson, vice president of human resources for the Chicago Cubs and a former GE employee, said that the Cubs organization has done its part to ramp up talent acquisition and a development culture through several transformative initiatives. For example, the Cubs partner with Northwestern University's Kellogg School of Management, where Robinson and his team of "strategic doers" participate in regular management and leadership development activities to bolster their own development and increase their organization's talent development prowess (Kalman 2015).

Consider, too, the example of Frances Hesselbein, former CEO of the Girl Scouts and now president and CEO of the Frances Hesselbein Leadership Institute. Hesselbein took a job with the Girl Scouts on July 4, 1976, when the organization was losing membership and struggling to attract volunteers. She approached leadership of the Girl Scouts as if it were IBM or GE, often persuading people at the top of their field to donate their services to her cause. She was convinced that high-level learning and development was required to build and sustain the transformation she believed the Girl Scouts needed. She engaged thinkers such as education and leadership pioneer John Gardner, leadership scholar Warren Bennis, and management guru Peter Drucker to speak to and work with Girl Scout leaders. She created partnerships with Harvard Business School faculty to help develop the strategic planning, finance, negotiation, and professional management skills of local council CEOs and national staff.

Because the Girl Scouts is a franchise organization, Hesselbein did not have the power to choose, fire, or promote council leaders, so she had to make the most of what she had to further her vision. During her tenure, the Girl Scouts' membership rose to 2.25 million girls, relying on a workforce of 780,000, most of whom were volunteers. A 1998 Presidential Medal of Freedom recipient, she is credited with leading a turnaround for the Girl Scouts and increasing their minority membership (Hesselbein 2013).

A partnership model, such as the ones the Chicago Cubs and Girl Scouts enlisted, can be invaluable for improving the effectiveness of the senior management team, especially for learning organizations with limited budgets and resources. This chapter's Case in Point gives another example of how a future-focused executive leveraged a learning culture to improve the effectiveness of his senior management team and create a sustainable leadership legacy.

Improve Leadership Development Programs

Truly sustainable learning organizations continually improve their leadership development efforts so that they remain relevant to changing business needs and evolving skill demands. Consider this: Organizations that take the time to invest in high-quality leadership development programs are more likely to benefit from engaged leaders and increased bench strength (Figure 4-2).

Figure 4-2. The Benefits of High-Quality Leadership Development Programs

Organizations with high-quality leadership development programs are:

7.4 times more likely to have leaders who are highly engaged and inclined to stay with the organization.	8.8 times more likely to have high-quality leadership and bench strength compared with those with low-quality programs.	3.0 times more likely to rank in the top 20 percent for financial performance, when leaders become more effective at leadership skills important to the organization.

Source: Mitchell et al. (2014).

To help senior leaders maximize their investments in leadership development, sustainable learning organizations focus on using the right approaches; targeting the right skills; distributing leadership roles, responsibilities, and skills across all organizational levels; taking the long view; and measuring development results.

Use the Right Approaches

Effective approaches for building leadership capabilities include the combined use of self-reflection exercises, 360-degree feedback, coaching, mentoring, action learning, and online learning platforms, such as massive open online courses and game-oriented simulations where participants are placed in real-world scenarios. By applying these approaches, learning organizations can engage executives and business partners as learning champions and begin to institutionalize a learning culture.

LEADERSHIP DEVELOPMENT AT A LARGE PUBLIC UNIVERSITY

The University of California, Davis, excels in public education and research, with a world-renowned faculty for more than 35,000 enrolled students and an academic ranking of 11 among public universities in the United States. Pressing talent management challenges include an aging workforce, a high percentage of retirement-eligible employees, and a number of high-demand positions at risk of attrition due to competition from the private sector. To sustain a leadership pipeline and upgrade skills as job demands get more complex, the university maintains a strong commitment to attract, retain, and develop talent.

The university's talent management team uses a mix of formal and informal methods to develop leaders and promote career mobility across a cross-functional, matrixed environment. Development programs for high-potential leaders have evolved into cache initiatives in which participation is highly selective and based on a nomination process. In addition to instructor-led training, sample approaches include:

- stretch assignments, in the form of actionable projects, completed by teams of three
- blended learning, including classroom, e-learning, writing assignments, and reading
- cohort programs
- "Day-in-the-life" sessions in which leaders share their expertise and lessons learned from their careers
- networking luncheons where high-potential employees can meet senior leaders and improve their visibility.

Senior leaders are highly involved and visible as mentors and learning champions, and they have worked closely with the talent management team to break down silo thinking, where some managers have been hesitant to develop their employees due to fear of losing them to other departments or organizations.

According to Carina Celesia Moore, director of the university's Talent Management Center of Expertise, "over 30 percent of recent cohorts have been able to experience increased mobility within their positions. Managers have begun to see the benefit of giving people the opportunity to move around so that we can keep our talent in house. These approaches have improved our metrics around engagement, retention, and mobility, and have been so successful that we've received institutional funding to continue running them. Meeting immediate and future needs for strong leaders has grown our learning culture and helped our learning organization to be more sustainable."

PRACTICE 2: DEVELOP AND DISTRIBUTE LEADERSHIP

From a design perspective, leadership programs are often run by traditional, ritualistic activities that have changed little over the years. For example, many leadership programs, particularly at the senior level, are structured as face-to-face, multiday events. Hybrid or blended learning approaches can increase field-based, action learning; reduce classroom time; and increase engagement. Leadership faculty can be project facilitators and observers of actionable projects, rather than simply "sages on the stage." Some best-practice learning organizations use a real-time redesign approach where leaders are asked at the end of a leadership development program to redesign the program for the next cohort of rising leaders. Elliot Masie, chairman and CLO of the Masie Center's Learning Consortium, challenges learning leaders to continually look at the design dimensions of leadership development programs to improve their efficiency and effectiveness (Masie 2011).

Finally, the right approaches for leadership development include providing the proper context for the use of learned knowledge and skills. Context is a critical component of a high-quality leadership development initiative because a leader may be effective in one situation but ineffective in another. Learning leaders can help grow leaders' capability by:

- ensuring the proper blend of formal learning, learning from others, and experiential learning
- putting a stronger emphasis on programs that foster creativity and innovation
- matching specific change skills to real-world demands for each leadership level (frontline, midlevel, senior level)
- expecting leaders to examine their own growth mindsets
- designing powerful learning journeys rather than traditional learning events
- focusing on growing collective leadership capabilities across the organization
- integrating networking tools for follow-up on development plans and post-training communication.

Target the Right Skills

The right skills for one organization may not be the right skills for another. For best results, leadership development should focus on the skills best aligned to the organization's mission, vision, and culture; its individual and organizational capability needs; and its leaders' strategic business goals.

For instance, here's how Twitter targets the right skills for development. In an interview with *Chief Learning Officer*, Melissa Daimler, head of learning and organization development at Twitter, said that every formal training program or team-based initiative is designed to be relevant "in the moment" and scalable globally (Whitney 2015). She said the philosophy and purpose of the learning and organization development function is to create an environment of learning where "we're not only setting Twitter up for success, we're setting Tweeps [Twitter's name for its employees] up for life. How do we help them develop the skills not just for Twitter but beyond?" To that end, Daimler said she worked with her team to develop the Twitter Core 5, five skills that all managers should learn and practice: coaching, delegating, deciding, directing, and developing.

Additionally, BNSF Railways says the right skills for its development initiatives focus on engineering safety and risk identification as part of its continuous improvement journey from compliance to commitment. To help the company turn a strong safety record into a stellar one, the learning organization has "completely revamped" itself by undergoing a four-year evolution to better align learning and development approaches with the right leadership skills needed by functional areas of the business (Salopek 2015c).

Distribute Leadership Roles, Responsibilities, and Skills Across All Organizational Levels

Distributed leadership, for our purposes, means pushing out and sharing leadership roles, responsibilities, and development opportunities with others. It's similar to good, old-fashioned empowerment and delegation, and the opposite of "command and control." Too many organizations restrict leadership development opportunities to C-suite executives or high-potential individuals, to the detriment of their other employees. David Ulrich, a partner in the esteemed RBL group and a renowned HR thought leader, has written that a major problem with leadership development today is that there is too much focus on the individual and not enough on the collective. Of course, growing collective leadership capacity will only work with the right:

- **leaders.** Leaders have to be willing to let go of always being the expert, solving problems, and making decisions.

- **employees.** Not everybody is ready for increased responsibility. Good candidates have a track record of seeking out new and bigger responsibilities, can handle ambiguity, and have strong problem-solving and decision-making skills.

- **organizational structure and systems.** Organizations that promote collective leadership and practice distributed leadership have processes that embed leadership into operational and talent management systems.

- **tools and resources.** Employees can't be prepared to lead without the proper information, tools, and resources. This includes relevant development opportunities and ongoing, accessible, timely performance support and feedback.

- **direction and values.** Managers at companies such as Johnson & Johnson, Google, Southwest Airlines, and Walmart have a lot of local autonomy but make decisions based on clear boundaries and a solid sense of mission, vision, and values.

Organizations that have successfully put those conditions in place for developing their leaders have achieved significant benefits. For instance, Telus, Haworth, and Vi demonstrate how developing and distributing leadership skills across all parts of the organization can lead to high performance and greater innovation.

Telus

Telus engages employees throughout the enterprise to "take pride in owner-ship" for world-class continuous learning opportunities that are not just about isolated leadership skills or product knowledge. This development approach has led to the highest engagement score globally for a company its size, along with proven success in client excellence and total shareholder returns, which the company attributes to the innovative leadership skills and attributes of high-performing, dispersed teams.

Haworth

Family-owned Haworth, of Holland, Michigan, designs, manufactures, and sells workspace components with 650 dealers serving customers in 120 countries. Following a 2010 partnership with the Center for Creative Leadership, the company launched the Haworth Leadership Institute to develop the leadership competencies considered vital for current and future success. The Institute promotes personal and development opportunities for managers, leaders, and executives, as well as aspiring leaders, to support the organization's goal of 70 percent promotion from within. Any employee seeking future leadership opportunities is eligible for the Aspiring Leader program, which seeks diverse, cross-functional participation (ATD Staff 2015b).

Vi

Chicago-based Vi operates residential retirement communities across the country. Vi's learning strategy strives to build its institutional learning and capability, and its leadership has a personal and extensive commitment to learning. Vi's head of learning sits on the executive management team and works with other executives to develop learning initiatives for the company. Employees chosen for Vi's frontline management development program receive personalized letters from Vi's executives congratulating them on their selection. Executives also meet with employees during the management development program to offer individual coaching, lead discussions, and share knowledge. In 2015, for the fifth year in a row, Vi was awarded the

LearningElite designation by *Chief Learning Officer* for its excellence in learning and development (Vi Living 2015). According to Sarah Kimmel, director of research and advisory services at *Chief Learning Officer*, Vi is the smallest company to reach the top 10 (it ranked number 7), which shows that even smaller organizations can make an impact. "It's not all about scale and size—it's about a passion for learning and the commitment of leadership to developing their people," said Kimmel (Vi Living 2015; Sipek 2015a).

Take the Long View

While there is no one-size-fits-all leadership development process, the most important thing to remember is that leadership development is a long-term cultivation process. So how can learning leaders address immediate leadership needs while still keeping an eye on the future? Consider the following example from another LearningElite winner. In an interview with *Chief Learning Officer*, Michael Molinaro, vice president and CLO at New York Life Insurance Company, described how he and his team created an accelerated leadership program to develop the next generation of leaders and tap potential earlier in employees' careers. This 14-month development initiative combines experiential learning with academics and challenges employees to go outside their comfort zone by applying leadership behaviors to real New York Life casework (Kahn 2013).

Molinaro said that during his first four years as CLO, the learning organization focused on building development programs in response to talent challenges. Subsequent efforts focused more on building the right infrastructures to fully integrate a development culture and ensure that all the parts worked together in an "easily understood, digestible way." The long view toward building a mature, sustainable learning culture is evident from Molinaro's comment: "We've got to have a sense of legacy and bring our important past forward, but we've got to make sure that we have a sense of permanence. That means looking forward to make sure that we are going to be here a hundred or more years from now" (Kahn 2013).

Measure Leadership Development Results

While investing in leadership development has been shown to pay off, many learning leaders continue to struggle with defining the business value of development investments. CEOs and sponsors want metrics that show how these investments relate to improvements in engagement, productivity, speed-to-proficiency, customer satisfaction, or sales. Yet as many as three in four organizations do not formally measure leadership development or attempt to link program success to important performance or business impact measures (Gurdjian et al. 2014). Of those that do measure program effectiveness, most report using general output data—courses, participants, hours of training—to justify training impact.

Learning organizations need to fine-tune their measurement to become a sustainable partner in business decisions. Measuring and evaluating processes for leadership development can help:

- Identify opportunities for improving individual and organizational capability.
- Demonstrate value that is relevant for your sponsors and stakeholders.
- Inform decisions that could affect future investments.
- Build confidence in your team's ability to contribute to organizational needs.
- Support supervisors in their efforts to improve team performance.
- Close gaps that prohibit the transfer of learning.
- Isolate factors that help or hurt job performance.

While the results from measuring a leadership development initiative might not be instantaneous, learning leaders need to raise the bar and follow the example of organizations such as American Express, Siemens, Accenture, and Caterpillar. In addition to demonstrating an active commitment to leadership development, starting with the CEO, these world-class organizations relentlessly monitor program success through business linkage and impact measures (Ray and Learmond 2013). Chapter 7 provides further examples of how learning leaders can use effective measurement and evaluation practices to demonstrate the business value of learning and cultivate support for a sustainable learning organization.

Improve Effectiveness of Frontline Supervisors and Managers

CEOs know that frontline supervisors and managers are vital to sustaining quality, service, innovation, and financial performance. Many learning professionals, including Peter Cappelli, director of the Center for Human Resources at the Wharton School, argue that frontline managers are more important today than ever before because "spans of control are bigger—each manager supervises a lot more people—and we also expect those frontline workers to do more, to be more responsive to customers, to cross-sell, to solve problems" (*Harvard Business Review* 2014a).

Here are a few reasons why equipping frontline leaders with better leadership skills makes good business sense:

- **Frontline leaders tend to manage 80 percent of the workforce.**
  In every performance metric, from customer satisfaction to employee engagement to productivity, frontline leaders are integral to business success in mission-critical ways.
- **There's a talent shortage.** Company growth, coupled with large percentages of retiring senior leaders, requires organizations to continuously expand their efforts to create talent pools for key positions. Most organizations do not do enough to "prime the pump" with first-line and emerging leaders. Identifying frontline and midlevel candidates for promotion and systematically preparing them to assume greater responsibilities and skill sets will improve the overall leadership pipeline.
- **Equipping leaders** at all levels with the skills needed to cultivate an engaged workforce will ultimately result in stronger, sustainable

capabilities for both individual job performers and the organization as a whole.

Improving the effectiveness of this vital group can take many forms, such as on-the-job training, classroom training, personality and leadership assessments, online learning, 360-degree feedback, coaching, and mentoring. Consider this example of how KPMG, a professional services company, has used mentoring to improve managerial effectiveness (Rouen 2012). KPMG worked to ingrain mentoring in its company culture through its Leaders Engaging Leaders program, which pairs the top 60 managers with members of the management committee, the board of directors, and national managing partners. Everyone in the organization has a mentor. The goal is to introduce mentees to available leadership opportunities. It also helps KPMG's leaders become familiar with managers that they might not otherwise meet.

Yet many organizations fail to provide enough leadership development. A 2014 *Harvard Business Review* report on frontline managers found that only 12 percent of 610 respondents said their organization invests sufficiently in developing frontline managers—first-level leaders whose direct reports are employees with no management responsibilities—to meet rising job demands, despite 77 percent saying that these managers are important in helping their organization reach its strategic goals.

In addition, leadership development at the frontline manager level tends to be ad hoc, sporadic, and too brief, with nearly 44 percent indicating a frequency of once a year or less (*Harvard Business Review* 2014a). Most described their development processes as "largely ineffective" in how they were administered.

Failure to properly invest in frontline manager development and the inadequacies of most current development efforts for this segment have contributed to serious leadership pipeline deficiencies. According to the *Global Human Capital Trends 2015* report, 86 percent of respondents, which included C-suite executives, said they are seriously worried about their leadership pipeline (Deloitte 2015). While organizations may differ in what they believe is most critical to leadership and business performance, prioritizing leadership behaviors that have broad relevance to *any* business situation is a good place for learning leaders to focus (Figure 4-3). These behaviors account for 89 percent of leadership effectiveness, according to McKinsey & Company's 2015 report *Decoding Leadership: What Really Matters* (Feser et al. 2015). By helping identify which skills or behaviors matter most, learning leaders can put their organization one step closer to restocking its talent pool.

Figure 4-3. Skills Associated With Leadership Success

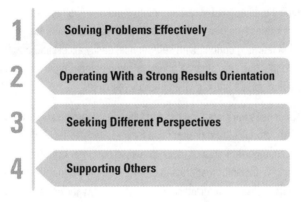

1 Solving Problems Effectively

2 Operating With a Strong Results Orientation

3 Seeking Different Perspectives

4 Supporting Others

Source: Feser et al. (2015).

Voices From the Field

In the technology industry, growing and retaining top talent is a mission-critical business need. Our talent development team continually works with senior leaders to identify key roles and positions that will most influence the company's ability to remain competitive in a global marketplace.

Our extended HR team works with senior leaders on a regular basis to get the right people in the right roles at the right time through our talent management software tools and ongoing dialogue between employees and leaders.

Leadership development is a top priority for individuals in these high-potential roles. Our senior leaders understand that talent development requires a long-term commitment in terms of investment dollars and sponsorship support, even at the expense of some other initiatives that may not be seen as equally strategic.

We've also worked with senior leaders to prioritize a commitment to frontline leadership development. Because we are hiring many Millennials, we want to ensure that their managers are equipped to work with them skillfully in the quest for productivity and optimal employee engagement.

We found increased expense and redundancy with customized development in each region or country. As a result, our talent development and organization development teams spent time in focus groups asking whether it was important that managers in one country had the same skills and tools as managers in others. We discovered that the answer was a resounding "yes"—a common language and a common set of management tools and practices were needed to properly develop and retain talent across all our locations. Meeting frontline expectations for career mobility and development support was critical to maintaining our talent pipeline. Since then, we've made great strides in creating robust, low-cost, blended learning options with self-service, easily accessible portals. Just-in-time topics such as conducting performance appraisals and delegating effectively are supported through self-service portals and our virtual library resources.

Our current challenge is balancing the need for low-cost learning solutions and skills development with strong cultural preferences for more face-to-face learning in high-touch cultures. This is an important area of focus for us, so our organization development teams have been working with senior leaders and other stakeholders to raise awareness about the issue and come up with optimized solutions. We're now looking at enabling business units to provide more face-to-face learning opportunities.

—Mary Ellen Kassotakis, Senior Director, HR Organization and Talent Development, Oracle

Improve Performance Management

Effective performance management processes, the hallmark of high-performance learning cultures, are critical in helping organizations face rising pressures to perform more effectively and efficiently, execute better on business strategy, and do more with less to remain competitive. Yet there is a growing wave of discontent with traditional performance management practices, and their future in the American workplace seems in question. For instance, a Deloitte survey found that 58 percent of companies did not think performance management was an effective use of time (Nabaum et al. 2014).

The consequences of poorly structured performance management processes are significant. Misaligned individual performance goals and business strategies can waste time and resources. Morale can suffer if there is no differentiation in performance ratings, development opportunities, or compensation between high and low performers. Inconsistent evaluation criteria and rewards can result in lower productivity, reduced engagement, and higher attrition. Decisions about learning and development priorities, along with decisions about learning resource allocations, can suffer if performance information is unavailable or difficult to access. Last but not least, legal issues can occur without proper documentation related to performance.

On the other hand, when effectively implemented, performance management can offer a wide range of benefits for employees, managers, senior leaders, and their companies. For example, when organizations effectively integrate learning and development with performance management, they are:

- three times more likely to report good employee results
- 55 times more likely to report strong overall talent management results
- 100 times more likely to report strong business results (Jones 2011).

Effective performance management processes also allow managers and leaders to evaluate and measure individual performance and optimize productivity by:

- aligning employees' day-to-day job tasks with strategic business objectives
- providing accountability around performance expectations
- tracking individual performance to support compensation and career planning decisions
- establishing focus for learning and skill development
- providing supporting documentation for decisions related to the annual performance appraisal.

A learning organization can increase its sustainability by helping leaders solve performance management issues. High-functioning performance management processes strengthen the links between strategic business objectives and day-to-day job behaviors. How can learning leaders help improve performance management and tighten these links?

Reconfigure the Annual Performance Review

In 2013, Corporate Executive Board research found that 86 percent of organizations were planning to make—or already had made—significant changes to their performance management system (Kropp 2013). Learning leaders can serve a vital role in revamping their organization's performance review process. Consider how three forward-thinking companies have done it:

- **GE** replaced its annual formal review process with a personalized and timely approach aimed to reflect the speed, flexibility, and collaborative spirit that drives the GE culture forward. The new approach emphasizes frequent conversations, coaching, and continuous development. Leveraging advances in mobile technology, GE enabled the process with a simple app to log priorities, capture conversation notes, and share feedback.

- **ConAgra** is testing a new ratings-free performance review process, which replaces a rated review with a series of conversations designed to engage managers with the projects employees are working on and how they are achieving their goals. In this way, managers become more like coaches than judges.

- **New York Life Insurance Company** created Real Talk learning programs as a way for managers and employees to engage meaningfully on performance management. Since program implementation in 2012, managers and employees have begun to set fewer but more strategic goals. Additionally, performance management favorability has increased 11 percent on employee satisfaction surveys (Staff 2012).

Rethink the Use of Peer Feedback

Many organizations have found real value in peer-based performance management. Facilitating peer feedback has been shown to improve workplace collaboration and provide increased visibility for employees' performance contributions. For example, Ceridian, a Minneapolis-based human resources software provider, leverages technology to aid in peer reviews and help make sense of the information being collected. It developed Conversations, a system that allows feedback to be solicited and gathered in real time, as opposed to traditional 360-degree feedback models that operate off set times for collecting feedback. Because traditional feedback approaches can be colored by experiences that occur between project completion and project review, in-the-moment peer reviews can collect performance feedback that is closer to what actually occurred.

Despite the great potential for peer feedback to improve current performance review models, there are common design and implementation challenges to keep in mind:

- Defining how the goals for a peer feedback approach align with greater organizational goals.
- Determining the rating criteria employees should use when evaluating a peer's performance. Many experts recommend eliminating a rating scale altogether so that employees can focus on comments about behavior instead of numerical values.
- Ensuring that employees are trained to provide credible performance feedback. However, some thought leaders like Marcus Buckingham contend that managers or peers are not credible or reliable raters of other people's performance, even with training and time.
- Identifying how to roll out the new peer review approach to the entire organization. GE rolled out its new performance management process using an iterative framework. Hearsay Social is on a five-year plan to integrate peer feedback into its performance management process.

Consider Fit

While there are many exciting innovations happening in the world of performance management, it's important to remember that what works for one may not work for another. As with any change in organizational structure, learning leaders need to ensure that a change to the performance management process fits with organizational culture and senior leaders' strategic goals.

Leadership Begins Within: Building Your Brand

A key feature of a mature learning organization is its sustainable brand as a pocket of excellence, a function that creates value and enables high performance. For a learning organization to become known as a pocket of excellence, its learning leaders must model a business-centric, results-focused approach. Consider Holbrook Hankinson, CLO for Delta Global Services. In an interview with *Chief Learning Officer*, he said he gained traction with Delta's new president and the rest of the leadership team by positioning learning as a key enabler for business success and by establishing himself as a vital member of the C-suite (Gale 2016). In meetings with business-unit leaders and chief executives, he asked business-focused questions related to finance, operations, and management challenges. From these meetings, he helped Delta implement formal metrics to evaluate compliance. He enhanced his credibility, value, and brand as a learning leader by partnering with the IT department to create integrated software for pulling and tracking compliance training. These measures are now part of monthly reports to stakeholders.

Credibility has many layers, but one common theme is to be believable in what you say and do. Credible learning leaders must exercise and leverage the same leadership capabilities that help their organizations survive and thrive in a competitive, global marketplace. After all, the message of a technically sound leadership development strategy is meaningless if people do not believe the messenger. To that end, learning leaders cannot expect to influence leadership behaviors without a commitment to shaping their own personal brand as a leader. And this means educating themselves on all functions of the business to determine how their learning organization can best engage senior leaders and contribute to effective leadership development efforts.

Supported by the many examples and best-practice behaviors from learning leaders in this chapter, here are some specific ways to gain credibility as a business leader and engage executives in effective partnerships:

- Be sensitive to others' needs.
- Build and share your knowledge.
- Exceed expectations.
- Think like a business leader, not a learning leader.
- Bring new ideas to the table.
- Promote achievements.
- Be accountable.
- Build relationships.

The sustainability and long-term value of a learning organization hinges on the business acumen and initiative of learning leaders who continuously strive to increase their personal brand and the credibility of their learning organization brand as a pocket of excellence. Remember, pockets of excellence are contagious and can spread throughout an organization.

Voices From the Field

To build and grow an engaged workforce and a sustainable learning culture, it's important to identify your high performers and make sure they have the support they need. Support means that employees have the opportunity to grow in a safe environment where it's OK to take risks, and even to fail, and where resources are readily available on demand.

A second sustainability challenge relates to how the value of learning is communicated and modeled in the workplace. Great organizations will nurture a learning and development culture starting with commitment from the top. They'll also make learning opportunities accessible across all levels of the organization.

The third challenge relates to how well performance improvement is linked to learning and development. Rewarding the desire to learn is important, but a sustainable learning culture is one that knows how to align learning to actual performance improvement, at an individual and organizational level.

—Kevin Sheridan, Employee Engagement Expert and
Bestselling Author of *Building a Magnetic Culture*

Voices From the Field

Credibility is a blend of personal characteristics and technical competence. You need both to be credible. Credibility comes from the confidence in knowing your own brand and knowing how to be an evangelist for your talents and strengths. Your brand represents what you stand for, what you're good at. With clients, it reflects how easy you are to work with, how fast you can get a contract turned around, how genuine you are. It's about how you manage the process as well as the consulting relationship. In a large, geographically dispersed, global organization, it can become more challenging to find opportunities to let people know about your brand. It takes a lot of work to earn it, but you can lose it in just minutes.

—Jason DeLeon, Integrated Service Manager, Intrepid/Xerox

Chapter Summary

CEOs continue to prioritize human capital strategies that focus on closing leadership gaps and improving leadership capabilities. Ineffective, out-of-touch leadership is a major concern because it leads to employee disengagement, poor customer service, high turnover, and, ultimately, loss of revenue. Learning leaders who can contribute to solving their organizations' top human capital challenges are more likely to enhance their strategic value and build and maintain executive support for a learning culture over time.

Research shows that closing leadership gaps and helping senior leaders better meet future challenges is largely accomplished by improving leadership development and performance management processes, practices, and programs. This can only happen with the visible commitment and active embodiment of learning by organizational leaders across all levels and functions. In best-practice, sustainable learning organizations, senior leaders view learning as part of leading and actively support a "continuous learning" culture. Embedding a learning culture with actively engaged senior leaders is not a "one and done" passive activity, but rather an ongoing development and cultivation process. To generate a commitment to continuous learning from the C-suite, middle managers, and frontline employees, learning leaders must also establish credibility as true business leaders, not just as learning and performance, talent management, or human resource experts.

Use the self-assessment in appendix 2 to identify patterns and possibilities for developing and distributing leadership capabilities within your own organization and learning function.

Figure 4-4. Key Actions

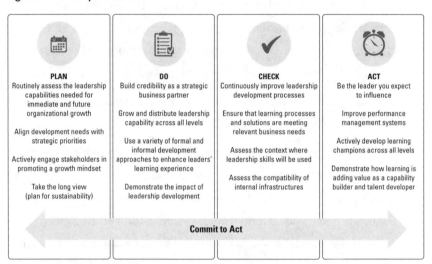

PLAN	DO	CHECK	ACT
Routinely assess the leadership capabilities needed for immediate and future organizational growth	Build credibility as a strategic business partner	Continuously improve leadership development processes	Be the leader you expect to influence
Align development needs with strategic priorities	Grow and distribute leadership capability across all levels	Ensure that learning processes and solutions are meeting relevant business needs	Improve performance management systems
Actively engage stakeholders in promoting a growth mindset	Use a variety of formal and informal development approaches to enhance leaders' learning experience	Assess the context where leadership skills will be used	Actively develop learning champions across all levels
Take the long view (plan for sustainability)	Demonstrate the impact of leadership development	Assess the compatibility of internal infrastructures	Demonstrate how learning is adding value as a capability builder and talent developer

Commit to Act

Chapter Highlights

Sustainable learning organizations have engaged and supportive leadership.

While what good leadership looks like varies, most experts agree that leadership matters, particularly to the success of a learning culture. Engaged and supportive executive leaders view learning as a strategic asset and a chief enabler of individual and organizational performance.

Engaged leaders are lifelong learners who champion and embody a commitment to learning.

The best executives consider themselves learning leaders and consider the developmental agenda to be their responsibility and part of achieving business results. They help remove barriers and empower learning capabilities across the organization to drive performance growth, engagement, and innovation. The more frequently, and authentically, that leaders model a commitment to learning, the more engaged and high performing the workforce will be and the more sustainable the learning organization will become.

Sustainable learning organizations cultivate leadership support by solving leadership problems.

CEOs across the globe have prioritized leadership development as a top human capital challenge. Learning leaders that can positively influence leadership challenges cited by C-suite leaders are more likely to enhance their immediate and long-term strategic value. Adding strategic value by helping resolve critical business issues wins the respect and appreciation of CEOs and builds executive support for learning as a key component of business success.

Sustainable learning organizations build and distribute leadership across all organizational levels.

The investment required to manage, coach, inspire, and build a leadership pipeline for the future depends on every level. Yet many organizations fail to provide enough leadership development to all managers. Frontline leaders, in particular, need special attention. Learning leaders can address these gaps by helping their organization move toward more collective leadership development efforts.

Sustainable learning organizations measure the impact of leadership development efforts.

CEOs have identified the need to close leadership gaps and improve leadership capabilities among their top human capital challenges. As such, investments in leadership development continue to rise, along with executive concerns that these investments are not paying off. While the impact of leadership development efforts may take time to mature, most organizations don't do enough to ensure that they are meeting strategic objectives, enhancing the effectiveness of the senior management team, or improving the effectiveness of frontline supervisors and managers.

You don't have to be big to have big impact.

Not all organizations have access to corporate universities, expansive budgets or staffing resources, or sophisticated technology options for best-in-class learning design or delivery. Many organizations meet this challenge through the use of partnership models with internal or external resources to distribute and grow leadership capabilities.

Be the leader whom you expect to influence.

Leadership starts from within. Turn your expertise into a personal brand and strategically expand the capabilities that define you and your learning organization. Emphasize your full range of talents and business acumen so that your learning expertise doesn't pigeonhole you. Continuously communicate and demonstrate the value of your brand.

Case in Point

The following Case in Point shows how a progressive executive focused on development as the catalyst for creating a sustainable leadership legacy. It's based on interviews with Bob Anderson, former CEO of Horizon House, and Ron Morey, president and CEO of Profound Results Consulting.

CREATING "GRACIOUS SPACE" FOR A LEGACY OF LEARNING

Bob Anderson began seriously thinking about his legacy as a leader more than 10 years ago. Anderson is former CEO of Horizon House, a retirement community serving more than 550 residents in the Seattle region. He envisioned Horizon House as a recognized leader and innovator in the creative aging industry, a model community of choice dedicated to dignified aging, life fulfillment, and service to the broader community.

To actualize that dream, Anderson enlisted the help of Ron Morey, president of Profound Results Consulting, along with the company's executive team (the chief operating officer, chief financial officer, health services officer, and chief marketing officer) and a board strategic planning group called the Futures Committee. They developed a 10-year plan (through 2017) for a sustainable future, which they monitored, refreshed, and annually reviewed. This plan modeled a framework of three pillars: strategy (key priorities and imperatives), tactics (resources and methods for executing strategies), and people (the role of all stakeholders in fulfilling the promise of the company's vision and mission). Collaborating with all stakeholders—the board, executive team, managers, directors, line staff, residents, and community members—was vital in crafting this preferred future vision to combat the growing competition from larger privately funded retirement communities emerging locally, regionally, and nationally.

Horizon House distinguishes itself from its competitors by providing residents with a "gracious space" of community living and quality of life. It engages everyone in creating a deep sense of hospitality. In much the same manner, Anderson and his executive team sought to create future-focused strategies that would promote this gracious space and a communal focus on learning, allowing communication and innovation to thrive. To focus on continuous improvement and sustainability, Horizon House aspired to become a learning organization where "teamwork, collaboration, and trust were our watchwords," Anderson says. In his view, there could be no growth or improvement without a solid foundation of personal, team, and organizational learning, and the strategic role of learning had to align with the three pillars of the 10-year plan. For example, learning became a strategic imperative; learning became a prioritized tactic for executing strategies; and learning investments played a vital role in creating a fulfilling environment for people involved in all levels of the company. Within this context, Horizon House worked with Profound Results Consulting to ensure that learning was consistently integrated with its strategic values, vision, and direction. Consulting services included the co-creation of strategic work plans and facilitation of quarterly executive team meetings to track progress against goals.

"It was important that everyone, from the board of trustees, to managers and employees from all departments, understood the big picture and how they fit in. It was also important that they had the right tools, information, and resources to succeed," Morey says. Leaders were firmly committed to a "loyalty strategy" of "preserving and protecting" talent investments so that capable people would "stay with us for the long haul," according to Anderson.

Nine years in, the plan, and its principles and practices, remain solidly embedded as a corporate compass, despite a number of challenging times and disruptions, including the 2008-2010 economic downturn. Yet during the downturn, Horizon House never lost a step because of its clear internal focus and ability to stay on its strategic course. While many organizations abandoned their strategic learning programs during the recession due to financial pressures, Horizon House maintained its investment in leadership and people development, which helped it remain financially stable and emerge from the recession stronger than ever. "During a period of time when many individuals were putting off decisions about retirement, and senior living occupancy rates were lower than they'd been previously, leaders' commitment to continuous learning, growth, and sustainability never wavered. Their unified vision and conviction to the 'long view' kept them focused on the 'vital few' imperatives instead of the 'urgent many,'" Morey says.

Another sustainability challenge around that time involved prolonged, contentious union negotiations. According to Anderson, "During all of this distracting and divisive activity, we held to the core leadership principle of gracious space and found a way to defuse the situation and come to a win-win labor agreement. We were a better organization for having to practice our commitment to 'learning in public' and 'inviting the stranger' and we kept our leadership integrity intact."

After 16 years of service, Anderson retired in June 2015, leaving "a very impressive halo across the organization, as well as into the senior living industry at large," says his successor, CEO Sara McVey. The executive team at Horizon House has been recognized, regionally and nationally, as one of the strongest executive teams in the industry due to a legacy succession plan that emphasizes leadership and professional development as a strategic imperative. Local, regional, and national residential living centers have identified the gracious space leadership model as a best practice in the industry. "Looking back over time, all milestones set over the past 10 years of strategic planning have been met," Morey says. Based on key industry measures—financial performance, occupancy rates, and resident satisfaction—Horizon House has achieved and maintained top-level results in all areas of performance. And that tradition of industry leadership is being sustained and enhanced now through the effective CEO succession planning process completed in mid-2015.

Anderson's three primary goals were to complete a legacy plan that was built upon strongly committed leadership, ensure a level of philanthropic support to sustain the company for decades to come, and install a strategic road map that aligned vision, mission, and values as the foundation for future growth and development. For example, Anderson promoted a culture of philanthropy to support the company's mission that no residents are left behind if they exhaust their resources for residential living expenses due to a longer life span. Philanthropic goals are achieved through annual fundraising efforts by executives, managers, employees, and residents alike, to support the company's endowment fund. In 2014, the five-year goal was to raise $9 million for the fund; within two years, $8 million had already been raised, prior to Anderson's retirement.

"The underlying story that has generated this success is the legacy planning and commitment to building a learning community where challenges were viewed as opportunities; where problems were openly addressed in a spirit of openness and genuine inquiry; and where creative solutions were achieved in a spirit of collaboration," Morey says. "If you look at their current occupancy rate—they've gone from 90 to 97 percent occupancy [from 2009 to 2015]—this is phenomenal within the context of industry standards and a true testament to Anderson's legacy of strategic leadership."

Anderson learned much during his 16 years leading Horizon House. When attending a national conference, he was struck by a mission statement he heard from the CEO of a for-profit company who was making a presentation. "When I heard his motto I thought to myself, 'That's me, that's what I believe and have tried to do all my working life," Anderson says. "And it goes like this: Love people, serve people, add value, have fun!" The last phrase may seem like a throwaway, but it is really about "sharpening your saw so you can reach back into your love of serving and add value to everything you do."

Case Review

This Case in Point shows how a future-focused executive leveraged a learning culture to improve the effectiveness of his senior management team, share and distribute leadership across all organizational levels, and create a sustainable leadership legacy. The commitment to a learning organization was based on understanding early (recognition stage) that there could be no growth or improvement without a solid foundation of personal, team, and organizational learning. As CEO, Anderson and his executive team worked with a consultant to interweave learning into the three pillars of their 10-year plan.

In addition, Anderson and his team committed to principles and practices of "servant leadership" to create responsive and collaborative structures that allowed movement in concert with shifting employee, resident, or business needs. The strong foundation of trust and shared leadership built by the executive team in the early stages of its 10-year plan helped the company withstand the pressures of an economic downturn and divisive union relations during challenging and disruptive times (resistance stage) from 2008 to 2009. To maintain its success (renewal stage), Horizon House developed a disciplined and rigorous system of managing to goals and objectives; initiated succession planning at key levels of the organization to assure continuity of leadership and effective management transitions; and achieved a targeted membership of prospective residents so the future residency pipeline could thrive. This example clearly illustrates how the visible commitment and active embodiment of learning by organizational leaders, collectively across all levels, can facilitate performance growth, engagement, and sustainability.

For more than 10 years, Horizon House's learning and leadership principles, practices, and structures have been progressively renewed and refined to the point where they are now fully integrated and optimized (refinement stage). Specifically, Horizon House exemplifies the following characteristics of a mature and sustainable learning organization (Table 4-1).

Table 4-1. Characteristics of a Sustainable Learning Organization

Characteristic	Examples	
C-Level Engagement	• Shared commitment and accountability to principles of "servant leadership" among senior leadership team. • Leadership viewed as a conscious choice to aspire to lead • Leadership owned and distributed from C-suite to every supervisor • All actively engaged in building a strategic vision based on shared mission, values, and goals, yielding a long-range plan and commitment to sustainability owned by staff, trustees, residents, and community partners	✓
Efficiency	• Consistent focus on ensuring that financial results were sufficient to realize strategic goals: "No margin, no mission" • Maintaining fiscal strength and stability integrated in quarterly dashboard review • Efficiency indicators of learning intrinsically linked to financial measures such as net operating margin, the fundamental driver of Horizon House's strategic plan	✓
Effectiveness	• Leadership and board effectiveness is measured by a Balanced Scorecard, where "vital few" qualitative and quantitative measures (operating margin, occupancy rates, staffing to budget, performance in the broader community) were assessed quarterly	✓
Investment	• Leaders committed to the loyalty strategy of preserving and protecting investment in equipping capable people with tools they need so that they stay with the company long term • Leaders continually choose to invest in customized versus off-the-shelf learning solutions to address desired outcomes and relevant business needs • Senior leaders actively engaged as training facilitators	✓

Table 4-1. Characteristics of a Sustainable Learning Organization (cont.)

Characteristic	Examples	
Utility	• A disciplined and rigorous system of managing to goals and objectives was used at every level of the organization • Utility reinforced with a continuity of leadership approach, where C-suite members and managers commit to monthly meetings for three to four hours of customized training to learn together • Leaders set expectations that participants will bring and apply learning to their departments between meetings • Vocabulary and principles associated with the principle of gracious space were used and modeled by all leaders, managers, employees, and board members • Strong system of performance management was used to connect individual employee goals to organizational goals	✓
Credibility	• Confidence and credibility were established through the gracious space leadership model, where leaders and managers committed to regularly learning in the same space to listen to one another's challenges and provide support • Horizon House has been recognized for excellence by local, regional, and national associations for its leadership model	✓
Demand	• The demand was high for the gracious space leadership model within a number of senior living communities	✓
Governance	• The board of trustees oversees operations and policy compliance with a Balanced Scorecard, a continuous process improvement approach to ensure that organizational goals are properly mapped and aligned • The board of directors applies the strong business discipline of a scorecard to govern work plans and increase accountabilities for their eight committees	✓
Continuous Improvement	• Continuous improvement and renewal were integrated into leaders' commitment to Stephen Covey's "sharpen the saw" principle • Horizon House adopted the Quality First Covenant set by LeadingAge, a national senior living trade association	✓
Resilience	• Resiliency bolstered by a culture of philanthropy and a firm commitment to fundraising to ensure that no residents are left behind if they exhaust their resources for residential living expenses • Expansion of its endowment fund is a critical piece of Horizon House's sustainability perspective and mission • Leaders are committed to maintaining and exceeding the debt service coverage ratio to ensure that the company's income and assets are sufficient to get a high borrowing rate • Leaders are committed to achieving a targeted membership of prospective residents so the future residency pipeline can thrive • Succession planning initiated at key levels of the organization to ensure continuity of leadership and effective management transitions	✓

Practice 3: Execute Well

"Without strategy, execution is aimless. Without execution, strategy is useless."
—Morris Chang
CEO of Taiwan Semiconductor Manufacturing Company (TSMC)

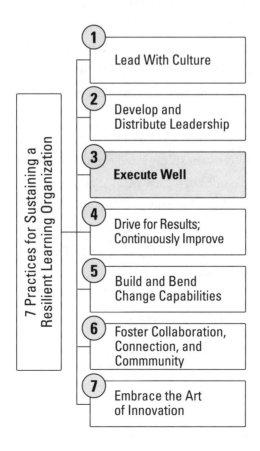

What's in This Chapter

- how effective execution translates business strategy into results
- why effective execution matters to the business of learning
- why execution unravels and what to do about it
- how a learning culture can help model and drive effective execution.

WHILE CEOS AND SENIOR EXECUTIVES TEND to have a clear idea of what strategy is and why it's important, they seem to know less about how to execute it. Most executives say they have little faith in their organization's capabilities to execute its strategy (PwC 2014). There are a number of reasons for this. First, organizations are often structured in a way that separates responsibility for setting strategy from implementing it. "Blue-sky" thinkers in a corporate office don't have much contact in this regard with divisional, functional, or geographic heads. Second, strategy development has historically been a static, linear process focused on the long term and heavily informed by an external (market and competitor) perspective. However, in today's complex, fast-changing environment, strategy development and execution must be dynamic, near term, and iterative.

PwC has conducted extensive research around why organizations struggle to close the gap between strategy and execution. Over the past five years, their studies have resulted in a database of 125,000 profiles representing more than 1,000 companies, government agencies, and nonprofits in more than 50 countries. Findings show that half of executive respondents consider setting a clear and differentiating strategy to be a major challenge (PwC 2014; Strategy& 2016). Of additional significance is that:

- 49 percent report that their company has no list of strategic priorities.
- 64 percent say that their biggest frustration factor is "having too many conflicting priorities."
- 56 percent say one of their biggest challenges is allocating resources in a way that really supports the strategy, while another 55 percent say the same about ensuring that day-to-day decisions are in line with the strategy.

- 82 percent say growth initiatives lead to waste at least some of the time.

This leads to important implications for learning leaders. The gap between strategy and execution provides ample opportunities for learning leaders to add sustainable value by improving execution capabilities for senior leaders and the organization at large. But how can learning organizations align learning and performance growth strategies to business priorities when strategic priorities are not in place, insufficiently formulated, improperly resourced or integrated, or perceived to be a waste of time? That can be a tall order when learning leaders face similar hurdles in linking strategy and execution in relevant, credible, sustainable ways.

In the learning and development space, best practices tend to focus on implementation tactics related to specific initiatives. For example, a great deal is written on designing or delivering implementation plans for specific learning strategies (such as leadership development), implementing change management steps for singular initiatives, or implementing learning transfer strategies to support and sustain performance related to isolated learning or performance solutions. But execution strategies that show how to embed a mature learning culture, versus a stand-alone learning solution, tend to be few and far between. What we know about strategy execution on a programmatic or systemic level is that it matters and it's difficult. With that perspective, a good place for learning leaders to start adding value is with a clear understanding of what execution is, where it tends to break down, and how to fix it.

DEFINITIONS

Implementation: the actions needed to execute or practice a plan, method, design, idea, model, standard, or policy. Implementation is the action, or series of actions, that follow preliminary planning. It is the building process of moving an idea from concept to reality.

Execution: the completion of actions into operation and effect. Execution is the manner, style, or result of performance. True execution is about measuring the impact of implementation actions on the results desired.

The What and Why of Execution

Many say that strategy is about deciding what to do and execution is about making it happen. Larry Bossidy and Ram Charan, in *Execution* (2002), contend that it's "a specific set of behaviors and techniques that companies need to master in order to have competitive advantage." In general, sound execution requires clear goals, regularly measuring progress toward those goals, and clear accountability for progress.

Beyond that, successful execution depends upon a disciplined, systematic, data-driven process. David Vance (2010) defines *disciplined* as a predictable process with clear rules and expectations, where methods for executing strategies are defined and optimized over time for consistent outcomes. This speaks to the notion of sustainability. A sustainable learning solution is one driven by a disciplined, data-driven process of planning and execution. This in turn leads to more optimal and consistent outcomes. A learning organization that can't execute data-driven strategies and processes for multiple learning solutions over time will not be sustainable.

Where Execution Breaks Down

Managers from hundreds of companies, from countless surveys, paint a remarkably consistent picture of where strategy to execution breaks down. Typical barriers include flawed information flow, faulty decision making, poor coordination, limited commitment and accountability, and failure to disinvest.

Flawed Information Flow

Senior executives are often shocked by how poorly their strategy is understood throughout the company. Many of today's middle managers complain that strategic objectives are not only poorly understood, but also poorly related to one another and seemingly disconnected.

Part of the problem is that executives believe that communicating strategy through an endless stream of emails, management meetings, and town hall discussions is a key to success. But the amount of information flow is not the issue. In fact, more middle managers find the number of organizational priorities to be the greater barrier to understanding strategy than a lack of clarity in communicating these priorities (Sull, Homkes, and Sull 2015). To help ease the flow of information about strategy and improve execution, executives need to isolate key priorities and focus on communicating them in ways all employees can understand. To paraphrase Stephen Covey, "Start with the big rocks when filling the jar."

While execution is typically driven from the middle, it needs to be guided from the top. Most managers are committed to doing their best to execute the strategy, but many say they are hamstrung in their efforts to translate overall company strategy into meaningful actions because top executives don't provide enough support (Sull, Homkes, and Sull 2015). Adding to the confusion is the tendency for business units to behave like silos when information does not flow across different parts of a company. Just 55 percent of individuals from organizations that perform well in execution find that information flows freely across organizational boundaries; that drops to 22 percent for organizations that perform poorly (Neilson, Martin, and Powers 2008). The end result is that the organization loses the opportunity to develop a cadre of up-and-coming managers well versed in all aspects of the company's operations.

Learning leaders often face the same level of confusion about where to focus and align learning and performance strategies when information is not flowing freely and messages about strategic priorities are mixed. A climate of moving targets and flawed communication from executives will ultimately erode any potential for immediate or sustained learning or performance impact. Executing learning strategies in the right way doesn't help if execution is focused on the wrong thing.

Faulty Decision Making

Faulty decision making interferes with information flow and prompts work-arounds that can subvert formal reporting lines and cause duplication of time and effort. A common decision-making issue within poor-execution companies is the tendency to second-guess decisions after they've been made. Whether someone is second-guessing depends on your vantage point. While a more senior, broader enterprise perspective can add value to a decision, managers up the line may not be adding incremental value; instead, they may be stalling progress by micromanaging subordinates' jobs and diminishing their own strategic line of sight.

Consider this example from a large learning organization serving a bi-state, third-generation retail company. Rapid growth due to new leadership and a corresponding increase in the depth and breadth of program offerings created additional strain on daily training operations. Many managers within this learning organization had come up through the ranks and took intense personal ownership of learning and development projects. Delegation of tasks, even at the most mundane level, was discouraged. As the organization grew, managers' inability to delegate led to decision paralysis and a lack of accountability. When there was doubt over who should make a decision, the default mode was to have a series of meetings in which no decision was reached. When decisions were finally made, there was generally no one person who could be held accountable because the decision had been vetted by so many parties.

An attempt to expedite decision making through providing regional managers with subject matter experts in newly established central and regional centers of excellence became instead another logjam. Key managers did not know how to take advantage of these centers of excellence, so they didn't. Ultimately, the learning organization's leadership team went back to the drawing board and brought in a performance consultant. The team developed a decision-making map to help clarify decision rights at all levels of management and identify where different types of decisions should be taken. There were some clear benefits. Delegation of standard operational tasks is now actively encouraged. Accountabilities increased once people had a clear idea of what decisions they should and should not be making. Clarifying decision rights and responsibilities brought renewed energy and strategic focus to the organization's service mission. And the organization is better able to track individual achievement, helping to chart new career paths and improve retention of learning and performance staff.

Poor Coordination

In large, complex organizations, execution often exists with middle managers who run critical business functions and with technical experts who occupy key spots in the informal networks that get things done. These organizations have at least one formal system for cascading goals downward, as well as methods such as cross-functional committees, service-level agreements, and centralized project-management offices that manage commitments across boundaries. But most managers believe those systems do not work well and that more structure is needed in the coordination processes across units. Coordination across boundaries is also complicated by conflicts that can arise when different units pursue their own objectives or when factions exist within the C-suite, making some agendas politically charged. These "turf wars" detract focus on what is best for the business.

At its fundamental level, execution is about the ability to seize opportunities that align with strategy while coordinating with other parts of the organization on an ongoing basis. Effective coordination is a critical element of effective execution. Learning leaders are in a key position to help executives develop structured processes to facilitate coordination and strengthen the capabilities of executives and other senior leaders in modeling cooperation and teamwork. Chapter 8 talks more about how learning leaders can grow collaborative skills across the organization and promote collaboration as a driver of execution excellence.

Limited Commitment and Accountability

Even if execution activities are well coordinated, commitment is another important factor that determines how well an organization achieves its strategies. Managers are far more likely to blame insufficient support from other units for missing performance commitments than they are to blame insufficient support from their own team (Sull, Homkes, and Sull 2015). Additional findings from a survey of 8,000 managers reinforce that resource support and performance commitments are lacking in many organizations (Figure 5-1).

Figure 5-1. Fast Facts

22%	20%	59%
Managers who say their organization effectively exits execution of an unsuccessful initiative	Managers who say their organization effectively shifts people across units to support strategy execution	Managers who can rely on colleagues in other departments all or most of the time when coordinating execution

Source: Sull, Homkes and Sull (2015).

Managers that intentionally duplicate efforts, let promises to customers slip, or purposely delay their deliverables are often compensating for poor commitment from their cross-functional colleagues. These dysfunctional behaviors can then escalate to more conflicts between functions and units, all of which undermine execution. How often have you witnessed the fallout? Learning leaders can add sustainable value by helping executives and managers identify and remove barriers that prevent individuals from working cooperatively across silos. As discussed in chapter 6, shaping an accountability culture is a key element of sustainable execution for learning leaders.

In addition, learning leaders can add value by assessing whether talent management processes help or hinder the coordination and commitment that is essential to effective execution. For example, when organizations make decisions related to hiring, promotions, and nonfinancial recognition, they are more likely to reward past performance than a track record of collaboration. However, while performance is critical, it can undermine execution if it comes at the expense of coordination. Most managers believe that their organization would tolerate managers who achieve objectives, but fail to collaborate with colleagues in other units. Daily team performance, and overall execution results, will suffer if companies espouse core values focused on teamwork, but then fail to recognize, reward, and model collaborative behaviors.

Failure to Disinvest

Organizations often struggle to disinvest from initiatives that continually drain resources and fall substantially short of their intended impact. Many managers complain that their companies fail to exit declining businesses or kill unsuccessful initiatives quickly enough. Knowing when to hold and when to fold is a big factor in effective execution. Consider LEGO Group, which went from losing a million dollars a day in 2004 to being the world's largest toy company in 2015 by cutting back in areas where it didn't have the capabilities to win and by investing more in the capabilities that mattered most to the global LEGO community. While a conventional approach may have been to go "lean" across the board, the company marshaled its resources to execute in strategic areas where it already had strength and a firm identity (Ringen 2015).

Yet many executives are reluctant to deviate from a strategic plan after investing an associated budget and enormous amounts of time and energy in its formulation. They view deviations as a failure or lack of discipline. In much the same way, learning leaders are often reluctant to let go of learning initiatives, policies, or processes that no longer serve them or their clients. But failure to exit a strategic plan or learning strategy that's not working has its downsides. First, the company or business unit is wasting resources that could be redeployed elsewhere. For example, top executives often devote a disproportionate amount of time and attention to businesses with limited upsides and then burn out talented managers who are sent in to save projects or plans that should have been shut down much earlier. Unless executives and learning leaders learn to screen opportunities against existing capabilities and capacity, they will waste time and effort on peripheral initiatives and deprive the most promising ones of the resources they need to achieve success. Second, the longer top executives drag their feet on cutting failing strategies loose, the more likely they are to lose the confidence of their middle managers, whose ongoing support is critical for execution. The same goes for learning leaders and their staff.

Of course, commitment flows the other way, too: Executives and learning leaders need to know when to follow through with a strategy and make sure it's executed properly. But very few organizations routinely follow through to track how they perform over how they thought they were going to perform (Mankins and Steele 2005).

In the end, it's difficult to know when to hold—or when to fold—without some measures of progress telling you where you're at in relation to where you want to be. Chapter 6 tackles how learning leaders can identify, influence, and track performance measures in more depth.

What to Do About It: Elements of Effective Execution

Companies that are effective at closing the gap between strategy and execution are ones that make exceptional execution part of their everyday work. While there are a host of approaches for improving strategy execution, proven best practices include consistency of purpose; disciplined, coordinated action; agility in response; leveraged expertise; and regular reflection and review.

Consistency of Purpose

Companies (and learning organizations) that are effective at executing great strategies focus their efforts on areas where their identity, value proposition, and purpose separate them from the competition. For these organizations, a stable, consistent purpose is required to support reliable execution. A consistent purpose can serve as a compass and beacon of light in the sea of constant churn and change. Consider Telus, a Canadian telecommunications firm, which transformed its business by adopting a clear, stable approach to strategy and culture. A global leader in total stakeholder value creation among telecommunications companies worldwide, Telus doubled its revenues from nearly US$4.5 billion in 1999 to US$9.2 billion in 2015. It has low customer churn rates, excellent customer satisfaction ratings, and strong employee engagement scores. Much of the company's success is attributed to traditional "good management" practices that focus on people, talent, and goal execution. But its main differentiator is a "consistency of focus" in its business strategy and culture. For example, the company's strategic imperatives, core values, and corporate responsibility initiatives have remained constant and been clearly communicated more than 15 years (Izzo 2015).

Why is consistency a key differentiator in strategy execution? Frequent changes in strategy and direction are common complaints among managers and employees who have trouble prioritizing tasks when companies continually move targets or subscribe to the trendiest execution tactics. In many organizations, there's a bias toward quick action at the expense of planned action. Many managers feel more productive when they're executing tasks and often perceive planning to be wasted effort, especially when under time pressure. This bias can be detrimental to talent management and overall performance results for a couple of reasons. First, constant, misdirected action can lead to workers who are too tired to learn new things or apply what they already know. (Chapter 7 talks more about the impact of change fatigue and the overwhelmed employee on organizational performance.) Second, always being ready for the next change doesn't give workers time to reflect on what they did right and wrong. And reflection is a key component of effective execution and the hallmark of a continuous improvement mindset, which we'll come back to later in the chapter.

Voices From the Field

There's one important thing I learned from a client that I use all the time. We tend to fix things that are broken and neglect things that are good, but could be better. Sometimes fixing that thing that's good, that could be better, is more valuable than trying to fix that thing that's broken. Maybe what's broken has no value and that's why it fell apart. This tends to resonate with leaders, especially if you can show a better ROI by improving something rather than reconstructing it.

—Ronnie Ashline, Experiential Learning Advocate at Google Fiber and Xerox

Disciplined, Coordinated Action

When multiple moving parts of an execution plan are effectively aligned to people processes, desired results are more likely to occur. Successful execution, in both the short and long term, relies upon disciplined, business savvy processes, where methods for executing strategies are clearly defined and optimized for consistent outcomes. Consider the following examples of intentional, disciplined, and coordinated actions taken by learning and talent management leaders as they executed culture changes within their learning organizations—one from a large, global environment, another from a small business environment.

A large, award-winning car rental company with more than 10,000 franchise locations in approximately 80 countries needed a centralized structure with global business processes to improve organizational effectiveness and drive market competitiveness. This transformation created an immediate need for a different HR model. To begin the shift toward a fully integrated global HR structure, the company's talent management function launched a disciplined, iterative execution plan that included removing functional silos and consolidating talent processes into one global operating system. The company deployed a diverse team of experts from each functional area to help coordinate the integrated "business-driven" talent management infrastructure. The infrastructure design evolved into a service organization, with service-level agreements that provided a basis for measuring and monitoring its financial contribution and service value. The transformation strategy incorporated regular use of evidence-based data and analysis to show how human drivers influence financial drivers. Through disciplined, coordinated strategy execution, the HR, talent management, and learning and development functions all proactively reinvented themselves as business enablers focused on continuous integration, adaptability, and flexibility, leading to their sustained impact and value creation (DeTunq and Schmidt 2013).

An industrial manufacturing company with 230 union employees wanted to migrate from batch processing to a single-piece flow process to adapt to changing market demands. The company brought in its first HR manager to help operational leaders execute this significant cultural shift. There were no people management systems in place, there was a backlog of almost 50 open requisitions, managers and supervisors were not trained to deal with employee issues, and the company was struggling under the pressure of accelerated growth. To support strategic objectives, the HR manager embarked on a comprehensive, strategically phased effort to support the transformation effort and create and nurture a pipeline of qualified machinists. Through strategic partnerships with the operations manager and his team, the HR manager executed several iterative business critical growth strategies during a 13-month period—for example, creating and launching a customized machinist trainee and master machinist training initiative designed to incentivize the internal, unionized labor pool to meet new performance demands and reduce attrition through the career ladder. The resulting machinist career paths were formally recognized as an innovative best practice among HR professionals within like industries in the Central Nevada region. The HR manager attributes the company's success in meeting its strategic goals to consistent, coordinated, and intentional actions between the operations manager and his leadership team, all of whom shared the vision of establishing a learning and performance culture. Additionally, the HR manager attributes her success as a member of the leadership team to the ability to speak the language of the business while selling and promoting people development and performance management solutions.

Incorporating proven project management approaches is also essential for disciplined, coordinated execution plans. Many learning leaders—such as those at Florida Blue, Florida's Blue Cross and Blue Shield Plan—manage and execute learning and performance projects in accordance with the ADDIE model (or some derivative), which has a long history as a framework for guiding the design and delivery of learning programs or projects. Both the project management (initiate, plan, execute, control, and close) and ADDIE (analysis, design, development, implementation, and execution) cycles propose a disciplined succession of iterative stages, where "execute" and "implement" represent a distinct phase of managing tasks in a project. Each phase offers an opportunity for self-correction before moving to the next phase. Practitioners over the years have made several revisions to the hierarchical versions of the project management and ADDIE models to make them more agile, interactive, and dynamic.

The performance improvement/human performance technology (HPT) model is another popular approach to project management and strategy execution used by many learning and performance professionals. The model, designed to be both linear and iterative, weaves in change management with every phase. The implementation and maintenance phase reflects the growing need for sustainable performance solutions. This model provides a solution-neutral process for managing performance consulting projects, as well as the performance consulting function, in an organization. A derivative of this approach is the human performance improvement model.

Many best-in-class learning organizations supplement their instructional design disciplines—or even their performance improvement disciplines—with proven project management methods to establish a shared vocabulary with business partners and allow for more flexibility in executing nontraining solutions that don't involve instructional design. Integrating project management disciplines into strategy execution begins with an approved project definition or business case and corresponding schedule, scope, and resource requirements. Planning elements usually include critical success measures; project milestones and tracking mechanisms; clearly defined roles and responsibilities; a work breakdown structure; routine communication tools and schedules; risk and contingency assessments; and resource requirements.

While it's not possible to anticipate every event that might help or hinder a project, most execution plans should assess and identify risks that might derail success. Typical risk categories include:

- **Schedule risks.** If a project plan or initiative has multiple critical tasks, risks increase exponentially, particularly if tasks flow into one another. Accelerating tasks to ramp up a schedule presents risks. If the time estimated to complete a task is overly optimistic or inadequate, there is risk. If tasks have been omitted from the planning schedule and work breakdown structure, there is risk.

- **Resource risks.** Resource allocation and logistics planning, key to the success of full-scale implementation of the solution, are often unstable and time sensitive. If a task completion is dependent on more than one person, there is risk. If a single group is expected to perform a large number of project tasks, there is risk. If there are limited to no resources (including technology) available to fully dedicate to a project, there is risk.

- **Scope risks.** "Scope creep" is a typical barrier to effective project management and successful execution in any business environment. If a project or initiative is more complex (or too big) than originally anticipated, there is risk. If there is new technology or unfamiliar development tools associated with project completion, there is risk.

A typical approach is to use a risk analysis matrix, in which potential risks are rated by their probability of occurrence, estimated impact (such as on cost or time), and the difficulty in detecting whether the risk is occurring. Most project managers use a high, medium, and low scale to rate risks. Finally, each risk is weighed and then prioritized, based on its probability, impact, and detection difficulty. Once the priority of risks has been assessed, the next step is to move on to planning risk management actions. Of course, one of the biggest risks to effective execution is the impact of change turbulence, which chapter 7 covers in more detail.

Other leading organizations use business management strategies and structured problem-solving tools, such as Six Sigma. This approach offers five main steps (define, measure, analyze, improve, and control) that can be used as a road map for any project or quality improvement effort. In the IT development industry, Agile methods have become another disciplined way of managing development teams and projects. Examples include DSDM, SCRUM, and XP (Extreme Programming). DSDM is probably the most complete Agile methodology, while XP focuses more on the software engineering process to address the analysis, development, and test phases in ways meant to enhance the quality of the end product. SCRUM is the most popular and widely adopted Agile method. Relatively simple to implement, it concentrates on how to manage tasks within a team-based development environment. In Agile software projects, project management relies far more on the project manager's skills in communication, facilitation, and coordination, with less emphasis on traditional project management skills in planning and control.

In short, failing to plan the execution of a business or learning strategy means planning to fail. Organizations with some formal, consistent system of execution typically outperform those with no system. Determine which execution methods work best for you and your organization and routinely apply them in a disciplined way. Rinse and repeat for every business-critical initiative or project. Consistent use of data-driven principles, methods, tools, and techniques for achieving business objectives will not only improve the sustainability of individual learning solutions, but it will also enable the sustainability of the learning organization as a strategic business partner and value creator. In other words, to add and create sustainable value, these processes must be consistently applied as a *way of doing business* rather than simply a way of doing projects. The Case in Point at the end of this chapter shows how one healthcare organization applied disciplined, coordinated execution practices to build and sustain a new way of doing business.

Agility

On the soccer field, tactics and adjustments to an opponent can make or break a victory. For example, World Cup teams often switch to new formations to seize new opportunities, push lines forward, or drop back and defend. If strategies don't work, they know how to quickly pivot, change positions, and bring in bench players. Success depends upon the ability to anticipate and assess what could happen next before it does. How well teams do this, and how fast they adjust tactics, can separate the good from the great.

Agility also provides a competitive edge in business—and learning and development. A lack of agility keeps many learning leaders and managers from effective execution. It's not so much a failure to adapt as it is the tendency to react so slowly that fleeting opportunities can't be seized or react so quickly that the "line of sight" to overall strategy is lost.

In volatile business environments, the allotment of funds, people, and managerial attention is not a onetime decision; it requires ongoing adjustment. Instead of focusing on resource allocation as a series of one-off choices, executives and learning leaders should concentrate on the fluid reallocation of funds, people, and attention. Many learning organizations, in particular, do not reallocate funds to the right places quickly enough to be adaptive, causing resources to be trapped in unproductive uses and stalling attempts to take advantage of new opportunities. Learning leaders can add sustainable value by helping executives and managers create processes that support flexible, agile coordination of resources.

Recognizing and rewarding agility and risk taking is also important. At Tata Consultancy Services, a six-time ATD BEST Award winner, agility is a core requirement in recruitment and hiring (ATD Staff 2015a). Yet many talent management processes fall short in how they recognize and reward agility and risk-taking during hiring or promotion decisions. Agility requires a willingness to experiment, and many managers fear that their careers could suffer if they pursue but fail at novel ventures or innovations. Few corporate cultures encourage the types of candid discussions necessary for fostering agility; less than one-third of managers say they can have open and honest discussions with their boss about difficult, risky issues (Sull, Homkes, and Sull 2015).

The most agile learning leaders, like the best coaches, are strategically prepared to adapt and change course when faced with the unexpected. Adding sustainable value means knowing how to anticipate and react to the nature and speed of change, act decisively despite surprises or uncertainty, and help senior leaders, managers, and employees do the same. More about that in chapter 7.

Voices From the Field

When we lay out a project plan as consultants, we lay out a timeline and project tasks as a guideline. But we also talk about the need to be adaptable as the need arises. Adaptability and flexibility are huge—they're key. For example, we might start with six critical tasks, and then determine that only two will be completed because the other four are no longer feasible, practical, or manageable given current conditions. It's better to say you're continuing to move forward than to stop everything because we can't get to step number six of this set of six.

—Sarah Thompson, Senior Manager of Learning and Development, Xerox Business Services

Leveraged Expertise

As Steve Jobs once said, "It doesn't make sense to hire smart people and tell them what to do; we hire smart people so they can tell us what to do." The common myth of a heroic CEO driving execution while perched on high is further dispelled in Larry Bossidy and Ram Charan's bestselling book, *Execution*. While frequent and direct involvement from the top may boost performance in the short term, top-down execution has many drawbacks, including the risk of unraveling after the departure of a strong CEO. It also diminishes an organization's capacity to execute over the long run because it diminishes middle managers' decision-making skills, initiative, and ownership of results.

Effective execution in large, complex organizations emerges from countless decisions, trade-offs, and actions across all levels and roles. Frontline employees, in particular—the people directly involved in creating, selling, delivering, and servicing offerings and interacting with customers—are frequently in the best position to spot and solve problems related to execution. Even in organizations that espouse "lean thinking"—a process-improvement approach that is intended to involve all employees—standard work practices seldom change, and only expert recommendations are implemented.

To that end, organizations sometimes define "expert" too narrowly, relying on indicators such as titles, degrees, and years of experience. Though experience improves efficiency and effectiveness, it can also make people more resistant to change and more likely to dismiss information that conflicts with their views. Different types of experience—including time spent on the front line, with a customer or working with particular people—contribute to understanding a situation and creating a solution. After all, as shown by the winning header by John Brooks for Team USA in the 2014 World Cup game against Ghana, some goals are made from the bench. Brooks might not have been a star player, but he proved indispensable. Effective learning leaders know how to help executives build and develop a winning lineup, not for one championship season, but for long-term growth and success. They empower and coach employees across all organizational levels to consistently cultivate their strengths and leverage their expertise for the greater good. And when all employees are empowered, the organization as a whole executes better.

Reflect, Review, and Learn

Once strategy has been translated into practice, it's important to identify what worked and what didn't. Applying lessons learned leads to continuous improvement for future action planning. Progress is not linear, and the best outcomes generally come from applying what was learned through mistakes and frequent, imperfect experimentation. Processes that support learning after doing and continuous improvement efforts include reflection and governance.

Through reflection, executives and learning leaders can identify execution bottlenecks and take corrective action. Some organizations are finding ways to incorporate reflection into their regular activities. One powerful approach treats reflection as a post hoc analytical tool for understanding the drivers of success and failure. The U.S. Army, for example, is well known for its after-action reviews. To ensure that a rigorous process is followed, facilitators, rather than the project's leader, conduct these reviews. An effective review involves comparing what actually happened with what should or could have happened and then carefully diagnosing the gap, be it positive or negative. From the private sector, British Petroleum reflects on past execution through a five-person post-project appraisal unit to review major investment projects, write up case studies, and derive lessons for planners that are then incorporated into the company's planning guidelines.

As learning organizations transition from service provider and cost center to more of a talent builder and driver of enterprise value, governance processes are increasingly used to review and prioritize learning investments. For example, many leading learning organizations use an executive governance committee or governance council to provide regular (such as quarterly) rigorous reviews and analyses of programs and processes. Best practices include incorporating a charter, adopting a vision and strategy for the future of learning, and identifying how engagement between the chief learning officer, business units, and senior management will be embedded in a company's overall culture, strategy, and business performance. Consider the following example of a governance process developed by a learning leader at a large home improvement organization.

Chapter Summary

Excellence in execution is a massive challenge for CEOs worldwide. In many organizations, translating strategy into execution is an exercise characterized by stalled initiatives, politically charged turf battles, opportunities that have fallen by the wayside, and important work that remains undone. Obstacles include a lack of accountability for project commitments, a lack of coordinating structures across boundaries, a lack of consistency in purpose, failure to disinvest from initiatives that drain resources, and a lack of agility to adapt to changing business conditions. While there are no quick fixes or fancy tricks that will help do the heavy lifting, keys to successful strategy execution include being:

- **Purposeful and intentional:** Dedicate resources to those strategies that reflect your organization's identity, value proposition, and core purpose.
- **Disciplined:** Practice routine follow-through and follow-up and address any deviations that might influence schedule, scope, or resource requirements.
- **Committed:** Believe in the soundness of your learning and performance strategies. Inspire confidence and commitment from leaders throughout the organization.
- **Agile:** Make adjustments to adapt to changes, risks, failed results, or faulty assumptions.

Use the chapter 5 self-assessment in appendix 2 to identify patterns and possibilities for improved execution of strategies and solutions within your own learning organization.

Voices From the Field

We have an interesting governance example here in my organization. One of the reasons I was hired was to help them evolve away from a "response to request" training organization to something that was much more consistent and much more business oriented. And so one of the things we did early on was create a kind of learning council for each major function inside the organization. Another thing we did was to put together standards, processes, policies, tools, and templates that communicated to stakeholders how we did business. As a result of doing that and working more closely with the executives, we got to much more business-oriented solutions. But we were still challenged in making sure our priorities were effectively aligned and balanced against the overall strategy of the organization, especially given the many shifts in the economy and in the company's leadership.

So in the last couple of years we worked with a consulting group and a team of 30 or 35 instructional designers to build a more robust set of processes, tools, templates, and policies to govern our work. The team accomplished this through an intensive, nine-week boot camp experience. Essentially, this consisted of a comprehensive action learning project where they went out into the stores to observe and analyze learning and performance processes that were working, and those that weren't—the focus was on "build, try, refine," "build, try, refine." Along the way they got coaching from the external consultants. We brought them back a month or two later, debriefed, and then refined the performance support tools and processes that needed improvement. For example, we streamlined an existing learning rubric used to evaluate our products by retiring 4,000 out of 6,000 elements.

What we got out of this was a really rich, upscaled set of processes and tools designed to meet the needs of various stakeholders and the five key executives at the C-suite level, including the chief human resource officer, the chief customer officer, the executive responsible for store operations, the chief supply chain officer, and the chief executive of our shared service organization. These templates and processes are still in use and are still being refined to this day. They represent a consistent, overarching philosophy and a set of clearly defined standards that govern how we execute our learning and performance solutions. They also give us a frame of reference or compass for measuring, monitoring, and continuously improving our work to ensure that those standards are being met and are still relevant to the needs of our clients.

—Director of Leadership Development, Large Home Improvement Organization

Figure 5-2. Key Actions

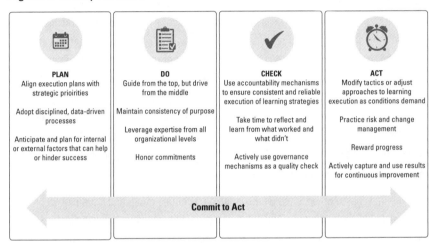

PLAN	DO	CHECK	ACT
Align execution plans with strategic prioirities	Guide from the top, but drive from the middle	Use accountability mechanisms to ensure consistent and reliable execution of learning strategies	Modify tactics or adjust approaches to learning execution as conditions demand
Adopt disciplined, data-driven processes	Maintain consistency of purpose	Take time to reflect and learn from what worked and what didn't	Practice risk and change management
Anticipate and plan for internal or external factors that can help or hinder success	Leverage expertise from all organizational levels		Reward progress
	Honor commitments	Actively use governance mechanisms as a quality check	Actively capture and use results for continuous improvement

Commit to Act

Chapter Highlights

The best aligned learning strategy is meaningless unless it is precisely executed.

Precise execution calls for disciplined, data-driven processes where methods for executing strategies are clearly defined and optimized over time for consistent outcomes. Managing and executing learning as a disciplined business process increases alignment to strategic objectives and adds sustainable value. Routine reflection and review, along with formal governance processes, are needed to help monitor how learning investments are aligned, prioritized, and executed.

Effective execution is guided by the top but driven from the middle.

Concentrating power at the top may boost performance in the short term, but it diminishes the organization's capacity to execute over the long run. In large, complex organizations, most execution exists with middle managers who run critical businesses and functions as well as technical experts who occupy key spots in the informal networks that get things done. Learning leaders can add sustainable value by helping filter information flow throughout the organization, develop leaders' ability to manage commitments and coordinate activities across units, and anticipate and resolve conflicts that may arise when different units pursue their own objectives.

Effective execution means knowing how to pivot, adapt, and change course as needed.

Learning leaders who know when to hold, when to fold, and how to pivot and change course when needed are more likely to add sustainable value to their organization and their own business unit. Executing learning strategies in the right way doesn't add immediate, or long-term, value if execution is focused on the wrong thing.

Sustainable learning organizations make effective execution part of everyday business.

Organizations (including learning organizations) with a formal system of execution outperform those with no system. Consistent use of data-driven principles, methods, tools, and techniques for closing the gap between strategy and execution will not only improve the sustainability of individual learning solutions, but also enable the sustainability of the learning organization as a strategic business partner and value creator over the long term. In other words, to add and create sustainable value, these processes must be consistently applied as a way of doing business rather than simply a way of doing projects.

Case in Point

The Case in Point from Community Health Care Association of the Dakotas shows how a bi-state primary care association used a performance improvement approach to project management to support strategy execution in a public sector environment.

COMMUNITY HEALTH CARE ASSOCIATION OF THE DAKOTAS

The Community Health Care Association of the Dakotas (CHAD) is the primary care association for federally supported health clinics in North and South Dakota. CHAD's membership includes 11 health clinics, four in North Dakota and seven in South Dakota. As the primary care association for two rural, frontier states with widely disbursed populations, CHAD serves a community health center network through consultation, technical assistance, training, resource development, financial management, and human resource advocacy for the purpose of increasing the capacity and sustainability of these centers. In general, community health centers play a vital role in providing high-quality primary and preventive healthcare to patients who might not otherwise have access to it, especially given the increasing number of uninsured Americans. Federally qualified health centers make up the largest national network of primary care providers. CHAD's mission is to lead the Dakotas in quality primary healthcare through public policy and community-driven health services. Its vision is to be recognized and valued for its network of services and expertise.

An expansion of health clinics in the Dakotas created an accelerated demand for CHAD to provide its members with more diversified and compliance-oriented training and technical assistance services. In light of increased pressures for utility and efficiency, and a political climate characterized by ongoing resource and budget constraints, the board of directors established strategic priorities around determining the value and payback of training and technical assistance services provided to network members. Improved outcome data were required to better meet member needs and to help focus CHAD efforts on those technical assistance services with the highest potential for value. In keeping with best practices for execution described in this chapter, the following issues were addressed during this two-year effort.

Clear Purpose

The key objective of the effort was to create, implement, and standardize an outcome-based evaluation model to ensure that CHAD's suite of educational and technical assistance services achieved desired results and made optimal use of agency and partner resources. Here, CHAD sought to ensure that any new model or process kept a clear and consistent link to its primary mission and purpose as a service provider. Desired results included enhanced methods for collecting, organizing, and presenting data about agency outcomes; improved resource allocation by defining the technical assistance services that add the most member value; increased member satisfaction with the agency's suite of technical assistance services; and the increased capacity and sustainability of community health centers to provide high-quality primary and preventive healthcare.

Disciplined, Coordinated Action

To meet its strategic goals, the agency enlisted a consultant to direct and coordinate staff action within this large-scale continuous improvement effort. The consultant applied a disciplined, data-driven performance improvement approach to help the learning organization adopt and integrate an outcome-based service model for its improved relevance, resilience, and value to sponsors and stakeholders. Figure 5-3 outlines the high-level phases and key actions associated with this approach.

Figure 5-3. High-Level Performance Improvement Approach

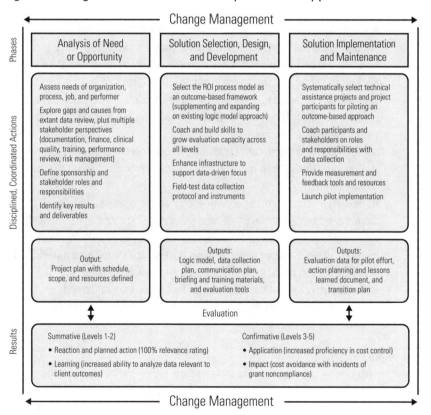

Agility

Internalizing a comprehensive business process into a service strategy or function, in any setting, is typically complex, requiring cultural changes to policies and programs across all organizational levels. In general, implementing a results-oriented focus in the public sector represents a fundamental, dramatic shift in business thinking, acting, and managing away from a focus on activities. Given the multiple variables and constraints associated with creating, implementing, and sustaining this results-oriented service model, the consultant worked extensively with agency stakeholders to frame implementation as an iterative change process. An evolutionary, flexible approach was especially needed here because ultimate outcomes may not be seen for many years and some desired outcomes were difficult to measure using traditional evaluation methods. To that end, the logic model linking immediate, intermediate, and ultimate outcomes with project activities and processes was a vital planning and communication tool. This visual approach helped staff stay focused on outcomes and kept underlying assumptions and influencing factors at the forefront.

During this two-year engagement, predictable change issues connected with stages of the Sustainability Cycle emerged:

- **Recognition:** driven by the board's push to prove technical assistance value through outcome-based, quantifiable data. *Enabling strategies:* define specific business and performance objectives; establish a shared purpose; adopt a disciplined, data-driven approach to strategy execution.
- **Resistance:** reflected in performance anxiety about how results data would be used; some hesitation by clients to adopt and apply new data collection tools used to measure individual or agency performance. *Enabling strategies:* acknowledge and openly address change issues or concerns; approach strategic change as a collaborative process; cascade major process changes to ease the transition.
- **Renewal:** reflected in resurgence of energy and commitment to using data for improved service delivery; renewed focus on using outcome data to add value due to positive results from pilot launch. *Enabling strategies:* identify and manage potential risks or negative impacts; reinforce shared accountabilities for results; establish processes to reflect on and review lessons learned.
- **Refinement:** not yet at this stage due to lack of full integration and struggles with resiliency due to leadership attrition, economic climate, and resource constraints.

Leveraged Expertise

Ongoing collaboration with experts and stakeholders, inside and outside the agency, was critical throughout each phase of analysis, solution design, development, implementation, and evaluation. Stakeholders with different types of expertise, experience, responsibilities, and tenure were actively sought out to contribute to building a better understanding of the situation and its needs. Sponsors maintained a continued emphasis on shared understanding of the overall purpose of the effort, shared commitment to continuous improvement goals, and shared ownership of results.

Execute, Reflect, and Learn

Following the initial pilot implementation of the outcome-based model, lessons learned and continuous improvement opportunities were identified using evaluation and feedback data collected, analyzed, and reported during each phase of the project. Evaluation data were collected across multiple levels of impact.

Reaction and planned action. Results were successful, with 100 percent of participants indicating that pilot participation represented a worthwhile investment of time, saying they would recommend the approach to others, and identifying planned actions they would take as a result of participation.

Learning. Using a five-point scale with 1 indicating "No Success" and 5 indicating "Completely Successful," participants reported the highest degree of success with the following learning objectives:

- Enhance methods for collecting data about agency outcomes.
- Enhance methods for organizing data about agency outcomes.
- Enhance methods for analyzing data relevant to client outcomes.

Application. Among the most frequently used behaviors, skills, resources, and materials gained from pilot participation were financial management (cost control) tools, document control and medical record management tools, human resource materials for performance appraisals, and risk management resources. Time and staffing constraints were reported as the most common barrier to using what was learned.

Impact. Impact data were collected through a questionnaire that asked pilot participants about the result of their actions on specific work measures, perceived cost benefits of applied behaviors upon defined work measures, and intangible benefits of applied knowledge and skills. These work measures were significantly influenced by the application of designated tools and resources:

- compliance with funding (grant) requirements
- cost control and cost conversions
- operational performance
- risk management
- compliance with health center program requirements
- customer (patient) satisfaction.

Improved compliance with funding requirements was the most frequently reported business measure influenced by applying new tools. This business benefit translated to cost savings related to rework and lost labor time associated with one incident of a grant noncompliance.

Case Review

This case illustrates how a disciplined, data-driven approach was used to carry out, execute, and assess the impact of an outcome-based service model for ensuring the efficiency and effectiveness of federally funded community education and partnership services. Execution was enabled by visible and active leadership support, extensive communication and collaboration across membership networks, and the dedicated commitment of agency specialists and task force representatives who exemplified the true spirit of partnership. Unfortunately, it has become increasingly difficult for the technical assistance organization to consistently execute data-driven methods and outcome-based processes for multiple learning solutions over time, thus compromising organizational success in achieving many of its desired, long-term objectives related to agency and members' sustainability.

Practice 4: Drive for Results; Continuously Improve

"Without data, you're just another person with an opinion."
—W. Edwards Deming, Data Scientist

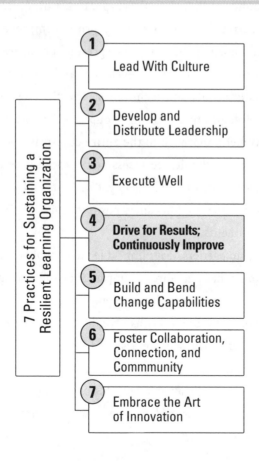

What's in This Chapter

- how a results focus drives a high-performing, sustainable learning organization
- how a learning culture can leverage measurement for continuous improvement purposes
- how learning leaders can build sustainable measurement processes and practices.

CREATING AND SUSTAINING A LEARNING CULTURE that supports organizational growth requires real-time data on performance and engagement. Yet many learning leaders who strive to measure organizational growth often lack support from key stakeholders responsible for providing and using performance data.

Does this sound familiar? Jim, the corporate training director for a global electronics firm, returned from a costly process improvement certification program endorsed by the senior vice president of operations, who said he wanted all processes analyzed, developed, and implemented using the program's signature tools and techniques. The firm agreed to introduce the new methodologies to a training group of 50 before it rolled out the process improvement approach to the entire enterprise. As the pilot project unfolded and the 360-degree assessment processes were identified as a program requirement, line managers got nervous and voiced fears about their job security if they couldn't show positive reviews from their peer and subordinate assessments.

"That fear led to barriers," says Jim. "It led to a lot of lack of support from the operations folks that were directly impacted by the learning program and by their operational managers. Instructional designers who were tasked to help customize program scenarios had trouble getting the right input from subject matter experts. The sponsor assigned key managers to help with the pilot effort, but the initiative never got off the ground or had the right internal support so it was eventually abandoned. One of the biggest barriers was actually from the human resources department, which claimed that integrating the assessment data with current performance management processes was too complex, despite the fact that we had another senior VP as our main sponsor."

Why is internal support so essential for a sustainable measurement program? Lack of internal support from stakeholders often holds learning organizations back from providing evidence-based data on learning effectiveness. And the absence of data may reduce the necessary funding support when an organization allocates annual resources.

Figure 6-1. Fast Facts

36%	80%	52%	46%
Talent development professionals who believe that their evaluation efforts are helping greatly to meet business goals	Talent development professionals who use Level 4 or Level 5 evaluation and believe that it has a high, or very high, value to their organization	Talent development professionals who use Level 3 evaluation and believe that it helps greatly in achieving learning goals	Talent development professionals who said a lack of access to data needed for higher-level evaluation was a major barrier

Source: ATD (2016).

A key part of maximizing existing learning resources, as well as building support for increased sustainability of resources over time, is to focus on where these resources, both internal and external, have the most impact and can do the most good.

Determining where learning resources have the most impact requires a dedicated commitment to achieving and assessing impact beyond the life cycle of a single program or initiative. Research shows that high-performing companies are more likely to consistently commit resources to measuring the impact of learning and talent management practices than lower-performing ones. High-performing companies exemplify a proactive, performance-first mindset in which evaluation is viewed as a value-added, integrated part of learning and talent management processes and a critical tool for continuous improvement—not a reactive, add-on, post-program activity.

Systematic methods of measuring performance success and capability add value because they help learning leaders and their organizations know whether:

- They are driving the right strategy for the right issue.

- They are executing to the best of their ability.
- Organizational constraints or cultural barriers are interfering with performance and retention.
- They have the right people in the right places with the right tools and resources.

Megan Leasher, director of talent assessment and measurement at Macy's and one of *Human Resource Executive*'s HR's Rising Stars for 2016, uses standardized metrics to help the 172,500-employee organization put the right people in the right roles. Leasher describes herself as a "scientist-practitioner" who combines psychology with "cold, hard data" to evaluate executives and predict their future leadership performance. In a company that has experienced major restructuring, along with drastic changes in the way technology and social media have altered consumers' shopping habits, reliable and consistent talent assessment and measurement practices ensure that leaders' skills are keeping up with dynamic business needs (McGraw 2016).

Alignment, Objectives, and Impact: The Basics Still Apply

The need for learning leaders, talent managers, and human resource professionals to establish a credible connection to performance impact has never been greater. For instance, 96 percent of CEOs want to see business data that show the impact of the learning organization on the broader enterprise, yet only 8 percent of them actually receive impact data. In addition, 74 percent of CEOs want to see ROI measures from learning, with only 4 percent actually seeing ROI now (Phillips and Phillips 2009).

CEOs are not the only ones who want more from their learning organization's measurement practices. In one study, a majority of the 330 chief learning officers (CLOs) surveyed reported dissatisfaction with the state of their measurement practice, and less than half reported that their learning enterprise was "fully aligned" with their learning strategy (Anderson 2015). This poor alignment led most CLOs to report that their strategic influence in shaping and contributing to organizational priorities was also weak. Business alignment is needed to ensure that all learning investments, not just isolated programs, drive relevant business results in both the short and long term.

As most seasoned learning and performance leaders know, achieving business alignment requires that solutions, programs, projects, and initiatives be positioned for success from the beginning and then evaluated accordingly. Building business alignment for impact-driven learning generally starts with clarifying stakeholder needs and desired outcomes.

For example, say your organization wants to increase sales performance among regional store managers. First, you identify the business measures needed to reflect improved performance, such as the number of monthly sales, the store profit margins, or the number of new customers per quarter. Next, you identify the performance measure needed to influence the business measure. With this example, one performance measure might relate to how well select employees could apply targeted sales skills, such as closing a sale, on the job. This performance measure would define the behaviors, actions, or changes needed by job performers. Drilling down, you would identify what employees need to know or learn to do to meet performance requirements. In this example, one learning need might be that employees know the steps associated with closing a sale. By gaining clarity about business needs as a first step, and then working through the process—from business need to performance need and then to learning need—you've increased the chances of identifying the right solution (or set of solutions) and the best investment opportunity for defined goals. In addition, you've set the stage for establishing meaningful objectives that will:

- Define measures of success.
- Communicate the what and why of a program or project to participants.
- Provide facilitators, team leaders, and program managers with direction around the key knowledge and behaviors needed to drive business outcomes.

By defining needs and developing objectives that reflect stakeholder priorities, learning leaders can better demonstrate that they understand the critical issues needed to support the organization. Well-defined, well-aligned objectives also lay the foundation for effective program evaluation that ensure that the right measures are taken. Finally, by developing these objectives, learning leaders create shared ownership of learning results, which can lead to being perceived as a business contributor, both inside and outside the learning organization. Consider this proactive message about collaborative evaluation from the Bill & Melinda Gates Foundation (2016):

> From the outset of the grantmaking process, we work with partners to define the overall results we hope to achieve and the data needed to measure those results. We call this approach outcome investing. To give our partners flexibility in how they achieve results, we do not require them to report on all of their activities. Instead, we focus on purposefully measuring the most critical metrics of progress that support continued learning, adjustment, and alignment. . . . Evaluation is another collaborative learning tool that provides us and our partners with feedback so we can improve, adjust, and decide how best to achieve outcomes.

A high-performing, sustainable learning organization plans and prioritizes its measurement strategies based on what outcomes are most important for the business and its business partners. While outcome measures tend to add the most stakeholder value, they are usually the least tracked by learning leaders, compared with other standard measures such as efficiency and effectiveness. Common efficiency measures include the number of programs and participants, as well as utilization rates, completion rates, and cost per learner or cost per hour. Typically, these measures don't tell the story of how efficient a program is unless they're compared with something else, such as historical numbers, previous trends, benchmark data, or the targets set at the beginning of a program. Effectiveness measures address the quality of a learning program or initiative. All organizations have standard measures that can be used to align learning programs, processes, or solutions with desired organizational results. Understanding and tracking these measures build support and credibility with the senior leaders who make funding decisions for learning.

Here's a snapshot of the various ways that award-winning learning organizations measure their efficiency and effectiveness:

- **Vanguard University** (VU) has used net promoter scores to assess learning effectiveness since 2009. VU's flagship course, Leading Crew to Success, has a net promoter score of 98 percent. When a score is deemed too low, the course is retooled. For example, when VU's Corporate Orientation program received a net promoter score of 73 percent, the program was successfully redesigned; the program's score rose to 81 percent after the redesign (Burjek 2016).

- **The Federal Deposit Insurance Corporation** is working to improve how it measures behavioral change related to learning outcomes. Its core school piloted a program for future bank examiners that assessed the writing and analysis in bank examination summaries before, during, and after the two-week school. To track and observe how changes occurred in actual practice, it conducted follow-up interviews with participants and supervisors.

- **Western Union** enhances the effectiveness of its high-profile, high-potential leadership development program with bi-weekly reviews on touch points that include milestone reports with senior leaders. This leadership development program trains leaders to identify new sources of revenue and is closely aligned to business needs around high-potential employee retention. Turnover rate for graduates of this program is reportedly 9 percent lower than the company average.

Knowing what and when to measure begins with evaluation planning. Measurement maps can be useful evaluation planning tools because they illustrate how learning and performance targets link to important business objectives. The measurement map represents the alignment and logical relationship between people investments and business goals so that the observable and measurable outcomes are clear to learning leaders and stakeholders. For best results when creating a measurement map, be sure to:

- Involve the right people (those with access to business data for impact analysis).

- Reach agreement on the strategic goals or priorities.

- Ensure that all indicators are measurable.

- Give equal weight to the process and the product.

- Focus on collaboration and relationship building when building a map.

- Use maps to both prove, and improve, the value of learning investments (Kelly and Pease 2015).

Figure 6-2 is a sample measurement map. Keep in mind that your measurement map will vary based on your learning organization and your learning investment.

Figure 6-2. Sample Measurement Map

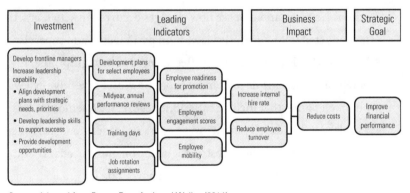

Source: Adapted from Pease, Beresford, and Walker (2014).

Voices From the Field

For more than the past 10 years, I've worked as a consultant helping organizations determine where they need to be to achieve exemplary performance. Whether in the L&D or talent management space, I've worked with client groups to figure out what their processes need to be. They're often at the very early stages of maturity and not sure what they need to do to move forward. To gain executive support it's important to show how learning will impact organizational performance. If you can tie the learning initiative, whether it's an onboarding or performance improvement initiative—if you can relate it to business goals and objectives, you'll get more support. For example, we use a measurement map to say, "Here's what you need from a learning perspective to tie it back to your goal of decreased costs," or, "Here's what you need from a learning perspective to tie it back to your goal of increased revenues." If you can show that kind of learning alignment, you can gain buy-in from business executives.

A recent example was with a redesign of an onboarding program. It was redesigned to be heavily experiential, "Less sage on the stage, more guide on the side." We established early communications with executives to show them how we were using "e-learning at your fingertips" to help employees get what they needed from the onboarding program to resolve real call center challenges. We tied the program challenges back to business objectives like decreased call time or increased sales with our measurement map. We had one senior executive say, "I want the measurement map at everyone's desk because it helps agents recognize how what they do impacts the business." It was really phenomenal to have the executive team so strongly supportive and alongside our design team throughout this initiative. We've continued to find that the measurement map is a key strategy in keeping executives engaged and programs aligned—we call it our North Star."

—Sarah Thompson, Senior Manager of Learning and Development
Xerox Business Services

Other more-detailed evaluation planning tools, such as data collection plans or logic models, also promote shared understanding of key objectives. They can illustrate:

- what inputs or investments are needed
- what outcome data will be collected
- how data will be collected
- when data will be collected
- who is responsible for collecting the data.

Sustainable learning organizations have typically standardized the use of measurement maps or similar tools due to their many benefits. First, driving alignment and defining business measures of success are critical to adding value. Second, every human capital investment is funded due to its promise to contribute to explicit business needs. Learning leaders who can effectively and consistently show how people strategies can deliver on their promise and link to important business strategies are more likely to be perceived as credible business partners. Third, adopting measurement tools and strategies can help learning leaders and stakeholders anticipate where future investments may be needed. Leveraging predictive analytics can help organizations optimize their investments and help learning leaders create more value as future-focused strategic partners. More on that later in this chapter.

The Rise of ROI

In a hypercompetitive market for knowledge workers, CEOs are looking to leverage their learning organization to provide strategic, data-driven, and analytical contributions to human capital challenges—and to determine whether talent investments are paying off. Yet despite these rising pressures from CEOs, learning leaders in the public, private, and nonprofit sectors still struggle to define and track measurable business objectives. Consider the following: In the 2015 AMA and i4cp global leadership survey, 87 percent of respondents said they do not measure the impact of L&D performance. Only 18 percent of respondents in the *Value of Learning* report (ASTD and i4cp 2014b) said their learning organization did a good job of evaluating overall learning effectiveness. This often stems from lacking the right technology to measure training efforts and improve communication and data collection (Anderson 2015).

Having the right tools and technology is important, but knowing what to do with them is another critical issue. Although some learning professionals are quite capable with data, analytics, and strategic thinking, learning and HR functions in general seem hampered by a lack of accurate workforce data as well as analytical and strategic planning skills; many seem unable to explain to CEOs what existing data say about the organization's ability to achieve its goals with the talent it has or can get. A 2015 survey of 362 CEOs and chief HR officers found that 24 percent reported a lack of analytical skills as their biggest obstacle to making and participating in data-based strategy decisions (*Harvard Business Review* 2015). No more than 30 percent said they had taken any positive steps to get better at it.

Given higher expectations for accountability, trends suggest that the use of return on investment (ROI) evaluation is on the rise. A 2015 measurement and metrics study suggests that almost 50 percent of the CLOs plan to implement ROI in the future. This increased use of ROI can be attributed to six factors:

1. increased competition for funds and resources
2. shifts in measuring the ROI for noncapital expenditures, using the same finance and accounting formula used for measuring the ROI for capital expenditures
3. emerging role of the chief financial officer (CFO) in monitoring the value of different organizational functions
4. shift to evidence-based investing, where executives want facts about the current or projected value of investments
5. accelerating cost of human capital investments in leadership development
6. growing emphasis on value, accountability, and transparency from internal and external stakeholders (ROI Institute 2015).

Voices From the Field

The business environment drove HR to really challenge itself around our culture of accountability. A big compliance issue helped us recognize that we weren't always paying people to be accountable. Our compensation practices and processes were in some cases really motivating and driving the wrong kind of behaviors. We expanded that and examined every component of talent management to ask questions about how all our work processes, approaches, and work products were meeting quality standards and producing the highest value.

We asked ourselves if we were being accountable as an HR organization. The work that came out of that was just very, very broad. My team was consulting with each one of the leaders including the head of compensation and benefits, the head of recruiting, the head of employee relations, and the head of compliance. I was on the team and led HR's efforts around how to use analytics to expose risk issues and define continuous improvement and accountability processes from a proactive standpoint.

—Senior Learning Analytics Consultant (Internal), Global Banking Institution

What's in it for learning leaders? Taking a more disciplined approach to consistent, versus ad hoc, impact and ROI analysis can offer significant payoffs. First, it can make programs better by showing where they add the most value. Showing where you deliver value can protect your budget during tough economic times. Second, demonstrating learning's contribution to the business helps to build key relationships with executives, because the number-one desired category of learning results is business impact. Third, a commitment to providing evidence-based data of effectiveness also strengthens the credibility, confidence, and morale of your learning and talent management professionals; most team members want to know how they make a difference to the clients and business units they serve.

While there are a variety of evaluation methods and approaches available, the Kirkpatrick and Phillips frameworks account for 80-90 percent of models used today (Phillips and Phillips 2009). As chapter 2 mentioned, their evaluation frameworks show how measurement data are collected at different times, from different perspectives, to show a value chain of impact across multiple levels of impact. In Phillips's ROI Methodology, the first is often referred to as Level 0 inputs. These data ensure that people cycle through the system efficiently. Level 1 is reaction, ensuring that participants react properly to the learning programs. Level 2 is learning, where participants acquire new knowledge and skills. Level 3 is application, where individuals take action after leaving a learning environment, using the content. The next two levels are Level 4, which is business impact, connecting learning to business measures, and Level 5, which is ROI, comparing monetary benefits with costs. While measurement can stop at any level along the way, more organizational clients and sponsors are demanding measures of application, impact, and occasionally ROI.

It's important to note that increased use of ROI does not mean that all programs need to be evaluated at the ROI level. Measuring learning and implementing an ROI impact study is usually recommended for only 5 to 10 percent of an organization's learning initiatives. Kimo Kippen, chief learning officer at

Hilton Worldwide, says that his learning team conducts one rigorous ROI study per year on a carefully selected program (ATD 2016)b. By carefully selecting the programs to evaluate at the ROI level, and using cost-effective, time-saving methods to collect and analyze data, learning leaders can fully integrate a comprehensive, results-based evaluation process into their learning organization with minimal resources. The Case in Point at the end of the chapter illustrates use of the Kirkpatrick and Phillips frameworks.

Measurement and Continuous Improvement

The disciplined, sustained practice of measurement and evaluation is critical to running a learning organization like a business. One of the best reasons for a results-based measurement focus is to ensure that you're delivering promised results and are continuously improving programs, processes, and products. To reliably demonstrate the business contribution of a learning investment, measurement methods must meet standards of quality and must be applied consistently. Some measurement methods are more credible than others. The hallmark features of best-in-class measurement methods include those shown in Table 6-1.

As measurement and evaluation processes become more mature, standardized, and visible, and as performance becomes more dynamic, continuous improvement mechanisms are needed to ensure that results generated from measurement practices consistently add value. One improvement mechanism that has worked well for many learning organizations involves using performance scorecards or dashboards to track micro- and macro-evaluation results for a single program, a series of programs, or the entire learning enterprise. Generally speaking, macro-level metrics are the overall organization or cross-functional metrics used to drive strategy and are typically reflected in a company scorecard or executive dashboard. Micro-level metrics track the success of a particular project, program, or initiative.

Table 6-1. Hallmarks of Effective Measurement Methods

Feature	Description
Relevant	Method is results-oriented and linked to strategically critical business objectives.
Comprehensive	Method identifies key issues and root causes, accounts for all relevant variables that influence results, and adequately tracks the whole solution result versus select parts.
Timely	Method delivers measurements at the right time.
Transparent	Method is open to those affected by it, not just collected privately for management's view.
Cost-effective	Method is realistic and easy to track using existing data for operating units.
Controllable	Method tracks outcomes created by those affected by it, who have a clear line of sight from the measures to the results.
Actionable	Method creates data that are easy to interpret and translate to management and employee actions.
Usable	Method serves the practical information needs of intended users.
Collectible	Method can be collected where effort to retrieve is proportionate to usefulness of the measure being tracked.
Specific	Method provides clearly defined measures for effective tracking, analyzing, and reporting.
Sustainability-focused	Method accounts for short- and long-term performance support needs.
Credible	Method provides valid, accurate information in the eyes of management and key stakeholders.
Ethical	Method is conducted with regard for the welfare of those affected by its results.
Continuously improved	Method can be monitored and updated regularly to ensure continued relevance.

Many resources are available to help with scorecard development. For example, the nonprofit Center for Talent Reporting has introduced Talent Development Reporting Principles (TDRp) as a framework for developing and implementing internal reporting and management standards for key human capital processes such as learning and development, leadership development, and talent acquisition. Founded by David Vance, executive director and former president of Caterpillar University, the center employs common industry measures to create three standard statements and three standard management reports to enable practitioners to run talent like a business, ensuring that planned, measurable outcomes are delivered effectively and efficiently.

Figure 6-3 demonstrates how addressing real evaluation challenges can help learning leaders support continuous improvement.

Figure 6-3. Addressing Evaluation Challenges

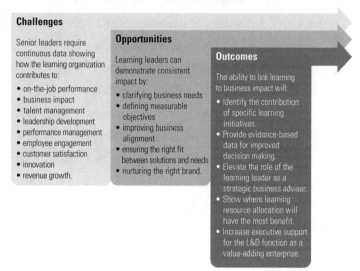

Challenges

Senior leaders require continuous data showing how the learning organization contributes to:

- on-the-job performance
- business impact
- talent management
- leadership development
- performance management
- employee engagement
- customer satisfaction
- innovation
- revenue growth.

Opportunities

Learning leaders can demonstrate consistent impact by:

- clarifying business needs
- defining measurable objectives
- improving business alignment
- ensuring the right fit between solutions and needs
- nurturing the right brand.

Outcomes

The ability to link learning to business impact will:

- Identify the contribution of specific learning initiatives.
- Provide evidence-based data for improved decision making.
- Elevate the role of the learning leader as a strategic business adviser.
- Show where learning resource allocation will have the most benefit.
- Increase executive support for the L&D function as a value-adding enterprise.

The Role of Analytics

If you read the book or saw the film *Moneyball*, you know that Billy Beane and Peter Brand transformed sports analytics by using an approach called sabermetrics. Instead of relying on their gut and old-fashioned scouting, they changed the way professional baseball teams recruit talent. Now, every team in the Major Leagues uses sabermetrics in some fashion. For example, the Oakland Athletics use empirical analysis baseball statistics to measure in-game activity and help predict future performance. The Chicago Cubs use a robust set of player data to make the best scouting decisions along with extensive social and networking data analysis, according to talent scout Alexander Levitt (Bowley 2015); data analytics are a core component in the team's decision making.

In much the same way, learning organizations are turning to talent and human capital analytics to help their organizations make smarter, faster decisions when recruiting and developing talent and when trying to structure work that aligns with strategic goals and employee capabilities. These analytics refer to the use of sophisticated data mining and business analysis techniques to explore human resources data. In today's data revolution, learning organizations are increasingly relying on advanced analytics to communicate their value and apply a data-driven lens to strategic decisions about talent acquisition, talent development, employee engagement, and retention.

The use of predictive analysis has been shown to improve learning and talent development processes, effectively link them to business priorities, and inform decisions about continuous improvement actions. Cheaper, faster technologies have made it more affordable than ever before to collect and analyze large data sets that go far beyond traditional measures, such as the number of applicants, number of programs, or number of people who were identified as high potentials. This can make the amount of big data available seem insurmountable. In fact, it takes years of incremental improvements and accomplishment for a learning organization to fully realize the potential of human capital analytics (Kelly and Pease 2015). Companies with leading capabilities in HR and people analytics have spent three years or more absorbing the technology, reskilling their teams, and bringing data to every major people-related decision (Deloitte 2015).

Here are two examples of organizations that are incrementally growing in their use of analytics as a strategic tool:

- **Footlocker** used predictive analytics to boost the company's effectiveness in hiring and to improve sales performance. The initial analytics team consisted of members from HR, finance, and sales, who implemented an 18-month pilot program for more than 300 stores. Despite some initial resistance from store managers, Footlocker rolled out the program to an additional 300 stores, and then across all its stores. Benefits include a streamlined hiring process, better prepared managers during interviews, dramatically reduced turnover, and improved customer feedback (Dixon 2015).
- **Intel** leveraged big data analytics to provide customer insights, leading to nearly $1 billion in incremental revenue and productivity

gains over a two-year period. The IT team and the sales and marketing team partnered to create a predictive analytics engine to identify customers with the greatest potential for high-volume sales; as a result, the sales team was able to grow Intel's reseller channel business. Through analytics, Intel improved the ways different business functions work together (High 2016).

Voices From the Field

We have a full-time person assigned to learning evaluation. So he brings some very sophisticated and nuanced tools to the table. Plus on the analysis side, we do a ton of qualitative and quantitative work to make sure that we're focused on the right things, the key indicators inside the organization. For example, we can translate employee engagement to a number of very valuable metrics inside the organization. We know that if employees go through our six-week blended, on-the-job store manager training program before transitioning into store management, then on average, that store manager's team will be 10 percentage points more engaged than managers who have not been through the program, even if they have much more experience. So for each percentage point of employee engagement, we know that there is a corresponding increase in customer satisfaction and in sales, and a corresponding decrease in shrink, breakage, and other things in the stores, and a corresponding decrease in safety incidents. So we use a wide range of qualitative and quantitative methods in order to evaluate what we're doing and show that we're making a difference."

—Director of Leadership Development, Large Home Improvement Retail Chain

No matter how sophisticated or advanced your current use of analytics may be, every learning organization needs to apply some standardized, consistent level of measurement and analysis to its goal setting and strategic decision making if it expects to remain relevant and resilient amid the changing needs of users and stakeholders over time. For example, the strategic use of human capital data has been a differentiator in the highly regulated industry of healthcare and pharmaceuticals for Massachusetts-based Biogen. Its global learning leaders and senior executives routinely rely upon measurement data to drive decision making and move the organization's performance forward (Locwin 2016).

Sustainability and the Measurement Continuum

Integrating a results-based measurement practice that consistently adds value over time is a unique sustainability challenge. While an impact study or scorecard may be used to measure the effectiveness of an individual program or series of programs, embedding a comprehensive set of measurement processes beyond the life cycle of a single program or impact study is an aspect of sustainability that is often overlooked. Here, sustainability goes beyond the learning transfer approaches designed to sustain the performance results from one initiative. Whether serving in a strategic or support capacity, or some combination, adding sustainable learning value means consistently following a metrics-driven approach to measure progress and make improvements to quality, speed, and cost-effectiveness for the duration of every learning scenario, not just single initiatives. The emphasis is on examining the long-term endurance and business value of the whole learning process instead of the business value achieved by a single program.

This approach requires full integration of credible, durable measurement standards, policies, and data collection systems with organizational and functional business processes. Supporting infrastructure is critical. According to one ROI professional, "Our biggest initial barrier was . . . we jumped to ROI without really having a solid base of measurement and evaluation within our organization." Here are some additional guidelines for building sustainable measurement processes and practices.

Identify Your Value Chain

As discussed in the introduction, a common mainstream approach to sustainability centers on the idea of lean thinking, in which all activities, products, or services surrounding the life cycle of a business process are examined for ways to improve value and efficiency and eliminate waste. Learning leaders who have successfully embedded, and gone on to sustain, a data-driven learning organization adapt lean thinking principles. They routinely examine how well learning and performance processes are integrated and viewed as a value-added, strategic business process, not simply as a learning and performance or HR process. They know what metrics, or key performance indicators, are most important to their organization.

Use It or Lose It

"I see so much data that gets gathered and then lies around like fertilizer in a sack. It sits there and nothing is done with it," says one seasoned measurement professional. Performance data that are not seen or used will have little perceived value to the organization or to the stakeholders responsible for supporting and funding the learning and development function over time. This means making sure that stakeholders get the information they need, at the time they need it, to make informed decisions. Sustainable learning organizations anticipate multiple uses and users of performance data and report not only on results achieved, but also on findings about poor outcomes. Utility of learning and development products and services, along with the utility of its performance data, is a defining characteristic of sustainable learning organizations.

Build Capabilities

Many learning leaders argue that they do not have sufficient resources to conduct consistent, comprehensive measurement practices. Yet available resources, in and of themselves, are not enough to drive sustainability. Resources are only an asset if they are capable and competent. Learning leaders should have some understanding of business and finance concepts to increase their evaluation capability and grow business acumen. For example, Jac Fitz-Enz advises individuals coming from a social sciences background to take an introductory accounting class so that they have a clear understanding of the underlying concepts behind income statements, balance sheets, and cash flows. He also advises learning leaders and HR professionals to have a good understanding of statistics so that they can look at data and understand when basic descriptive statistics should be used—not necessarily how to use them personally, but to know when they are needed. "The function should be about providing strategic insights. While the inward facing HR metrics is interesting, in terms of large contributions to the organization, the initial focus needs to be on strategy," he says (Gilbert 2015).

Developing the capability of internal resources is also critical because many organizations have turned to core teams of subject matter experts to initiate and lead comprehensive evaluation efforts. Sustainable learning organizations build capability by:

- conducting briefing sessions and workshops with mid- and senior-level managers on the importance of learning and performance impact on the business
- inviting subject matter experts and managers to participate as reviewers and evaluators
- establishing a cross-functional advisory group or measurement community of practice.

It's important to provide continuing education and performance support for measurement teams to promote collaboration and innovation. According to one measurement professional, "Now we're holding the business units accountable for doing impact studies. We have a two-year plan mapped out to try to institutionalize this."

Increase Accountability Mechanisms

As shown in our opening scenario, many learning leaders encounter problems assessing and reaching performance targets because those responsible for providing performance data are not always held accountable for enabling easy access. Alternatively, there may be limited accountability within the organization, or within individual business units, for managers or supervisors to improve or change their performance. Or the message of holding individuals or departments accountable for meeting performance goals may be positioned in a punitive light, leading to fear and negativity about supporting performance improvement efforts. Yet employees want to be part of an organization that holds them and others accountable. Companies that enable and challenge employees to take responsibility for learning and performance are more likely to improve productivity and engagement. A 2015 Towards Maturity benchmark study found that top-tier learning organizations are twice as likely to assign accountability for learning to business leaders and managers in comparison to the average. The better the approach to accountability, the better the ability to hit performance indicators and achieve desired results.

Use Proven Project Management Approaches

Effective project management means that evaluation plans remain manageable, flexible, and appropriately aligned with identified business needs. Best-practice recommendations include being realistic and starting small. One ROI professional says, "I think, off the bat, if I look back, selecting five programs for ROI evaluation was probably too much." Others have said that trying to implement too much too fast is another problem. As discussed in chapter 5, effective project management also means that implementation plans include situational assessments and risk management assessments that address such contingencies as attrition of staff, changes in leadership, resource constraints, or unexpected change demands.

Ensure Alignment With Other HR and Talent Management Processes

In this case, alignment extends to integrating the mission, values, strategies, processes, practices, and standards of the entire learning organization with other functional parts of the business for increased effectiveness, value, and sustainability. A measurement coordinator for a large government health-care agency describes its alignment strategy as follows: "The whole evaluation process—its infrastructure, philosophy, standards . . . is interwoven in all the ways we do business. It is built into a philosophy of accountability and evidence-based decision making. Evaluation skill sets are seen as a core competency for demonstrating customer value and meeting customer-driven requirements."

Use Data to Tell Success Stories

Sustainable learning organizations routinely present success stories to the organization in the form of case studies or project reports. As one ROI professional says, "We keep [ROI] alive and visible within our organization and in front of our leaders so that they can, in turn, be champions. . . . I will always share impact studies with our project manager, instructional design and community practices [groups] because that is part of our internal sharing." Another senior evaluation leader approaches communication sharing in this way: "We [have] shifted from working with individual projects in the field to . . . talking about [ROI process] on a more strategic level . . . at higher-level committees and planning meetings."

Using evidence-based data as a form of storytelling has been shown to win funding and sponsor support, gain added commitment of stakeholders, inform decisions about a program's value, and help identify improvement opportunities. Robert Brinkerhoff (2003), evaluation expert and founder of the Brinkerhoff Evaluation Institute, created the Success Case Method as a structured evaluation approach for sharing stories about learning effectiveness.

Share Responsibilities for Results

As chapter 2 discussed, subject matter experts, participants, and line managers are needed to provide technical expertise when defining business impact measures and converting those measures to monetary value. Participants and managers are typically the primary source for providing data about learning gains and on-the-job application of learning through questionnaires, surveys, interviews, focus groups, and follow-up sessions. Sustainable learning organizations set expectations with stakeholders so that they understand the commitment required to build the culture and capabilities needed to support improved accountabilities and fully integrated measurement practices. A "Transfer Strategy Matrix" is a useful tool for documenting the "before, during, and after" responsibilities among learning leaders, sponsors, managers, and participants throughout a measurement effort. It also helps dispel the myth of evaluation as simply an add-on, after-the-fact task (Burkett 2008). Sharing responsibilities for defining, collecting, analyzing, and reporting performance data not only validates measurement work, but also secures sustained support and cooperation for learning and performance solutions.

Assess the Effectiveness of Appropriate Learning and Nonlearning Solutions

Resolving a performance gap or problem usually requires more than one type of solution. Leading organizations generally choose several blended solutions, phased in or used concurrently, to address the many aspects of an issue. Types of other solutions used in combination with learning or training solutions may include work design, organizational design, performance support, or performance management. Subsequently, an effective measurement process must be able to evaluate the effectiveness of each solution applied to an issue, as well as demonstrate the relationship between each solution and the intended performance goals of an initiative.

Emphasize Measurement as a Long-Term Process-Improvement Tool

Sustainable learning organizations create value by using results data as a tool to continuously improve and make decisions, and to drive innovation. For example, Apple continually takes what it learns from one product launch and applies it to create a new and better product. When implemented properly, high-quality measurement processes can:

- Lay the foundation for organizational learning.
- Provide methods for a learning organization to track its progress.
- Enable data-driven decision making.
- Help prioritize resources.
- Contribute to increased organizational performance.
- Provide evidence of a program's value.

Embrace measurement and evaluation for what it is and what it can do for you and your learning organization. Practice routine benchmarking to continually assess whether human capital expenditures and related success measures are realistic and well used. Ultimately, a high-quality measurement system is best viewed as a living process and should be maintained, nurtured, and improved to ensure that data, lessons learned, and findings remain relevant over time.

Figure 6-4. Key Actions

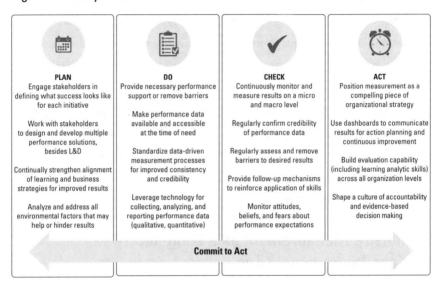

PLAN	DO	CHECK	ACT
Engage stakeholders in defining what success looks like for each initiative	Provide necessary performance support or remove barriers	Continuously monitor and measure results on a micro and macro level	Position measurement as a compelling piece of organizational strategy
Work with stakeholders to design and develop multiple performance solutions, besides L&D	Make performance data available and accessible at the time of need	Regularly confirm credibility of performance data	Use dashboards to communicate results for action planning and continuous improvement
Continually strengthen alignment of learning and business strategies for improved results	Standardize data-driven measurement processes for improved consistency and credibility	Regularly assess and remove barriers to desired results	Build evaluation capability (including learning analytic skills) across all organization levels
Analyze and address all environmental factors that may help or hinder results	Leverage technology for collecting, analyzing, and reporting performance data (qualitative, quantitative)	Provide follow-up mechanisms to reinforce application of skills	Shape a culture of accountability and evidence-based decision making
		Monitor attitudes, beliefs, and fears about performance expectations	

Commit to Act

Chapter Summary

Learning leaders are facing increased pressure to show how learning investments contribute to critical work measures such as productivity, cost, quality, and time. While most learning leaders agree that strong measurement strategies and practices are important, most L&D measurement remains stagnant and centered on tactical, present-focused metrics such as courses, students, and hours of training rather than evaluating learning impact and anticipating future needs. Higher expectations for evidence-based success metrics, including those based upon the use of analytics, have only increased dissatisfaction with current measurement practices from both CEOs and learning leaders themselves. Still, this is an exciting time for learning leaders because they have more opportunities than ever to demonstrate how the learning organization adds appreciable value to the business. Use the chapter 6 self-assessment in appendix 2 to identify patterns and possibilities for an improved results orientation within your own learning organization.

Chapter Highlights

Measurement cultures and learning cultures go hand in hand.

Measures and methods for assessing learning and performance impact are critical for a relevant, sustainable learning or HR organization. For instance, a learning organization may have perfectly aligned strategies that are flawlessly executed. But if it lacks data-driven processes and practices for communicating the tangible and intangible value of those strategies to key stakeholders and investors, support for learning will wane. In many ways, a strong commitment to measurement lays the foundation for organizational learning. It generally takes years to build and integrate measurement and analytics capabilities into a learning organization.

Sustainable learning organizations consistently measure and monitor learning investments.

Learning leaders must be able to clearly articulate the relationship between learning investments and business goals. Using evidence-based data to show that learning resources are being used effectively is one of the best ways to build and sustain senior-level commitment for continual learning and development. More CEOs and CFOs are demanding measures of business impact and return on investment to justify learning expenditures. Predictive analytics can be used to add statistical rigor and optimize decision making for high-stake investments.

Best practices in measurement and metrics are built around a culture of accountability.

Don't assume leaders know how to hold others accountable. Adopt a model of empowering accountability that can be trained, coached, and hired against. Help ensure that leaders model accountability in all their interactions. Align learning and performance improvement efforts to accountability standards.

Measurement is best framed as a value-added business process.

Measurement is a strategic business process and should carry just as much weight as budgeting and financial governance. While the costs related to human capital are often a company's largest expense—and talent is typically seen as an organization's most important resource—many companies do not sufficiently fund or support evaluation efforts. Those that do allocate funding tend to spend resources toward Levels 1 and 2 measures, with only 25 percent of resources at the average organization devoted to Levels 3 and above (ATD 2016a). Dedicating funds to higher levels of evaluation is associated with increased learning and business effectiveness, as well as increased maturity and sustainability for the learning function.

Case in Point

This chapter's Case in Point shows how FlightSafety International's learning organization applied a systemic metrics-driven approach to support and sustain its culture of safety and continuous improvement. The organization's evaluation strategy focused on fidelity and efficacy. Efficacy refers to the power or capacity to produce a desired outcome. Ensuring efficacy meant that learning leaders took a rigorous, evidence-based approach to achieve optimum effectiveness.

Establishing the fidelity of outcome data provided necessary evidence to senior leaders about what was or wasn't done to affect strategic outcomes. Don Highley, former creative direction supervisor of courseware support, and Chad Raney, director of programs, volunteered to share their story, present their results, and describe how their journey mirrored stages of the Sustainability Cycle.

ENSURING LEARNING FIDELITY AND AGILITY AT FLIGHTSAFETY INTERNATIONAL

FlightSafety International is the world's premier professional aviation training company and supplier of flight simulators, visual systems, and displays to commercial, government, and military organizations. The company provides more than a million hours of training each year to pilots, technicians, and other aviation professionals from 167 countries and independent territories. For more than six decades, the company has invested in technology, personnel, and an expanding worldwide network of learning centers. Its network consists of more than 1,800 highly qualified instructors who provide more than 3,500 individual courses for 135 aircraft types, using more than 300 advanced simulators. FlightSafety operates the world's largest fleet of advanced full-flight simulators at learning centers and training locations across the world.

The corporate philosophy of FlightSafety is "The best safety device in any aircraft is a well-trained crew." Since pilot error causes about 80 percent of all aviation accidents, according to the National Transportation Safety Board, it is mission critical that products and services evolve as quickly as possible to ensure that clients' safety needs are being met. To that end, FlightSafety partners with regulatory authorities to ensure that training products, programs, and processes produce the highest degree of safety outcomes possible. Operating in a continuously changing business environment, FlightSafety faces constant challenges to update products to match the technological advances in avionics and integrated aircraft systems. A culture of continuous learning and improvement, along with a strong culture of metrics and measurement, are vital elements to the company's sustained success and competitive edge in the industry.

Recognition Stage: Project Conception

Operational Day Flow (ODF) is a new "classroom to cockpit" methodology applied to pilot ground-school training. Compared with traditional, lecture-based pilot training that focuses learning on how each aircraft system works independently of other systems, ODF focuses learning on how integrated systems are simultaneously used while operating the aircraft. Based on two years of research and both customer and client feedback, the methodology enhances instructor qualification and training requirements to match technological advances. Specifically, it is designed to help reduce pilot errors by guiding each client to a deeper understanding of aircraft systems and integrating crew resource management and aeronautical decision-making skills in the classroom. The result is a much higher level of learning versus simple rote memorization.

Strategic objectives aimed to increase:
- product differentiation and competitive advantage in the marketplace
- revenue and lower discounts applied to pilot programs
- client engagement, satisfaction, and loyalty
- learning effectiveness, efficiency, and applicability on the job.

Multiple stakeholder groups collaborated on ODF courseware design, prototype development, and an enterprise-wide, staged implementation process that integrated desired competencies with compatible structures and communication plans (Figure 6-5).

Figure 6-5. ODF Working Group Analysis

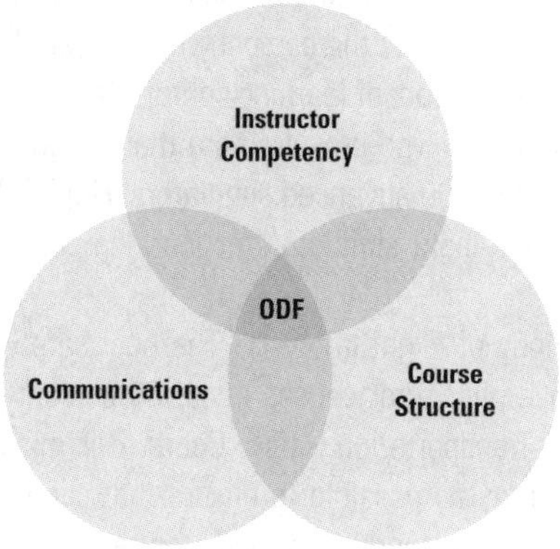

Adapted from FlightSafety International. Used with permission.

"When trying to introduce something like ODF that changes our end product, it was extremely important from the very beginning to have an executive sponsor that supports the idea and the plans for executing it," says Raney. "We're an industry leader in pilot training with extremely high client satisfaction ratings. Our clients are vocal and we're very responsive to their feedback. It was a high-risk proposal to take something that's already very good and then change it."

Development and Design

To develop a corporate training standard that remained adaptable across various aircraft types, six prototype courses were created. Three were initial training courses and three were recurrent training courses, each representative of a major segment of the training within FlightSafety. The training content for each session was organized into two major sections called Systems Review and Flight Scenario. Flight Scenario presented real-world aircraft systems and performance malfunctions in the context of potential weather, environment, and external pressures. Each scenario has fixed learning objectives that go through periodic refreshments and updates. Systems Review ensured that instructors:

- Evaluated strengths and weaknesses of participants' current knowledge and experience level.
- Provided content to overview the prescribed systems (electrical, hydraulic, fuel, and so on) to be discussed in that session. The subject matter expert were allowed to reuse content (such as graphics) from each respective systems-based lesson.
- Used instructor interface tools and resources as required to review knowledge gaps.
- Allocated approximately 30-50 percent of the session time to Systems Review.

Finally, each format and content area provided customized toolsets designed to help instructors guide interaction and facilitation. Any new and customized toolset was automatically integrated into FlightSafety's rigorous Pilot Instructor Training and Qualification protocol to ensure that learning experiences adhered to strictly defined quality standards.

Evaluation Plan

Operational fidelity, the cornerstone of FlightSafety's brand and mission, refers to the degree of similarity between the simulated training experiences and real-world operations (Table 6-2). The higher the operational fidelity, the greater the training effectiveness, efficiency, and transfer.

Table 6-2. Operational Fidelity

Type	Definition	ODF Examples
Physical	Visual and spatial representation with real aircraft and its avionics systems	• Cockpit posters • Instructional materials • Projected images • Client data terminal set with common connectivity device (if appropriate)
Functional	Accuracy with system operations	• Schematics • Dynamic slide presentations • MATRIX training system (if available)
Psychological	Degree of perceived realism with crew resource management and decision making	• Scenario details (weather, realistic context, airport charts)
Task	Degree of scenario realism with a real-world operational trip	• Scenarios match line-oriented flight training experience

Adapted from Thomas (2003).

To ensure fidelity and promote data-based decision making, a comprehensive evaluation plan was used to determine whether the six prototype courses achieved the intended strategic objectives of the ODF methodology (Figure 6-6). Evaluations occurred at each independent learning center to account for potential variations among locations, pilot groups, and types of aircraft operations. The goal was to collect a comparable sample, per condition, to evaluate the value of ODF compared with traditional learning methods.

Figure 6-6. Evaluation Process Model

Adapted from FlightSafety International. Used with permission.

The evaluation plan assessed program fidelity and effectiveness across four levels of impact: Level 1 (extent of client reaction), Level 2 (extent of knowledge, skills, and attitude gains), Level 3 (extent of improved pilot performance and flight preparedness), and Level 4 (extent of business impact through increased pilot safety and reduced risk of pilot error).

Measurement categories included descriptive data, hard data, and soft data. Specific data collection methods for each of the above levels of evaluation included:

- **Level 1.** FlightSafety measured client and stakeholder satisfaction with ODF observation surveys provided to pilot trainees immediately after ground-school training and at the end of simulator training. The focus was on how well the ODF training experience met expectations and achieved its stated objectives.
- **Level 2.** FlightSafety captured learning gain measures in a number of ways during ground-school and simulator training. In ground school, instructors gave a series of multiple-choice questions to learners to assess knowledge gains; these questions were designed to link to the knowledge areas (environmental conditions, preparation requirements, decision-making criteria) being taught experientially in simulator training. FlightSafety designed simulator training to increase skills and critical decision-making capabilities around how to operate

the aircraft in different environments, such as cold weather or high altitude. Data collection methods included ground-school pre- and post- test scores (Figure 6-7) and a simulator checklist that rated observed pilot performance during standard maneuvers.

To FlightSafety, specific, measurable learning objectives were critical. "By the time [pilot trainees] get to simulator, that's [the] closest they come to actually flying the airplane," Raney says. "We evaluate how quickly and accurately they complete their preparation checklist before flight, and then during flight we tie it back to job performance. Time to startup, accuracy, and time in the simulator are all progress indicators and important predictors of future pilot performance." FlightSafety used comparison groups to statistically test pre- and post-differences in scores during prototype development (Figure 6-8).

- **Level 3.** FlightSafety conducted pilot interviews 30 days after training to collect hard performance measures and soft data. An ODF observation summary survey was also sent as a 30-day follow-up to trainees' supervisors. "We wanted to see if ODF helped them perform their job better, not just whether it helped them perform better in training," Raney says.

- **Level 4.** FlightSafety captured operational metrics on an ongoing basis with a very robust client survey system used across the enterprise. It continually collected data through surveys, interviews, and observation from three groups— instructors, clients, and customers—and compiled the data into one record to enable various queries. The system could sort on any of the variable data entered into the records. In addition, FlightSafety conducted an evaluation study one year after the final ODF design was integrated with each program. "The purpose of the study was to validate that we had a successful long-term transition," Raney says. There was a lot of emphasis during the change process to make sure a quality product was maintained, but it is important to know that people's behavior changed and the mission was properly carried out to the customer's satisfaction."

Figure 6-7. Abbreviated Sample Post-Assessment Checklist

Instructions: Please rate your ability to perform each item at this point in time.

No.	Item	Poor	Fair	Acceptable	Good	Excellent
1.	Operate all common connectivity device (CCD) functions, including trackball, select switch, menu key, data set know, and enter keys.	1	2	3	4	5
2.	Use the CCD to configure the primary display units and multiple display units for each phase of flight.	1	2	3	4	5
3.	Initialize the avionics system.	1	2	3	4	5
4.	Build a flight plan in the proper sequence with minimum mistakes.	1	2	3	4	5
5.	Correctly insert data into each principle of flight within the flight management window.	1	2	3	4	5
6.	Interpret the difference between optional and mandatory entry fields in the flight management window.	1	2	3	4	5

Adapted from FlightSafety International. Used with permission.

Figure 6-8. Before and After Ground-School Ratings

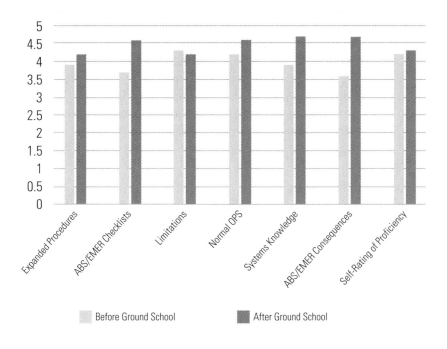

Before Ground School   After Ground School

Risk Assessment

In addition to developing an evaluation plan, the training operations team worked with sponsors and stakeholders early on to identify potential risks of creating, delivering, and sustaining ODF courses. After identifying risks, the team presented recommendations to resolve them (Table 6-3).

Table 6-3. Potential Risks and Recommendations

Potential Risk	Recommendations
Insufficient systems review	• Change knowledge check to a brief systems review.
Confusing subject flow	• Improve transitions between content about various systems. • Update scenarios to include malfunctions relevant to the various phases of flight.
Unclear understanding of ODF	• Produce visual job aids for instructors and clients.

Unprepared or unsatisfactory instructors	• Update qualification requirements for instructors to include:
	  ◦ a solid grasp of the ODF methodology
	  ◦ proficiency in navigating resources
	  ◦ demonstrated facilitation skills
	  ◦ ability to teach initial systems-based course.

Lack of customer or client awareness	• Develop customer support talking points. • Develop electronic information sheet for customers and clients.

Anticipating and proactively planning for implementation risks was a key element in establishing credibility with sponsors. No matter how well defined results targets may be or how well designed an implementation plan may look, no project is risk-free.

ENABLING STRATEGIES

1. **Get sponsors on board.** For a project of this size and scope, FlightSafety needed an executive sponsor at the vice president level. "We had a number of briefings with our sponsor before prototype design, at several points along the way, and during regular progress reports," Raney says.

2. **Link strategies to critical business measures.** FlightSafety determined what metrics were important to the organization and focused on learning strategies that link to

critical business measures. It was specific about how success will be measured. It set expectations with stakeholders so that they could understand the commitment required for completing evaluation strategies and projects.

3. **Use data to inform strategy.** FlightSafety takes metrics and measures very seriously. "Our sponsors are very smart people; they're not easily swayed," Raney says. "We needed good, proven data early on to prove the value of our plan and show success measures with our strategy. It wasn't enough to just say, 'I think it should be this way or I'd like it to be that way.' We had to have data to say, 'This is what clients are saying,' or, 'This is what we've seen in reduction time to set up aircraft in simulator,' or, 'Here are survey results.'

4. **"Include a risk assessment in evaluation project planning.** For FlightSafety, helping its clients and stakeholders get a full picture of potential roadblocks or risks was an important part of defining the implementation plan and determining resource needs.

Resistance Stage: Implementation Challenges

During early implementation of the ODF prototypes, the training and courseware operations teams experienced some expected challenges. For some flight instructors, the change in training methodology was uncomfortable. Many learning centers had trouble allocating subject matter experts to refresh and update new scenarios for ground-school and simulator training. Performing updates to the base curriculum required more time and resource support than originally projected. There were also operational concerns about taking an instructor away from daily duties to build scenarios. Learning centers had trouble meeting operational demands when instructors were pulled for up to three months of instructional design and development. When performing course updates, enterprise designers and stakeholders lacked consensus about flight scenario content, which caused longer cycle times for development until a consensus was reached. Finally, the technology needed to increase standardization across learning centers was sometimes lacking or in need of maintenance.

To stay on top of change issues and enable a more seamless conversion, the working group staged its implementation into two phases. The first was a fully supported stage in which working group members were on the front line, answering questions and walking people through the transition. To meet business demands, instructors' teaching time was reduced by half to allow more time to ramp up ODF design and development. This was operationally acceptable because once the course designs were in place, courses could be repurposed at a later date and instructors' development time would be reduced. The second phase was to review results over time using the survey systems and other metrics in place.

When ODF prototype training fell below client or faculty expectations, the working group team took time to evaluate whether it was a methodology issue or a facilitation issue. "What we learned was that instructors with a higher level of facilitation skills delivered a better product," Raney says. "Instructors that struggled through or rushed the training process didn't deliver ODF as it was intended." By using evaluation as a continuous improvement tool, the team was able to go back and augment instructor training for improved consistency and quality.

In addition, during monthly progress meetings with the vice president or directors, evaluation data were critical to explaining why specific programs or groups were not satisfactory. "In the end, we were able to show statistical data that ODF had been rolled out successfully in 10 to 12 settings, and that instructor or courseware gaps with the one to two lower-rated programs had been adjusted quickly and correctly," Raney says.

ENABLING STRATEGIES

1. **Prepare for challenges.** Don't be discouraged if not everyone is receptive to change. FlightSafety knew to expect resistance along the way, at all different levels. "Be prepared to deal with that through training and education," Raney says. "Give people a chance to vent concerns, ask them to try it, and to participate in designing and refining as you go."

2. **Ongoing evaluation is critical.** "Having good numbers and data helped us to continually justify the change strategy and keep senior leaders bought in," Raney says. "We used results to make ongoing adjustments to our products and processes and to identify where we had issues that needed to be resolved. We needed consistent and continual data to tell us if our clients and customers were truly happy with the new product."

3. **Use a transition plan during implementation.** "Using a two-pronged change management approach to roll out the ODF methodology was critical to our success," Raney says. "Taking extra time up front to work through issues with instructors, learning centers, and clients helped us meet expectations and ensure that we were delivering a quality product. Hands-on assistance and ongoing communication between all parties during the transition helped build support and commitment across the enterprise."

Renewal Stage: Customizing, Standardizing

Phase one of the ODF transition plan focused upon addressing and mitigating operational issues and challenges around integrating the ODF methodology. With effective transition planning and successful prototype results, blanket approval was granted to standardize ODF into "the way we do business," according to Raney. Specific results were as follows:

- **Level 1.** Client and stakeholder satisfaction with the ODF approach was overwhelmingly high, with some saying, "This was the most engaging learning that I've had" or "I've flown airplanes for over 20 years and never realized several of the things that I learned."

- **Level 2.** Survey feedback from instructors and clients confirmed that the ODF learning experience was considered substantially better and more relevant than previous training experiences. Ground-school scores and simulator checklist ratings showed that pilots were better prepared to operate the aircraft in variable environments.

- **Level 3.** Pilot observation reports and survey responses from pilots, supervisors, clients, and instructors showed that pilots demonstrated more accurate and timely preparation of the aircraft before flight thanks to ODF participation. In addition, pilots' ability to perform procedures in compliance with regulatory standards and make all the decisions that go into the operation of the airplane have increased as a direct result of ODF participation.

- **Level 4.** Business impact results (collected after prototype rollout and on an ongoing basis) confirm that integrating ODF methods into standard business practice contributed to its strategic objectives around increasing competitive advantage and market or product differentiation. This, in turn, resulted in increased sales revenues, customer satisfaction, and customer loyalty and retention. "We've proven over and over again that you'll be a better pilot going through this courseware," Raney says. "It's helped us recover contracts that we may have otherwise lost. It's given us an edge and been a deciding factor in many marketing and contract negotiations with clients and customers." Other impact measures included reduced costs for curriculum deployment and updates.

ODF also offered many intangible benefits, including increased engagement at instructor levels, enterprise program standardization by aircraft class, and enhanced training effectiveness, efficiency, and learning transfer. As the ODF methodology became more mature and established, phase two efforts focused on renewing activities to make the product more scalable and sustainable across the enterprise. For instance, the original ODF concept grew out a specific field office and design elements were tailored specifically to the aircraft at that location. Thus, the focus during this stage revolved around refining courseware design and delivery, beyond its initial migration, to improve customization for different aircraft at different locations.

ENABLING STRATEGIES

1. **Speak the language of the business.** "We spoke to our sponsors, clients, and customers about results and business impact," Raney says. "Most of the working group didn't know anything about 'evaluation levels' or measurement 'jargon.' But we all knew what we were trying to accomplish, why it was important, and how we planned to monitor our success."

2. **Practice the art of flexibility.** "We invited people to be part of the refinement process, which meant we had to be flexible and release control, especially when unexpected things came up," Raney says. "The end product is different than the original, but the concept was spot on and it's a better product because of all the input."

Refinement Stage: Refreshing, Sustaining

Success from this initiative has helped FlightSafety innovate its core product and standardize learning and performance goals across multiple locations. While most of FlightSafety's new courses have now been transitioned to ODF, not all programs have been converted because of the quantity of programs present. Legacy airplanes in particular are still due for migration to the new methodology.

"We are at the mature stage, with second- and third-generation products facing sustainment," Raney says. Regulatory requirements demand that courses be refreshed every one to two years, so FlightSafety is updating decision-making scenarios from original prototypes so that it "can continue to adapt to changing conditions."

Throughout FlightSafety, the message is out about the value of ODF and the value of the courseware support team as a mission-critical learning organization. "In the beginning, it's always easy to say it's Don's idea or Chad's idea," Raney says. "But there's a point where something takes on a life of its own and people just grab on. I know that's where we are now. We're creating value with what we're doing."

And the courseware support team has caught the eye of FlightSafety's CEO, who "will stand up and say, 'This is why ODF is important to FlightSafety, this is how we do business, this is what helps us be better than our competition, this is what helps us develop safer pilots.' That's why we do what we do and how we continue to stay relevant to changing industry needs," Raney adds.

ENABLING STRATEGIES

1. **Talk to your customers.** "This project came from a combination of customer and instructor feedback. It originated from frontline employees," Raney says. "Customer feedback along the way helped us refine it and make it the standardized product it is today. We put our customers at the center of everything we do, helping them operate their aircraft to the highest level of safety."

Case Review

This Case in Point shows how a mature, customer-centric learning organization leveraged its measurement capabilities to assess the business value of a new training methodology, developed in response to technological advances in avionics and integrated aircraft systems. Learning, performance, and impact results showed a positive link between applied use of the methodology and desired business objectives. In addition, the ability of the learning team to successfully partner with business units in the design and delivery of an innovative, evidence-based training solution led to the increased credibility, leadership support, and sustainability of the learning enterprise. Table 6-4 illustrates the characteristics of an adaptive, sustainable learning organization that enabled these accomplishments.

Table 6-4. Characteristics of a Sustainable Learning Organization

Characteristic	Examples	
C-Level Sponsorship	• Senior leaders actively engaged during planning, definition of business needs, strategy development and targeted pilot, prototype implementations • Senior leaders actively committed to measuring the impact of new methodologies upon safety and customer satisfaction • Leaders reinforced accountability for learning centers to participate in testing, evaluate new instructional design, clearly communicate purpose behind the new methodology and its evaluation effort, as well as the importance of sustaining performance gains	✓

Characteristic	Examples	
Efficiency	• Regular monitoring of time, usage, and cost indicators through statistical data analysis	✓
Effectiveness	• Design team uses a variety of qualitative, quantitative measures to continually assess the fidelity and effectiveness of new, existing methodologies (pre- and post-tests, simulator scores, performance observations, follow-up surveys, interviews) • Specific success measures, aligned with key performance indicators, are used to drive results	✓
Investment	• Senior leaders invested in two-year research, design, delivery, evaluation, and continuous improvement of innovative methodology to maintain and sustain instructor qualifications, competitive advantage	✓
Utility	• Sponsors and stakeholders (clients, instructors, customers) across all locations regularly utilize flight training data to inform strategy • Performance data are visible and available to multiple users as requested or needed	✓
Demand	• Sponsors and stakeholders (clients, instructors, customers) across all locations regularly request flight training data for informed decision making and continuous improvement	✓
Credibility	• Confidence and credibility established through an evidence-based approach to learning methodology • Collaborative design and delivery enabled credibility • Customer feedback and results data reinforced credibility of solution and its impact	✓
Governance	• Cross-functional governance committee (ODF design team) engaged as governance group	✓
Continuous Improvement	• Pilot execution results, continuous data collection, and customer feedback were regularly used to inform iterative adjustments and improvements in the moment of need • Improvement activities were integrated beyond initial migration to make the product and process more scalable, customized, and sustainable across the enterprise	✓
Resilience	• Risk factors, contingency plans addressed in evaluation planning • Design team conducted two-pronged, phased rollout of new methodology to reduce risk, minimize disruption • Flexible, scalable learning and performance framework designed to withstand changes in the compliance and safety environment	✓

Practice 5: Build and Bend Change Capabilities

"The greatest danger in times of turbulence is not the turbulence—it is to act with yesterday's logic."

—Peter Drucker

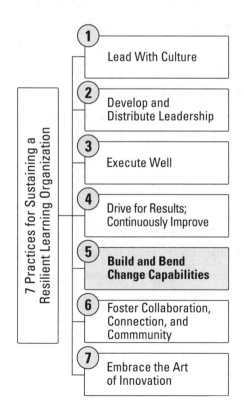

7 Practices for Sustaining a Resilient Learning Organization

1. Lead With Culture
2. Develop and Distribute Leadership
3. Execute Well
4. Drive for Results; Continuously Improve
5. **Build and Bend Change Capabilities**
6. Foster Collaboration, Connection, and Commmunity
7. Embrace the Art of Innovation

What's in This Chapter

- how a learning culture can drive organizational adaptability and change readiness
- how learning leaders can add sustainable value as strategic change agents
- how learning leaders can build their own change capabilities
- how an adaptable, change-capable learning organization adds sustainable value.

DOES THIS SOUND FAMILIAR?

"Change management is a real issue in sustaining a learning organization. When I started as director of our corporate university, I reported to one senior VP. Within two years, my job changed three times and the senior VP changed. I was constantly being aligned with different lines of business. I was told that if I had success in one line of business, I could replicate it with other business units. It was like management by chaos. It was very tumultuous with too much change, too fast. We could never get any traction in gaining leadership support since leaders and their priorities were constantly shifting."

Gaining traction is a unique challenge in a learning landscape characterized by volatile, uncertain, complex, and ambiguous times. How often have you witnessed revolving chairs with CEOs that come or go or moving targets that shift with the latest urgent decree or flavor of the month? All of this makes sustainability more difficult. In fact, learning leaders and HR professionals say that managing change and cultural transformation is among their top five challenges and it is the one area in which they are most likely to partner (SHRM 2014). CEOs want help getting their organizations to be more proactive, adaptive, and productive when confronted with change, because most organizations today are implementing one or more change strategies, whether incremental or radical. These include organizational growth strategies designed to improve short- or long-term sustainability; organizational turnaround strategies that can include downsizing, rightsizing, and demergers; or organizational termination strategies, which can include closures and operation shut downs, among others. Whatever form these initiatives take, there is usually a lot riding on them.

This turbulent landscape, combined with the amount of knowledge needed to sustain high performance amid growing complexity, requires sophisticated learning capabilities and evolving change capacity across an organization. More than ever before, organizations need leaders who can anticipate and react to the nature and speed of change; act decisively without always having clear direction and certainty; navigate through complexity, chaos, and confusion; and maintain effectiveness despite constant surprises and a lack of predictability. To respond, learning leaders need to rethink how they develop change-capable leaders and prioritize change capabilities.

In chapter 5, we talked about the role of effective execution as an enabler of a sustainable, mature learning organization. One of the biggest barriers to execution of any strategy, learning or otherwise, is change turbulence and the resulting change fatigue generated by its accelerative pace and disruptive nature. In other words, change is not only picking up speed, but it's wreaking more havoc than ever before. The number of disruptive changes—"a severe surprise or unexpected shock"—that impede core operations, necessitate a major shift in strategy, and threaten long-term viability are on the rise (AMA 2006). When greater volatility produces more fluctuation in strategy, there's more risk in strategy execution. As Lou Gerstner (2003), former CEO of IBM, writes, "You have to be fast on your feet and adaptive or else a strategy is useless." Periods of business stability are now the exception rather than the rule for most organizations. Change volatility is the new normal.

Change Capability as a Strategic Imperative

The complexities of perpetual change are part of every organization's DNA, and change leadership is a vital capability that plays into everything that leaders, learning professionals, and employees do every day, regardless of their role. Executives have identified critical gaps in competencies related to leading change, thinking strategically, creating a vision, and rallying others around a vision (DDI 2015). According to a survey of almost 800 learning and business leaders, not enough organizations are prepared to handle these complexities (Figure 7-1). As a result, organizations are turning to the learning function for guidance and development support.

Figure 7-1. Fast Facts

48%	17%	63%
Business leaders who say the pace of change is faster and more unpredictable than in recent years	Business leaders who say their organization is highly effective at managing change	Business leaders who rate their organization's learning function as highly effective in providing change training

Source: ASTD and i4cp (2014a).

Despite a proliferation of books, research, and best practices on how to effectively manage change, attending to change issues remains an elusive leadership practice for most. In fact, mismanagement of change is often the number-one factor in the firing of CEOs (Herold and Fedor 2008). Many lessons can be learned from the last several decades of mistakes that dominant companies have made by not adapting to change or managing change well. Consider the case of JCPenney, which is still attempting to recover from a disastrous 17-month period in which it alienated customers, enraged employees, and suffered abysmal sales, due to aggressive, mismanaged retail and cultural changes launched under the regime of former Apple executive Ron Johnson. Another example is BlackBerry, which almost went under in its efforts to become another Apple. Its apparent strategy now is to become a better BlackBerry by focusing on what it does best. Its current phone, the Android-based PRIV, was met with strong reviews, and many tech reviewers believe that BlackBerry would still be a leading smartphone maker had it done something like the PRIV 10 years ago. It should be no surprise, then, that one of the biggest factors separating high- and low-performing organizations is their success in managing change.

Learning leaders have great advantages and opportunities in this area because, ultimately, all strategy is executed by people, who need to be supported, trained, and equipped to fulfill the strategic vision of change. Learning leaders can provide immediate and sustainable value when they can leverage their role as a strategic change agent.

DEFINITIONS

Adaptability: The ability to change (or be changed) to fit changed circumstances; the ability to adjust yourself to different conditions.

Agility: The ability to move quickly, decisively, and effectively in anticipating, initiating, and taking advantage of change; the ability of an organization to renew itself, adapt, change quickly, and succeed in a rapidly changing, ambiguous, turbulent environment.

Change agent: A person who acts as a catalyst for change. In broad terms, change agents help organizations sustain and grow performance by empowering people to work effectively as they plan, implement, and experience change.

Change capability: A feature, ability, or competence that can be developed or improved. Organizational change capabilities represent the collective skills, abilities, and expertise of individuals. They are what turn know-how into action and results.

Change capacity: The ability of individuals and organizations to accommodate new change demands.

Change leadership: Focuses on the transformational actions, skills, attributes, and mindsets needed to empower, inspire, and innovate during a change (or series of change processes), typically on a large scale.

Change management: Focuses on the transactional actions, tools, and techniques needed to control, facilitate, and administer a change process, typically in a series of steps.

Resilience: the ability to recover from setbacks, adapt well to change, and keep going in the face of adversity (Ovans 2015).

The Learning Leader as Change Agent

Many factors influence the capacity of an organization to accommodate and internalize complex change. One key factor is the initial readiness of the organization and its employees; as a result, organizations need change agents to lead them toward effective readiness. However, change initiatives often fail because organizations and their leaders think that being a change agent is the same thing as being a project leader. In reality, acting as a change agent requires a different set of skills and strategies. A change agent is someone who not only leads a new project, but also helps an organization transform itself for the better. A change agent should aim to make the organization better able to meet future challenges while moving forward with increased efficiency, effectiveness, and profitability. Often, that means thinking outside the box and trying new ideas, both strategically and tactically. It also means placing projects, especially learning and performance projects, within the context of broader change. While change agents typically wear many different hats, the most common for today's learning leaders are those of change architect, change strategist, and change catalyst (Figure 7-2).

Figure 7-2. Change Agent Roles

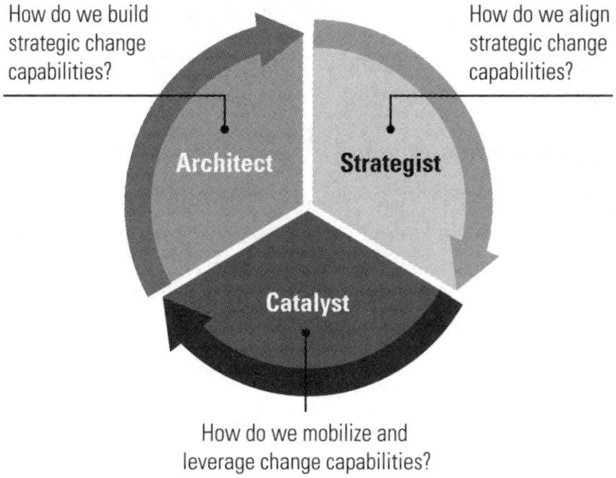

Source: Burkett (2015a).

Change Architect

Learning leaders add sustainable value as effective change architects by assessing and aligning capability needs and gaps, continuously improving leadership development, and leveraging capabilities to build a change-ready culture.

Assess and Align Capability Needs and Gaps

Learning leaders can start building change capabilities by focusing on the foundational strengths and gaps within existing talent pools. Most organizations consider managing change, demonstrating adaptability, and enabling teams to navigate change to be essential leadership competencies, yet often those behaviors and attributes are ill defined. Change capability can't be developed if it's not clearly defined. This is where learning leaders and stakeholders can work together to identify the characteristics and competencies needed to drive change in their organization. It's also important to define the role and capabilities that frontline managers need to make change happen. Note that change management capabilities vary greatly from one organization and business unit to another.

There is no universal profile for a change-capable leader. But it helps to have a shared frame of reference during conversations with leaders about building change-capable talent. Table 7-1 highlights common characteristics used to assess and develop effective change leaders (Burkett 2015b).

Table 7-1. Common Characteristics of Change-Capable Leaders

Characteristic	Definition
Emotional intelligence	The awareness of their emotional makeup; the willingness and ability to understand the varied emotional responses that people may have to change (fear, resentment, excitement); the know-how to help others deal with their reactions in a positive way
Empathy	The willingness and ability to fully appreciate another person's experience of change and to not attach a value judgment to it
Curiosity	The willingness and ability to probe for understanding and meaning
Flexibility	The willingness and ability to modify their style and approach based on situation, context, and the needs of the team, group, and organization
Change adaptability	The ability to tolerate ambiguity, accept new ideas, and show interest in new experiences
Coping skills	The ability to be positive and work productively during pressure situations or setbacks, and to handle criticism while keeping emotions in check
Teach ability	The willingness and ability to learn from every situation
Comfort with risk	The willingness and ability to try new things and balance risk and reward

Identifying and nurturing individuals with these competencies, attributes, and mindsets is essential to change leadership success and to the role of learning leaders as strategic change agents.

Once critical capabilities and gaps have been identified, it's important that they be integrated into the talent management functions guiding the attraction, development, management, and retention of leaders. As shown in Figure 7-3, this includes workforce planning (talent acquisition and retention), performance management, rewards and recognition, learning and development (especially leadership development), succession management, and career development. For example, prioritizing and aligning change capability with recruitment processes might include hiring leaders who demonstrate change adaptability and resiliency. Screening for adaptability can help reduce the potential cost of replacing a bad hire, which can be up to five times a person's annual salary (SHRM 2014). Screening applicants for fit in terms of change adaptability and resiliency also improves engagement and retention. Change capability should thus be assessed not just on current needs but also on future potential. In general, talent, and the organizational needs for talent, should be re-evaluated regularly so that learning leaders can identify and address the impact of dynamic or disruptive change upon talent needs.

Of course, successful integration of change capabilities starts with a solid understanding of the internal and external business environment, including such factors as business strategy and future trends. Key questions here include:

- What are the most critical business, strategic, and capability needs for leaders during the next three to five years? What is the gap between current and desired capabilities?
- What is the business context in which capabilities (including change capabilities) will be used? How will the context evolve over time?
- How can elements of change capability be aligned with current talent management strategies and frameworks?
- What competency tools and processes can help define the profile of a change-capable leader?

- How will you measure your progress in growing individual and organizational change capability? How will you know if you've successfully closed capability gaps?

Figure 7-3. Integrating Foundations

Workforce Planning
Performance Management
Rewards and Recognition

Learning and Development
Career Development
Succession Planning

Voices From the Field

Change is a very critical capability. If we're not focused on delivering learning solutions designed to create sustainable change, then I don't think we're doing a full job as a learning leader. When we develop learning strategies, we're constantly thinking about change: "What's the current state, what's the future state, where's the gap, how do we keep people moving forward?" Learning leaders need to think of themselves as change practitioners and look at the learning function as a change enabler.

—Lisa Nunes, Senior Director of Performance and Learning, Blue Shield of California

Continuously Improve Leadership Development

Many change initiatives flounder because leaders lack the skills to initiate and sustain change. While change capacity relates to the ability of individuals and organizations to accommodate new change demands, change capability is a feature, ability, or competence that can be developed or improved. Leveraging leadership development remains a key strategy for building change capability at the middle and senior leadership levels.

Building change competence is high on the agenda for CEOs around the world, who have identified managing complexity, leading change, and having an entrepreneurial mindset as skills critical to leadership success. Behaviors that characterize entrepreneurial and innovative leadership include questioning, networking, observing, and experimenting, which have been termed "discovery skills" associated with identifying new opportunities at the front end of the innovation process. Innovation also calls for a "leapfrogging" mindset, in which creating or doing something radically different produces a significant leap forward (Christensen 2013). These capabilities are critical for driving organizational change initiatives around operational excellence and performance. Yet few organizations currently focus on developing innovation and creativity among their leaders (Mitchell, Ray, and van Ark 2014). Chapter 9 talks more about the role of innovation as a lever for a sustainable learning organization.

Learning leaders can add sustainable value by ensuring that methods and processes for developing leaders' strategic change capabilities are in sync with evolving business needs. As discussed in chapter 4, effective development methods include the combined use of self-reflection exercises, coaching, mentoring, stretch assignments, action learning, and game-oriented simulations in which participants are placed in real-world scenarios and roles where they must lead change. Best practices include contextualizing and customizing leadership development approaches to fit the capabilities required of specific change roles and responsibilities, such as:

- change sponsors (those who lead change strategy)
- change managers (those who manage the change plan)
- change agents (those who build commitment and advocate for change efforts).

Developing the change capability of high potentials who are frontline leaders or individual contributors also increases access to future talent. Chapter 4 described hallmarks of effective leadership development for current and future talent. In general, leadership development will increase leaders' change capability when it:

- provides the proper blend of formal learning, learning from others, and experiential learning
- puts a stronger emphasis on programs that foster creativity and innovation
- matches specific change skills to real-world demands for each leadership level (frontline, midlevel, senior level)
- expects leaders to examine their mindsets toward change
- designs powerful learning journeys, rather than traditional learning events
- focuses on growing collective change capabilities across the organization.

Building change capabilities includes providing relevant learning and performance support across all organizational levels. For example, the presence of a designated change management team is strongly linked to both learning and change management effectiveness, but most organizations don't have teams in place. Available resources, while important, are not enough. Resources are only assets if they are capable and competent.

Leverage Change Capability

Ongoing, highly adaptive change capability is about more than stand-alone leadership development programs. Change capability is about nurturing change responsiveness and innovation throughout an entire organization so that it resides within the organization's culture, systems, and practices, including its learning function. Change architects should rewire the cultural aspects of their organization for increased change readiness and responsiveness. A change-ready culture enables an organization and its workforce to be more adaptive and resilient to change, be more innovative, think critically in complex or ambiguous situations, and continuously learn and improve. It also promotes a culture defined by flexibility, empowerment, and connectivity, which are key factors associated with employee engagement. Findings from a 2013 culture and change management survey with more than 2,200 global participants show strong correlations between the success of change programs and whether culture was leveraged in the change process, pointing to the need for a more culture-oriented approach to growing change capabilities (Aguirre, von Post, and Alpern 2013).

Learning organizations can help leaders facilitate a change-ready culture through enabling mechanisms (employee networks, performance management systems) that support the new culture. Examples of how sustainable learning organizations have enabled a change-ready culture include a "change academy" approach and a "change network" approach.

Change academies educate executives, managers, and change advocates in how to lead and manage change projects using consistent, field-tested, and standardized approaches. For example, a large manufacturing firm embarked on a major transformation program designed to solidify the company's market position through no fewer than 64 change initiatives affecting productivity, asset management, workforce development, safety, customer service, contractor management, and systems and data. The impact of these changes on the daily performance of its 5,000 employees was significant. To help build internal change capability, the firm established a dedicated change academy to customize capability development at three levels of leadership: the senior executive team, managers, and a group called "change supporters," who were especially influential people across the business who agreed to actively support change. In light of the importance of the transformation, and its impact, the goal was to do more than simply train people to work in new ways. The firm used the academy approach to help employees understand the nature of change along with how to lead and manage an effective change effort. Thanks to its efforts, the firm saw more distributed and capable change leadership, improved productivity, increased operational performance, and a rise in overall engagement.

Change networks build up an organization's collective capacity to navigate change and filter change management expertise among business units that need it most. An energy company with operations in 47 states, for instance, shifted from viewing change as a series of isolated events to viewing it and employees' change capability as a constant strategic imperative. To build internal change competency, the company embedded more than 50 change management tools and templates into existing Six Sigma frameworks. It also provided enterprise-wide training in problem-solving, process improvement, and change management concepts, principles, tools, and skills, which were immediately applied to projects. The company leveraged a change network of 60 to 200 advocates (depending on the project) to help integrate change capabilities and transform the way critical knowledge and skills were transferred among employees.

Change Strategist

From a strategic standpoint, change-capable leaders need a realistic assessment of the broader corporate culture to ensure that their learning strategies properly address everything that can help or hurt the rollout of a change effort, such as employees' readiness for change. Senior management often has trouble getting a true read on an organization's culture because of distorted views from the top, where executive leaders receive information only after it has been filtered through multiple layers of management. Learning leaders can add value as effective change strategists and business partners by helping leaders assess change readiness, identify the nature of change, define change capacity as a strategic readiness issue, assess risks of change fatigue, and measure change impact.

Assess Change Readiness

Change capability and responsiveness is about being ready to act during disruptive, uncertain, or complex circumstances. Learning leaders can influence change strategies by helping senior leaders stay in touch with the day-to-day elements of the workplace that influence readiness. These include structural, cultural, and human elements.

Structural elements influence how the organization's internal systems, processes, and infrastructure will be leveraged to operationalize a change strategy. Senior leaders need to ensure that these structural processes remain adaptive, resilient, and responsive to changing needs. Learning leaders can advise senior leaders to replace archaic systems that are poorly aligned, too complicated, or too isolated with technology-enabled, adaptive structures.

Cultural elements represent organizational norms and values in such areas as communicating, making decisions, measuring success, and rewarding achievement. Cultural integration is a critical success factor with any transformational change effort. According to Lou Gerstner (2003), "Culture is everything," a motto he leveraged while leading IBM's historically successful business transformation. Learning leaders can help senior leaders facilitate cultural integration through enabling mechanisms (employee networks, performance management systems, communities of practice) that support the new culture.

Human elements, at the heart of successful change, are often the most challenging to manage. Learning leaders can help senior leaders successfully mobilize the organization around new change demands by incorporating these principles when planning and implementing transformational change:

- Motivation increases when employees are confident that they can meet change expectations.
- Resistance may be more related to performance anxiety than negativity.
- Change expectations should allow for a learning curve after change is introduced.
- Additional resource support provided right after a change can minimize performance declines and ramp up proficiency.
- The more that individuals are involved in the change process, the more engaged they will be.
- Change volatility saps motivation, erodes confidence, and depletes goodwill.

Learning leaders add value as change strategists by emphasizing that structural, cultural, and human elements need to be aligned and that alignment requires time to be sustainable. Marcus Buckingham equates this kind of leadership savvy to the difference between checkers and chess. In checkers, the pieces all move the same way, whereas in chess all the pieces move differently.

Through a consultative role, learning leaders can help educate senior leaders about how each change piece fits with current organizational structures, systems, and processes—and how each piece is moving and contributing to the overall game plan.

Identify the Nature of Change

Not all change is created equal. Common types of change include developmental (improving skills and processes), transitional (putting new designs in place), and transformational (directing restructures, mergers, acquisitions, and new systems). Largely unpredictable and messy, transformational change requires change readiness and continuous adaptability across all organizational levels.

Traditional "step-by-step" change management approaches work best with developmental or transitional changes that have low to moderate organizational impact. However, one-size-fits-all change management approaches won't work for complex, transformational changes. Instead, transformational changes are best managed with an iterative process of staged changes, not a single event with a distinct beginning, middle, and end. By sharing knowledge and expertise about the nature of change, learning leaders can build their credibility as strategic change agents and ensure that senior leaders match their change strategy to the type of change demands at play.

Define Change Capacity as a Strategic Readiness Issue

An integrated, well-planned change strategy is meaningless if an organization lacks the capacity to execute it. In reality, capacity is finite; people can only do so much and there are only so many people. Capacity becomes a strategic issue when senior leaders demand that there be more capacity than there actually is or can be, or when they add major change on top of normal operating requirements and don't take anything off people's plates. In his book *How the Mighty Fall*, Jim Collins (2009) warned about the risk of frenetic, undisciplined change that goes beyond what leaders or companies can manage. Consider what happens when a metal spring is pulled. Initially, the material stretches to accommodate the increase in pressure. Yet when a metal spring is repeatedly pulled, there comes a point when the material yields to support increased pressure, often resulting in a damaged, but intact spring. Over time, pulling will cause the material in one area of the metal spring to narrow, causing a neck that becomes smaller and smaller until it can no longer sustain any pressure and breaks.

In much the same way, the people involved in the early stages of a change initiative will usually agree to stretch and tackle all necessary tasks. However, many individuals and teams struggle to maintain an intact change focus when they are repeatedly pulled to accommodate new initiatives, new tasks, and competing change demands. Multiple, change-after-change demands have become standard for most organizations, and studies show that demands are on the rise. When individual employees have trouble yielding to the pressures of constant change without damaging or breaking, it threatens the capacity of the whole organization to withstand the pressure of perpetual change without breaking.

Learning leaders can add sustainable value by helping senior leaders understand that all change requires an expenditure of physical, emotional, and cognitive resources that should be prioritized like any other organizational asset. One way to prioritize change tasks and resources is to assess the capacity gaps among the jobs, employees, and business units targeted by change:

- High-priority jobs may include those that are mission critical, hard to fill, highly paid, revenue generating, close to the customer, or filled by executive search.
- High-priority employees may include high performers, innovators, leaders or potential successors, hard-to-replace individuals, revenue generators, diverse employees, or those who be at risk of leaving.
- High-priority business units may include those that represent high profit and margin, high growth, or high criticality to business performance.

Learning leaders need to be proactive in anticipating the effort required for new changes under consideration to ensure that the organization has the capacity to take them on. It's also important to make sure that senior leaders are in tune with the realities of all change efforts, including workload, time commitments, and non-value-added work.

Assess Risks of Change Fatigue

Change fatigue is a major risk to a successful change effort and the effective execution of any new business strategy. Change fatigue sets in when people feel pressured to make too many transitions at once or when change initiatives have been poorly thought through, rolled out too fast, or put in place without adequate preparation. Change fatigue is one of the biggest barriers to change readiness. It drains support no matter how well planned or executed the change may be, or how motivated or capable the workforce (Figure 7-4).

Figure 7-4. Fast Facts

#1	#1	#2
Barrier that prevents sustainable change is change fatigue from too many competing priorities	Reason employees resist change is due to skepticism due to past failed change efforts	Reason employees resist change is because they do not feel involved in the process

Source: Aguirre, von Post, and Alpern (2013).

As change strategists, learning leaders can alert senior leaders to the impact of constant change on employees' motivation and their overall capacity to perform. Some organizations manage change turbulence by using a vetting process, in which proposals for significant change are subjected to rigorous "war room" screenings by key stakeholders and then prioritized according to their importance to business strategy, financial impact, and probability of success.

Measure Change Impact

Many organizations involved in transformation efforts declare victory too early and fail to measure success before moving on. Failing to assess what worked and what didn't deprives senior leaders of valuable information about how to adjust next steps and support the change process throughout its life cycle. Because many senior leaders envision change as a driver of revenue growth, innovation, cost savings, or talent development, learning leaders need to measure the efficiency, effectiveness, and outcomes of change efforts so that decision makers have credible data for determining whether to continue the investment.

Action-learning projects are one way to help measure the extent of on-the-job application and business impact of select change efforts, such as those focused on increasing sales, improving business processes, or increasing a leadership pipeline. For instance, many executive leadership programs include action-learning projects designed to support business objectives such as increased sales revenues, improved efficiencies, and enhanced leadership pipelines. Action learning is an approach that has teams attempt to solve real problems and reflect on the results. Teams generally report their recommendations for projects to other senior leaders within the organization, who can then provide a qualitative assessment of the project's success in meeting the key business objectives of a designated change. Chapter 6 provides more details about effective measurement processes for learning and performance solutions, all of which are intended to influence change, on some level, within the work, workers, or workplace.

Change Catalyst

Effective change leaders cannot create participation and commitment to change by decree. To develop and model change capability, learning leaders need to catalyze the hearts and minds of multiple stakeholder groups through open, collaborative, and iterative conversations about emerging opportunities and compelling new futures. And creating change commitment and growing organizational change capability is not a one-and-done event. Instead, change agents and change leaders must develop new ways to deepen a sense of shared ownership in both the day-to-day implementation of change and the outcomes of change efforts.

As change catalysts, learning leaders can use coaching opportunities, programs, and processes to elevate executives' change performance and productivity and level their expectations of change. They can also add sustainable value by helping leaders plan and execute change strategies, anticipate and manage risks of change, and continuously improve change capability across the organization.

Provide Mentoring and Coaching Support

From a coaching perspective, senior leaders often have trouble balancing operational and strategic leadership roles when attempting to drive change. Both managing and leading competencies are important to strategic change leadership because creating the inspiration for change also means ensuring that the proper management practices are in place to support it. However, senior leaders tend to be least proficient in the interaction skills required to lead change, and have actually expressed a desire to spend more time and effort on improving relationship building and interaction skills with others (Mitchell, Ray, and van Ark 2014). Many learning organizations fail to invest enough time or resources in mentoring, coaching, and supporting leaders' long-term progress. As change agents and catalysts, learning leaders build change capabilities by coaching and mentoring change leaders in the key skills needed to foster collaboration, build trust, and tap into the "wisdom of crowds" for wholesale commitment to change.

Help Leaders Plan and Execute Change Strategies

Prevailing wisdom, backed by an abundance of research, shows that most change initiatives fail at an alarming rate of 70 percent. The costs are high when change efforts go wrong—they include lost opportunity, wasted resources, and lowered morale. When an initiative is launched with great fanfare, only to fizzle out, cynicism sets in among employees who have endured the upheaval and added work pressures for another fleeting change. Planning and driving execution properly is especially critical because most change initiatives are so far-reaching, frequent, overlapping, and open-ended that they can no longer be successfully managed as discrete events.

As change catalysts, learning leaders can help senior leaders effectively plan and execute change strategies by adopting a standardized change management model—with matching language, tools, and techniques—that can be used strategically and interchangeably over time, across business units. While there is not one best approach, there are many prevalent change models and techniques available, such as ADKAR or Prosci. Learning leaders can add sustainable value by helping executives identify the strengths, weaknesses, and cultural fit of available tools and resources. No matter what change approach or tool is used, however, the following 10 success factors reflect universal guidelines for implementing any major change strategy:

1. Communicate a compelling vision about a new future (make a rational and an emotional case).
2. Develop a change strategy that includes milestones, timelines, and success measures.
3. Encourage appropriate, meaningful involvement before, during, and after a change process (engage, engage, engage).
4. Provide resources, remove barriers, and act as change advocates.
5. Deliver information, direction, and focus throughout a change effort.
6. Reward progress and quick wins toward defined success measures.
7. Adjust, adapt, and accelerate processes, policies, and practices to support change.
8. Create accountability mechanisms that show leadership is serious about the effort.
9. Model the behaviors expected.
10. Follow up and follow through to ensure ongoing attention to a change effort.

In particular, follow-up and follow-through are often underestimated as critical success factors in change implementation. Many efforts fail because leaders jump too quickly from one change effort to the next or because they try to make too many changes at once and fail to cascade them effectively through the organization (Moran and Blauth 2008). Consider the example of Luke Skywalker in the Star Wars trilogy. Luke is frequently impatient, steers off course, and in the *Empire Strikes Back*, ignores the advice of Yoda and Obi-Wan to rush off and face Darth Vader before completing his training. It's a bad decision that costs him his sense of identity, his confidence, and his hand. He recovers and learns from the experience. But what ultimately gets him through is the completion of his Jedi training, where he learned enough to successfully confront Darth Vader and the Emperor later in the trilogy. Change agents can add significant value by helping leaders recognize that there are few quick fixes, it takes time for major changes to take hold and be sustainable, and—as Luke found out the hard way—it's important to finish what you start.

Anticipate and Manage Risks of Change

In any major change effort, some level of discord, fear, and failure is inevitable, especially in times when quick decisions are needed and information is incomplete. Common risks associated with transformational change include staff attrition, changes in leadership, flawed communications, resource constraints, employee resistance, lack of follow-through by change leaders, scope creep, and lack of accountability. As change catalysts, learning leaders can support senior leaders' strategic change capabilities by helping them anticipate and remove common barriers to change progress and by helping to manage risks that occur. Promoting a culture in which both setbacks and successes are viewed as learning experiences, and innovation, improvisation, and risk taking are encouraged, is one way of the best ways that learning leaders can increase executives' change readiness and reduce the risks associated with performance anxiety or fear of failure.

As discussed in chapter 5, executives need information about risks to determine whether to continue or alter the course of a change project and whether to continue allocating resources to its progress. Critical risks that could derail change goals should be prioritized, and response strategies should be formulated to deal with them. Sustainable learning organizations have proper risk controls in place, along with identified practices for uncovering real or potential performance threats. Learning leaders can add sustainable value by helping senior leaders avoid the risk of overcomplicating improvement solutions designed to create change.

Voices From the Field

Change issues are significant. For example, we had one client with over 200 managers using our software to complement the learning transfer and application of skills from targeted learning programs. The level of application significantly increased among groups using the software compared to those that were not. Sadly, their budget was cut due to changes in the economy and the financial downturn. So they sacrificed the support software in the cost-cutting process.

But I think we as learning professionals sometimes overcomplicate things. For example, in another situation, we worked with a client to institute an induction process where learners routinely reported to their managers about how a learning experience benefitted them, their team, the company, or the customer, and what they planned to do with what they learned. Something as simple as this can shift cultural norms and withstand the forces of change because it's focused on the mindset of the learner and the manager. This wasn't an onerous or expensive process like a software investment. However, it did become institutionalized as a way to informally capture learning impact and it's proven less susceptible to organizational changes over time.

—Patrick Taggart, Managing Director, Odissy Ltd.

Continuously Improve Change Capability

Creating change commitment and growing organizational change capability is about more than the actions of a single charismatic leader or a stand-alone leadership development or change program. True change leaders help people feel connected and engaged through a sense of shared ownership in both day-to-day and large-scale changes. Consider the example of UPS, which is known for empowering its drivers to do whatever it takes to deliver packages on time. When Hurricane Andrew devastated Southeast Florida in 1992, many people were forced to live in their cars because their homes had been destroyed. Yet UPS drivers and managers sorted packages at a diversion site and made deliveries just one day after the hurricane, even to those who were stranded in their cars. UPS has credited its critical thinking, its adaptive skills, and a shared sense of purpose among employees for its ability to keep functioning amid the chaos of the catastrophe and its aftermath (Coutu 2002).

As the speed of change increases and the market for high-skill talent tightens, learning leaders can add sustainable value by continuously improving the way their organization grows, recognizes, and rewards collective change capabilities. Developing a network of change-ready employees across the entire organization will not only meet capability challenges, but also accelerate business performance. Studies confirm that high-performance organizations (based on revenue growth, profitability, market share, and customer satisfaction over time), strengthen their change effectiveness by extending change management training to senior leaders and all employees at a rate nearly 1.5 times that of lower performers (Morrison 2014). Chapter 8 looks more closely at the important role of networks and connections in growing and sustaining a resilient, high-performance learning culture.

Learning leaders can't expect to influence organizational change capabilities without also examining the flexibility and adaptability of their own learning models, processes, and practices. A learning organization that is not strategically aligned and responsive to the changing needs of the business and its clients is not sustainable. This means ensuring that learning processes and practices are adding continuous value to their operational and functional counterparts. It also means taking corrective or innovative action to improve or replace archaic systems that are poorly aligned, too complicated, or too isolated with technology-enabled, adaptive structures.

From Institutional Agility to Individual Resilience

It's important to remember that an organization's change capability and resilience ultimately reside in the change capability and resilience of its individual members. While change agents can help create the conditions needed to enable change readiness, they cannot inspire confidence and commitment in uncertain times unless they embody and model adaptability and resilience. Resilience is one of those elusive traits that most people want, but are not quite sure how to get or even explain. There are different ways to define resilience. For some, resilience is the ability to recover from setbacks. For others, it is about adapting well to change. And for still others, resilience is tenacity, perseverance, or grit, the ability to focus on completing tasks and solving problems, even in the face of limited or flawed resources. Regardless of how you define it, knowing what resilience means to you, and what strengthens and diminishes it, will allow you to be more effective in your role as a learning leader.

While some people seem to be naturally resilient, it can also be learned. In her book *Team of Rivals*, historian Doris Kearns Goodwin (2006) describes how Abraham Lincoln learned to adapt to uncomfortable situations to gain the support of legislators and win passage of the constitutional amendment that outlawed slavery. The ability to do what is required in a situation, and to adapt, evolve, and sometimes display energy and confidence not really felt, characterizes Lincoln and many other great leaders.

Some common techniques that can help you foster personal resilience include:

- Focus on a sense of purpose in your life.
- Develop a strong social network.
- Embrace change.
- Keep working on your skills (Cherry 2015).

Any number of obstacles can challenge a commitment to building change resiliency in the workplace, from company politics to the balance between compromise and goal setting to general resistance to changes in structures and policies that may be familiar or entrenched. Becoming a more effective change leader means taking the time to assess underlying, or "iceberg," beliefs that influence change commitment and serve as a precondition for behavioral change. For example, many organizations have a history of failure with past change efforts, so addressing such mindsets as "this is just another flavor of the month" or "this too shall pass" is an important part of change planning and communication that's often underestimated, dismissed, or overlooked.

In this regard, learning leaders need to monitor their own beliefs and aversion to change, especially underlying attitudes concerning resistance. Many learning leaders equate resistance with negativity. Yet some researchers have challenged prevailing wisdom about change resistance. Herold and Fedor (2008) contend that much so-called resistance can be attributed to performance anxiety about learning readiness: "Can I do what's expected of me?" To minimize performance anxiety and increase commitment during change efforts, consider providing more up-front training, removing environmental or on-the-job barriers, providing appropriate resource support at the time and place of need, and improving incentives for performance improvement.

Change is more successful when individuals are confident that they can attain change goals, give and receive feedback, and meet performance expectations. Strategic change agents can help level senior leaders' change expectations by helping them prepare for a learning curve or slight performance dip after a change is introduced. Change leaders can also minimize performance declines and increase proficiency by ensuring that additional resource support is provided during and immediately after changes are introduced.

To consider how well you and your team apply best practices associated with strategic change agent roles, complete the chapter self-assessment in appendix 2. Use the results to identify areas of strength and prioritize way to improve your own, or your team's, change capabilities.

Chapter Summary

Whether your organization is targeting a new growth agenda, refocusing its strategic priorities, or building its leadership pipeline, the ability to navigate change is the ultimate competitive advantage in today's global market. The pressures for change are real, change is here to stay, and the lackluster state of change leadership today shows that the world needs better change leaders.

Yet managing and leading change is not easy. As learning leaders, we have a responsibility to fully embrace our strategic change agent roles. This means we must continuously monitor our own aversion to change so we can best support the change strategies, processes, and practices needed to help leaders drive high performance and operational excellence. Only by transforming our own skills and capabilities can we deliver on the promise and opportunity of dynamic change.

Figure 7-5. Key Actions

PLAN	DO	CHECK	ACT
Define change-capable competencies and characteristics across all levels	Customize and contextualize leadership development programs and processes to build capability across all levels	Continuously monitor risks, especially change fatigue	Embrace your role as a strategic change agent
Routinely assess the talent pool for change capability needs and gaps	Use a consistent, disciplined, and planned change process for initiating and implementing significant change efforts	Monitor and measure the impact of major efforts	Leverage individual and collective change capabilities
Align change capabilities with talent attraction, retention, and development priorities	Cascade multiple or overlapping change efforts	Assess the business environment for current and future change demands, threats, and opportunities	Provide immediate and accessible performance support during and after change
Engage stakeholders in defining the success measures of change initiatives	Follow up and follow through with change efforts for improvement purposes	Monitor your own bias and aversion to change	Partner with senior leaders in defining change capacity as a strategic readiness issue

Commit to Act

Chapter Highlights

Rapid change poses a continuous threat to successful strategy development and execution, no matter how well supported, designed, and executed the strategy may be.

The business environment is changing faster than strategies can be devised or executed and the pace keeps accelerating. Change plays into everything that leaders, talent managers, and employees do. CEOs are turning to learning leaders for help creating adaptable, responsive, and agile organizations that can withstand the pressures of perpetual change.

Organizations (including learning organizations) cannot thrive in today's business environment without change capability, capacity, and readiness.

The future belongs to change-capable leaders and agile organizations. Whether targeting a new growth agenda, refocusing strategic priorities, or building a leadership pipeline, the ability to navigate change amid growing complexity and uncertainty is the ultimate competitive advantage. Organizations that are change capable are more likely to have strong financial performance and a strong leadership bench.

Learning leaders play a key role in building individual and collective change capabilities.

Building change capabilities is about more than stand-alone leadership development or change programs focusing on the actions of a single charismatic leader. Change capability is about nurturing change responsiveness and innovation throughout an entire organization so that it resides within the organization's culture, systems, and practices, including its learning function.

Building change capability is not a one-and-done event.

Creating change commitment and growing organizational change capability takes time and perseverance. A key role of learning leaders and internal change agents is to continually assess the environment for any barriers that may get in the way of desired changes. Follow-up and follow-through are important, often overlooked, elements in creating sustainable change.

Institutional resiliency begins with individual resiliency.

An organization's adaptability and change capability ultimately resides in the change capability and resilience of its individual members. The best leaders continually adapt their behaviors and mindsets to grow their personal resilience. As learning leaders, we have a responsibility to fully embrace our strategic change agent roles; to be the change we seek.

Case in Point

This Case in Point from the U.S. Army shows how one learning organization is transforming its strategies, processes, and practices to meet mission-critical needs for increased adaptability and change readiness. Richard Ayers, former deputy commandant of the U.S. Army Warrant Officer Career College (WOCC) in Fort Rucker, Alabama, volunteered to share his story about how he and his learning team built and adapted change capabilities in their journey to sustainability. (Ayers is now an organizational psychologist with the Army Capabilities Integration Center.) Their transformation process and change journey mirrors aspects of the Sustainability Cycle.

BUILDING INSTITUTIONAL AGILITY IN THE U.S. ARMY

The future success of the U.S. Army depends on its ability to be more prepared, innovative, and adaptive than its adversaries. For decades, the army has relied upon advanced technology for its source of competitive advantage. Yet technology has greater potential to be compromised by the enemy, or outmoded, in today's military landscape. A 2011 capstone report outlined a future vision of the army where the "human dimension" was emphasized as the best way to out-adapt, out-think, and out-innovate current and future adversaries. In the report, the army identifies cognitive dominance and institutional agility as mission-critical elements of the human dimension (U.S. Army Training and Doctrine Command 2011). In this context, cognitive dominance involves leader competencies such as critical thinking, mental acuity, perception, and intelligence that will enable army leaders to make sound judgments in complex environments where clear answers are not readily available. In addition, the future army will be smaller, so leaders must have the cognitive tools to support rapid, effective decision making with fewer resources. Learning is a chief enabler in growing the army's 21st-century soldier competencies.

Helping leaders gain critical capabilities in areas such as cognitive dominance occurs primarily through structured education at the WOCC. The term *institutional agility* refers to the learning institution's ability to adapt to leaders' educational needs, particularly because warrant officers only attend the college once every five to six years. The army's model for leadership development is based on three pillars: training, education, and experience (Figure 7-6).

The WOCC is the only army organization dedicated to training and educating army warrant officers from all specialties, with approximately 25,000 officers across the total force (active, guard, and reserve). About 70 full-time faculty provide "institutional" army education for three schools:

- The Warrant Officer Candidate School is a six-week program that averages 1,500 candidates a year. New classes of 60 student start every two weeks. At any given time, there are 120 to 180 candidates on campus.
- The Warrant Officer Intermediate Level Education is a five-week program designed to prepare candidates for positions of increased responsibility. It is held 18 times a year, every two to three weeks for 50 to 60 candidates each.

- The Warrant Officer Senior Level Education is a four-week program held six times a year for 60 students each. It is the most academically rigorous of the three.

Figure 7-6. 3 Pillars: Training, Education, and Experience

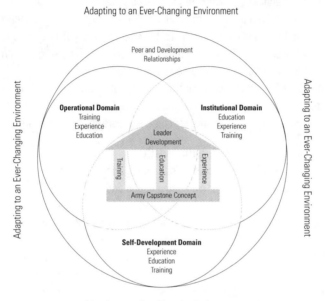

Adapting to an Ever-Changing Environment

The Army Leader Development Model

Current Challenges

These are challenging times for the military, according to Ayers. For starters, the U.S. Army defines its future operating environment as one that is highly complex, ambiguous, and uncertain. The complexity stems from a future that is unknown, unknowable, and constantly changing. Unlike the Cold War era from 1950 to 1990, when the United States' enemies were well known and threats were familiar, today's enemies are "new, nowhere, and everywhere." During the Cold War period, the army knew Soviet doctrine and strategy, the systems capabilities and limitations of Soviet weapons, the number of troops the Soviets had, what uniforms they wore, and what languages they spoke. In contrast, 21st-century soldiers are unsure about what region of the world they will go to next, and what will face them when they get there.

National policy goals add their own challenges. For instance, army leaders are not politicians, yet they know that war is an extension of politics, and winning a war is a political outcome. To that end, the United States must often engage in war and other military operations to achieve national policy goals while operating with tighter budgets, leaner personnel, and drastic reductions in new materials or programs.

Given the changing nature of war and the growing dangers and complexity of military service, the U.S. Army faces unprecedented problems in attracting and retaining recruits. Many recruits lack basic mathematical, reading, or writing skills. "I've read articles saying the cognitive preparedness of college grads coming into the military has been on a linear and steady decline for 30-plus years, from 1980 to 2014. One statistic I've seen said that up to 72 percent of military-age men and women between the ages of 17 and 24 are not fit for military service," Ayers says. Those that may be eligible or fit for duty are often dissuaded by the prospect of long stretches of overseas deployment time.

Further complicating the skill shortages are significant budget cuts; the military will soon see its force reduced by almost 100,000 active-duty soldiers. Essentially, the army is being asked to do a lot more with a lot less in an environment that's more complicated than ever before.

Recognition Stage: Transforming the WOCC

The WOCC is the army's primary resource for building adaptive leaders who can solve complex problems in an environment of increasing chaos and uncertainty. The capstone report issued a call to action for improved adaptability at the "human dimension" level of leadership and improved agility at the institutional, learning organization level (U.S. Army Training and Doctrine Command 2011). This report was the catalyst for WOCC transformation efforts, which resulted in a major overhaul of the college's learning strategy, its instructional design and delivery approaches, and its monitoring and evaluation processes. Gaining collaboration and buy-in from such stakeholders as the director of education and training, chief of academic instruction, chief of academic operations, and registrar was critical to the transformation strategy, which had an adaptive learning model at its core.

The continuous adaptive learning model provides a framework for outcome-based learning, focused on 21st-century soldier competencies in a learner-centric learning environment. The model is founded on two principles:

- "Improving the quality, relevance, and effectiveness of face-to-face learning experiences through outcome-oriented instructional strategies that foster thinking, initiative, and provide operationally relevant context."
- "Extending learning beyond the schoolhouse in a career long continuum of learning through the significantly expanded use of network technologies" (U.S. Army Training and Doctrine Command 2011).

The adaptive learning model, which originated in response to the capstone report, has been progressively honed and developed to improve methods for teaching critical-thinking skills in the context of "what's happening in the current operating environment, whether it be the Middle East or in the Pacific," Ayers says. "The operating environment changes so quickly that officer education has to change with it. We can't educate today's soldier with techniques used for yesterday's war. Soldiers have to be adaptive, so training has to adaptive." The evolution of the learning model included a shift from content-driven approaches to more experiential, learner-centered approaches emphasizing relevant action learning, simulations, case scenarios, artificial intelligence, e-learning, and virtual modalities.

ENABLING STRATEGIES

1. **Develop a learning strategy.** One of the first steps for the WOCC leadership team was defining the characteristics of a learning organization and researching what works and what doesn't in terms of using learning to foster adaptability and innovation. The team then developed a learning strategy to align with strategic objectives around building an adaptive learning organization. The strategy was fully endorsed by senior leaders.

2. **Engage sponsors.** When Ayers joined the WOCC in 2014, he and the WOCC commandant instituted a daily "stand up" exercise to reinforce the importance of informed and engaged leadership. Here, multiple service personnel are chosen at random to come stand in a circle in the middle of a room with the commandant. The commandant asks a few questions: "How's it going?" "What are you working on?" "How can I help?" This process is grounded in norms of open, honest, and transparent communication that have been distilled through WOCC training and reinforced by senior leadership. Enlisted personnel know that it's acceptable to talk freely to their "boss," and their "managers" encourage the exchange by telling them that it's OK to say you need more time, money, or help with an initiative. This horizontal and vertical communication approach has helped further a shared sense of purpose among military personnel and has strengthened the collaborative networks needed for improved problem solving, innovation, and adaptability. "When everyone knows what everyone else is working on, or what challenges they face, it can spark creative, 'out-of-the-box' thinking. Good ideas are able to emerge," Ayers says.

3. **Encourage risk.** To meet demands for increased innovation, the WOCC emphasizes risk taking in its experiential learning design. Without risk, a "high degree of mediocrity" will

prevail, says Ayers. Risk involves being open to disparate points of view and examining issues from multiple perspectives. For WOCC participants, it was initially a risk—and a paradigm shift within army culture—to openly disagree with superiors. Through formal and informal instruction, learning leaders emphasize that disagreement is not equivalent to disrespect. It is only through risk that innovation can occur.

Resistance Stage: Overcoming Challenges

The early stages of strategy implementation represented a slow process of transforming bureaucratic processes and entrenched practices across 70 locations and a million-person workforce. Faculty that had been using lecture-style methods needed time to adapt to experiential-based, action-learning approaches focused upon the learner. To help enable shifts in instructional mindsets and change instructors' behavior, the WOCC leadership team focused on providing the right conditions and performance support for new learning philosophies and methods to take hold. Performance support included advanced faculty development programs; self-directed learning options (such as watching TED talks); peer coaching and on-the-job observations of instructors applying a student-centric, facilitative teaching style; and student feedback showing that participants viewed the new approaches to be more relevant and satisfying. Also essential to the early transition process was constant communication from the leadership, both horizontally and vertically, on the importance of the change necessary to become a more effective learning organization.

In addition, creating the space and environment needed to support the adaptive learning model posed occasional roadblocks. For example, there were considerable technology gaps in terms of outdated equipment, broadband constraints, and videoconferencing capabilities. Communication protocols between the military and nonmilitary bodies needed to be approved, designed, developed, and monitored. Ultimately, a team of IT experts was given sole responsibility for upgrading the technology so it could be "seamlessly leveraged" during the learning experience. "Of course, technology is useless if instructors don't know how to use it," Ayers says. Because future army learners are expected to be expert users of digital technologies, the WOCC faculty had to develop technological expertise as well.

In addition to changing long-held beliefs and behaviors associated with Socratic learning methods, many faculty were anxious about integrating technology and blended learning approaches into their instructional practice, which in turn created additional challenges for the WOCC leadership team. The process and lead time involved in converting faculty to new learning structures, processes, and methods, and increasing instructors' proficiency levels, took longer than anticipated.

ENABLING STRATEGIES

1. **Provide support, build capability.** The WOCC leadership team made a deliberate effort to provide all the tools and resources faculty needed to be successful in adopting the new learning model. The team listened and openly addressed concerns, questions, and fears about meeting new performance expectations.
2. **Keep the "end in mind."** Senior officers were, and remain, actively involved in reinforcing the importance of faculty's role in building a smarter, better, and more adaptable workforce. Alignment with the purpose of the change was critical to gaining faculty engagement and support.

Renewal Stage: Continuing to Improve

"Sustained adaptation is tough," Ayers says. Maintaining the relevance of the curriculum given rapidly changing world threats, economic instabilities, and ongoing resource constraints has continued to be a challenge. The WOCC frequently needs to change instructional materials to ensure that they remain relevant to emerging operating-environment changes and military priorities. Continually adapting the curriculum places a huge burden on institutional faculty, who must demonstrate not only subject matter expertise, but also personal attributes of flexibility and agility amid disruptive conditions. Developing this agility is especially challenging because the range of desired outcomes for each college audience can be very broad: Faculty may one day be teaching brand new officer candidates who are just starting their career, and then the next day be instructing senior officers with 25 years or more of army experience. Critical-thinking skills required for junior officers differ greatly from those required for senior officers, heightening the demands on faculty to ensure that experiential learning content and context remain relevant.

"They have to constantly be at the top of their game," Ayers says. "Every time a class comes through the operating environment may change. It really puts the WOCC in a challenging position. How can instructors facilitate critical thinking and interactive discourse on current or emerging events when they may have little knowledge or experience about the topic? That's where we've really learned to leverage technology. We only need one expert who can distribute their knowledge about the operating environment to everyone through video teleconferences or through online access to real-time speeches before Congress given by senior officers."

Ensuring curriculum relevance also factors into motivating reluctant participants, who are not always eager to attend the college and be away from home for four to five weeks after returning from long deployments overseas. Relevant instructional materials foster student engagement, while enhancing their capabilities.

In addition to maintaining program relevance, the WOCC works toward enabling the continuing development of past attendants. Participants who have attended the college before assume a great deal of responsibility to maintain ownership of their continued development. After all, they attend the WOCC every five years. To stay current and connected to operating environment "experts" in a rapidly changing world, graduates are given multiple resources, tools, and follow-up support to stay engaged with their self-development. The WOCC builds in a degree of accountability through annual efficiency reports (or annual performance reviews), which ask soldiers to articulate what they've done to improve themselves and their unit. The reports often lead to recognition of and rewards for professional development efforts. "Most soldiers and their superiors know that learning and development is the right thing to do, that they need to be informed, to be a life-long learner," Ayers says. However, the WOCC continues to assess ways to improve follow-up support.

Current Status

In response to these challenges, the WOCC implemented a range of value-adding renewal approaches designed to ensure the sustained success of the learning organization in meeting its core mission of institutional agility. For example, the WOCC offers annual development opportunities for facilitators, in which they continue to enhance instructional skills in the adaptive learning model.

"You can't provide a world-class education without a world-class faculty," Ayers says. "This sends a powerful message about our commitment to help soldiers succeed both in the classroom and in the battlefield. It also provides more internal collaboration and knowledge sharing among facilitators and leads to a more rigorous accreditation process."

To assist with quality control, quality assurance monitors, who report to the WOCC commandant, routinely visit each classroom to ensure that criteria from the adaptive learning model are being met. They meet openly with faculty to debrief and share observations and findings to promote a spirit of transparency and continuous improvement.

Finally, the WOCC team has embarked on an extensive quest to learn and apply best practices to refine and better integrate current WOCC approaches. For example, Ayers and his team have traveled to military academic institutions such as the Army War College, Navy War College, the Military Academy at West Point, and the Command and General Staff College to establish networking relationships and share best practices. According to Ayers, "We are fully supported with our resource requirements because the army knows we won't have the capability to out-adapt, out-think, and out-innovate our adversaries without investing in the development of our human capital." These connections will allow the WOCC to prepare the next generation of army officers with the most relevant and highest-quality materials to meet the complex, ever-changing challenges of modern warfare.

ENABLING STRATEGIES

1. **Maintain the long view.** "It's important to always remember what stakeholders want. What is the mission? You've got to have alignment in any learning strategy or change approach, to tie methods to desired outcomes," Ayers says. "Keeping our eyes on the overall mission and the outcomes we're trying to achieve has kept us all focused and working together towards the same 'end in mind.' We also know that it's a journey and not a destination."
2. **Focus on continuous improvement.** WOCC team members are at the point where they "keep raising the bar" and expecting more from themselves. Best practices in learning and management are routinely shared across the organization, and the learning organization is viewed as a value-added, mission-critical enterprise. Ayers says, "We're growing and sharing our intellectual capital because 'a rising tide lifts all boats.'"

Case Review

This Case in Point shows how a learning organization within the U.S. Army is successfully transitioning to a more change-ready culture in response to labor shortages, advanced technology, increased complexity of global threats, and increased demands for more flexible and accessible learning modalities. Table 7-2 includes the characteristics of a sustainable learning organization that enabled these accomplishments.

Table 7-2. Characteristics of a Sustainable Learning Organization

Characteristic	Examples	
C-Level Sponsorship	• Senior leaders actively engaged as sponsors of an adaptive learning model and the transformation of the learning organization • Senior leaders are actively involved as learning champions	✓
Efficiency	• Partial monitoring of time and usage indicators (some automation challenges) • Learning outcomes integrated with efficiency reports generated by graduates after training	✓
Effectiveness	• Partially measured by instructor and participant feedback • Quantitative measurement targets in development are not currently utilized	In Progress
Investment	• Significant investment of dedicated resources, especially technology, to transform the learning institution • Dedicated investment in benchmarking activities, including travel to best-in-class military institutions	✓
Utility	• Sponsors and stakeholders (clients, instructors, customers) across all locations regularly utilize learning data to inform decision making	✓
Demand	• Flexible, blended curriculum development provided relevant, accessible learning on demand, at the time and place of need	✓
Credibility	• Learning team is seen as credible subject matter experts • Strategic partnerships with senior leaders increased the credibility of learning team	✓
Governance	• Quality assurance monitors are utilized to ensure consistency and quality around adaptive learning standards of instruction	✓
Continuous Improvement	• Continuous benchmarking conducted with other military learning institutions • Consistent pursuit and application of best practices in military education	✓
Resilience	• Renewal and development opportunities incorporated to help instructors remain resilient • Integrated use of on-demand technology to distribute critical information about changes in the operating environment at the time of need	✓

Because the WOCC is continuing to work on its effectiveness measures, and those measures are not yet fully integrated or operationalized, this learning organization has not reached the refinement stage of maturity. The learning team continues to evolve its measurement practice beyond satisfaction

(Level 1) and learning measures (Level 2) of effectiveness. The WOCC team acknowledged the need to develop more robust and quantitative measures of on-the-job application and business impact.

Practice 6: Foster Collaboration, Connection, and Community

"If you want to go fast, go alone. If you want to go far, go together."
—African Proverb

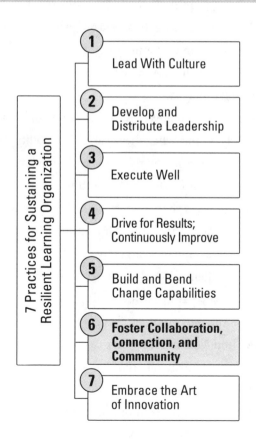

7 Practices for Sustaining a Resilient Learning Organization	**1** Lead With Culture
	2 Develop and Distribute Leadership
	3 Execute Well
	4 Drive for Results; Continuously Improve
	5 Build and Bend Change Capabilities
	6 Foster Collaboration, Connection, and Commmunity
	7 Embrace the Art of Innovation

What's in This Chapter

- why a climate of collaboration promotes engagement and high performance
- how a learning culture can drive collaboration for increased sustainability
- how learning leaders can increase collaboration, foster connections, and build networked communities for the good of the business.

WE LIVE IN A TRULY CONNECTED WORLD. The average adult has 338 Facebook friends, 44 percent of whom actively "like" content published by those friends at least once a day (Pew Research 2014). That's on top of an estimated 500 million active Instagram users (Statista 2016a), 313 million active Twitter users (Statista 2016b), and 450 million active LinkedIn users worldwide (Statista 2016c). People's lives are increasingly played out in a digital world. Outside the workplace, people use comments and ratings from sites such as TripAdvisor, OpenTable, and Yelp to influence their decisions about where to eat, how to travel, or which hotel to stay at.

Inside the workplace, employees want the same kind of accessible choice and connection in how and what they learn. The ability and flexibility to connect with others play a major role in overall employee satisfaction and retention. Employees at all levels are drawn to peer networks that challenge and support them, projects that connect with their strengths and abilities, and managers that support them through team-based training and development. Among the newest, and now largest, generation flooding the workforce, some "88 percent of Millennial workers prefer a collaborative work culture to a competitive one" (Asghar 2014). Millennials place a high priority on a cohesive, team-oriented work environment that emphasizes a sense of community, more so than their non-Millennial counterparts (PwC 2013).

Beyond the increased demand from workers, jobs simply require more collaboration among people from different units and supervisory levels than they did in the past. Changes in traditional hierarchical structures reflect these increased demands for connection and collaboration. In today's knowledge economy, where the half-life of knowledge progressively shrinks each day, it's become even more important for organizations to design structures and processes that enable fast and free information flow across boundaries.

Social learning experiences and peer-learning networks have gained prominence as effective ways of enabling employees to quickly connect with others to solve problems and focus exactly on what information they need, when they need it, with minimal interruption to their daily work flow. At its core, social learning is about sharing knowledge, information and experiences through interactive discussion and peer collaboration. For example UL, a safety consulting and certification company, has a global leadership program that builds a global network of leaders through conversation and facilitation. During program sessions, cohorts work together on important company issues, with recommendations presented to senior leadership. The program is designed to provide a powerful, collaborative experience as a social learning tool with a focus on how learners can succeed when working across cultures and time zones (Graber 2016).

Why Collaboration and Connection Matter

It makes good business sense to encourage collaboration. It also pays off (Figure 8-1). Effective collaboration can lead to more meaningful connections, both formal and informal, among teams, leaders, and employees. Connection can be described as an intangible aspect that reinvigorates the positive bonds between individuals, teams, and organizations. Connection meets the basic human need to belong and helps make people more trusting, cooperative, empathetic, enthusiastic, optimistic, energetic, creative, and innovative. From a business perspective, a connected environment is one where people want to:

- Collaborate with their colleagues.
- Create ideas that stimulate innovation.
- Share information that helps decision makers become better informed.

Figure 8-1. Fast Facts

Up to 1.8x	Up to 3.1x	Up to 4x
Increased individual productivity from enhanced collaboration	Accelerated rates of innovation from enhanced collaboration	Higher productivity in meetings from enhanced collaboration

Source: Filigree Consulting (2012).

Landmark research from a 2006 Gallup study with nearly 8,000 business units over seven years showed that business units with higher connection scores experienced higher productivity, profitability, and customer satisfaction, as well as lower employee turnover and fewer accidents. The study examined measures of connection through questions that assessed how caring a work environment was, how much learning and development was encouraged, and how the work environment enabled individuals to be heard, collaborate, and contribute. Similarly, a 2010 IBM study found that high-performing organizations are almost 60 percent more likely than low-performing ones to provide collaborative and social networking tools to their global teams. The bottom line is that connection plays a critical part in improving organizational performance and creating a new source of competitive advantage.

Connections can vary tremendously across organizations, and across departments in the same organization, depending on leadership and cultural norms. We all know it when we feel it and, when it's absent, we experience neutral or even negative feelings toward a person, place, project, or event.

The need to connect is powerful. In recent years, neuroscientists have discovered that connection reduces stress levels, provides a sense of well-being, and makes us more trusting. An organization with a high degree of connection has employees who are more engaged, more productive in their jobs, and less likely to leave the organization for a competitor.

DEFINITIONS

Collaboration: A process governed by a set of norms and behaviors that maximizes the contribution of individuals by drawing on the collective intelligence of everyone involved. Collaboration requires the understanding and application of key behaviors that are increased through learning and practice.

Community: A feeling of fellowship with others as a result of sharing common attitudes, interests, and goals. Collaborative partnerships are alliances used to improve the health of a social or business community.

Connection: Connection is considered a powerful force that creates a positive bond between people and contributes to bringing out the best in them—it energizes people, makes them more trusting, and builds their resilience in the face of difficulties. Generally described as something intangible, it can be the outcome of successful collaboration and a key driver in fostering employee engagement (Stallard 2015).

Cooperation: Collaboration should not be confused with cooperation. Cooperation is when individual goals are developed and shared through give-and-take discussions, which often lead to outcomes that promote new ways of working. Individual actions and achievement remain the focus rather than a collective strategy (Ashkenas 2015).

Teamwork: Teamwork involves individuals with different knowledge, skills, and abilities working together toward a common goal. Teams can be formed but collaboration is not guaranteed.

Challenges With Collaboration

Most executives understand the value of collaboration and say that making workplaces more collaborative is a high priority. Yet as employees become more scattered across multiple locations, budgets shrink, and workloads expand, collaboration and connection remain a challenge: In 2011, 86 percent of more than 1,400 surveyed executives and employees cited a lack of collaboration or ineffective communication for workplace failures (Fierce 2011). Many best-practice learning organizations have met this challenge by using social media tools to help connect employees with colleagues, coaches, or mentors who can answer a question, share information, or collaborate across space. For example, employees at Salesforce collaborate by sharing ideas on a social networking application called Chatter. This program allows employees to analyze data, compare drafts of documents, and share ideas in real time. Real-time collaboration and knowledge sharing eliminates the lag associated with using email or other forms of communication.

While social technologies play a vital role in enabling the speed and access of connections, the real value of effective collaboration and networking does not lie in more robust project management tools or advanced technology. These are simply means to an end—a collaborative and connected culture ultimately resides in the social fabric of organizations and how people do their work. In a truly collaborative environment, everyone has a voice, can contribute, and understands how their contributions fit with strategy and purpose.

A key cultural challenge is that many senior leaders continue to view collaboration as a skill applied to a single project or activity. When collaboration is focused solely on teams or a single level of an organization, it is extremely difficult to sustain and benefits are fleeting. Learning leaders must help organizations move beyond this narrow definition to redefine collaboration as a cultural value that should be embedded as part of an organization's DNA.

In short, a truly collaborative environment involves all organizational levels and is a part of the organization's cultural identity. When organizations consistently apply collaborative approaches to improve cross-functional connections and break down silos, even in a limited manner, they have achieved many sustained benefits, including:

- fully engaged workers eager to take on new projects
- improved organizational agility and flexibility
- more productive, energized meetings
- competitive advantage attracting top talent
- higher retention rates
- improved performance and profitability.

Gear Up for Collaboration

Collaboration doesn't always come naturally to organizations and their employees, even with the best messaging or learning and performance support. For example, many individuals have ingrained beliefs about the value of competition and see collaboration as a sign of weakness. Some view collaboration as too slow or ineffectual, especially when dealing with the pressure of fast-paced environments. Others believe that "if you want something done right, you have to do it yourself." In addition, many organizations inadvertently sabotage collaboration by emphasizing short-term competitive behaviors and quick fixes at the expense of the future vision of a collaborative culture. To make collaboration a true part of an organization's culture, learning leaders can add sustainable value by helping organizations power and grease three levers (Figure 8-2).

Figure 8-2. 3 Levers for Effective Collaboration

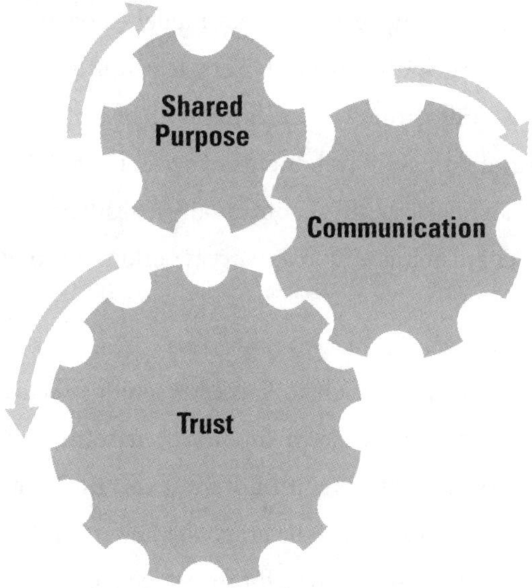

Trust

Trust is the foundation of effective collaboration. Leadership expert and bestselling author Simon Sinek (2014) says that trust offers a sense of psychological safety—the feeling that our leaders have our interests at heart. This means creating an environment where employees can feel free to take risks and openly express concerns, fears, and differences of opinion without reprisal or retaliation. When former Campbell Soup Company CEO Doug Conant took over in 2001, he transformed a "toxic culture" into one that valued fresh ideas by making it safe to challenge the status quo (Duncan 2014).

Cultures that build trust and increase risk taking enable more rapid innovation because employees can dare to experiment and fail. Adobe is a company that is intentional about trusting employees to experiment and do their best. Employees are given challenging projects and then provided the trust and support to help them meet those challenges successfully. Continual training that promotes risk taking without fear of penalty is part of the company's culture (Patel 2015).

Learning leaders play a key role in leveraging leadership development to help executives understand, promote, and model the value of trust-building and risk taking. As strategic business advisers, learning leaders can also demonstrate that trust is built through small moments of consistent, daily interaction rather than grand mission statements or sweeping proclamations. Finally, learning leaders can help executives continually assess and improve trust levels through such mechanisms as employee surveys or one-on-one interviews.

Communication

For cross-functional collaboration to succeed, senior executives and managers must communicate goals clearly; modify their communication approach to meet the needs of individuals with different communication and collaboration styles; and recognize how to leverage the talents of those with different communication styles to pave the way for increased engagement. The majority of leaders fail to clearly communicate their strategy through the organization, which slows down projects, hurts performance results, and hinders engagement. To nurture cross-boundary collaboration, the best executives view every interaction as an opportunity to invite input and fresh ideas about strategy.

Doug Conant made it a practice to interact with as many employees as possible, at every level, during daily walks around Campbell Soup's headquarters in New Jersey and production plants in Europe or Asia (Duncan 2014). Conant has said that these interactions enabled people to put a human face on the company's strategy and direction and helped keep him informed about goings-on throughout the company.

Most employees prefer workplaces where communication is open and issues are discussed effectively. Listening to and inviting diverse input brings in more valuable information, builds bridges of trust, and promotes shared accountability. Chapter 3 highlighted other examples of best-practice communication processes used by both executives and learning leaders who are building and sustaining a cohesive, high-performing learning culture.

Shared Purpose

A collaborative work environment is one that works across boundaries to build connections and shared purpose. Having a purpose associated with work produces better performance and engagement than pure financial rewards do. Most people want to feel like they are part of something bigger than themselves. Companies that help employees focus on the meaning and purpose in their work have shown a decline in absenteeism and a reduction in turnover. Pixar University, created to build connections across the company, bears the Latin phrase *alienus non dieutius*, which translates to "alone no longer," on its crest. Every employee, from the janitors to the CEO, spends four hours a week in classes with colleagues learning about the arts and animation, and most important about one another. By having all employees go through this learning experience, Pixar can embed a shared sense of purpose in its culture that resonates across all collaborative efforts (Stallard 2015).

The Role of the Learning Leader

To make collaboration a true part of an organization's culture, learning leaders can add sustainable value by consistently taking the following actions.

Teach Collaboration

Many organizations expect employees to work well together without properly teaching them how or defining what collaboration looks like in terms of daily practice and behavior. In addition, collaboration often fails because it's viewed as an activity instead of a skill or because collaboration is a mandated performance requirement focusing on compliance instead of commitment.

Preparing leaders for collaborative leadership requires a different teaching approach, because the goal is to unlock the capacity for everyone to contribute. Frequently, collaboration skills are only offered to senior leaders and high-potential employees, which is detrimental to creating an organization-wide collaborative environment. Employees need to speak the same collaborative language, learn collaborative behaviors in the business context where collaboration occurs, and consistently practice collaborative behaviors that receive appropriate reinforcement, recognition, and rewards. Collaborative skills are often incorporated among the following professional development skill sets:

- how to ask for input from others
- how to listen for understanding
- how to reach consensus
- how to provide constructive feedback
- how to share information with others
- how to use negotiation skills
- how to lead change.

When teaching collaboration, it's also important to encourage healthy debate, creative tension, and constructive criticism. Collaboration is often stymied because of norms that encourage people not to criticize, which can be counterproductive when it comes to cultivating collaboration. As employees work through conflict, they become more comfortable and fluid, ideas flow more freely, and results become more successful. The process of learning and collaborating together is as important as the content components. Chapter 4 described how sustainable learning organizations have used approaches such as action learning or simulation methods to create powerful, collaborative learning experiences to close leadership skills gaps and foster creative thinking.

Ensure That Talent Management Processes Enable Connections

Connections to a group are strengthened when employees' role and work duties are a good fit with their skills, their work is believed to be worthwhile and meaningful, and they have control over their work. Connection is also enhanced when employees experience personal growth. Subsequently, high-performing, sustainable learning organizations build and leverage integrated talent management processes (recruiting, onboarding, engagement, rewards and recognition, performance management, succession planning, knowledge management and learning) to enable connections across organizational levels, outside direct reporting relationships and across functional boundaries. Consider the following:

- **Onboarding.** Radio Flyer's six-month onboarding and assimilation process, New Flyer, incorporates multiple elements that foster connection, community, and shared purpose from day one. One element is a connections phase, in which new hires meet with their team and various groups and committees within the organization. Learning and knowledge content around products, customers, or the company's mission, vision, and values is taught by employees who act as coaches. The company's CEO also facilitates two courses in the series, which includes a specific element devoted to teaching new employees and managers team communication skills, both in and out of the office. The final element of the New Flyer onboarding process is follow-up, which includes five yearly check-ins regarding employees' progress, concerns, or suggestions. The evolving focus on connections and community as part of the onboarding process has had a positive influence on retention at Radio Flyer. Turnover rates have decreased and employee satisfaction with the organization has significantly increased since the inception of the program (Dixon 2016b).

- **Performance management.** To gather better perspective about the talents of the people on the team, leading organizations create mechanisms for employees to recognize the collaborative efforts of their co-workers. A recent study from human resources research firm Mercer on performance review practices suggests that 35 percent of companies with more than 1,000 employees collect peer feedback in some capacity (Sipek 2015b). Hearsay Social, a San Francisco–based computer software company, has taken steps to integrate peer feedback into its performance review process because teamwork and collaboration are core values of its company culture. Training is provided in how to give constructive feedback and a Facebook page is available for employees to give and receive feedback. While there is great potential for peer feedback to increase collaboration and improve engagement, however, there are significant challenges to implementing and integrating the process, the greatest of which is execution. Chapter 4 provided some guidelines and considerations on this topic.

- **Recognition and rewards.** Job descriptions and work design often tend to emphasize individual accountability while overlooking the critical importance of an employee's collaborative skills. Every organization has people who influence and energize others without relying on their title or formal position in the hierarchy to do so. To foster collaboration, recognize and reward informal connectors who share knowledge and contributions, especially managers who promote collaboration. They are a powerful, informal resource in spreading a critical few behaviors from the bottom up.

Break Down Silos

Despite the fact that most work today is collaborative, work flows and decision processes are typically not designed to reflect the collaborative nature of work and innovation. Siloed work environments, where departments operate as independent fiefdoms, work at cross-purposes with collaboration and stifle the free exchange of information and expertise across the organization. It's important to routinely assess how and where collaboration is breaking down, as well as areas where collaboration is working well for teaching and continuous improvement purposes.

For example, as highlighted in chapter 4, Hesselbein transformed the Girl Scouts in a number of ways. But of critical importance were her efforts to dismantle a fairly entrenched hierarchy during her tenure as the agency's CEO. Like many other youth organizations, the Girl Scouts had adopted a military structure where "the brass" in the national organization was mostly insulated from the realities in the field. There was a wide divide between those in authority who made decisions and those who executed them. Hesselbein instituted a comprehensive restructuring with new organization charts that used concentric circles to, as she put it, "free people from being stuck in little boxes." This was later described as a "web of inclusion" designed to foster communication across levels and divisions and enable cross-functional teams to come together and make their own decisions (Helgesen 2015.)

Engage Senior Leaders

Ensure that senior leaders understand their role in promoting collaboration as a cultural value and in modeling behaviors that support an open, transparent, and collaborative environment. A.G. Lafley, former CEO of Procter & Gamble (P&G) and current executive chairman of the board, used the power of collaboration and connection to boost the performance of P&G. When he first became CEO, P&G was performing poorly and morale was low. Lafley actively and regularly connected with employees and encouraged people to "get the moose out of the closet" before problems grew bigger. Within his first 12 months, these efforts resulted in a two and a half times increase in employee approval of P&G's leadership, matched with increased profitability and stock price, which then enabled P&G to acquire the Gillette Corporation (Stallard 2015).

Define Success Measures

Define indicators that will help leaders map progress and establish accountability measures in support of a collaborative work culture. Collaboration measures can be tracked at the organizational and individual level. For example, at the organizational level, collaboration can be tracked by monitoring how well talent and ideas are flowing across boundaries. Are people moving freely from one area to another; are ideas and practices openly developed, shared, and applied across business units? Some organizations measure collaboration by cost savings in administration through shared services, which has been shown to produce a 15 to 25 percent savings in employee administration costs (Ulrich et al. 2009). It's also important to ensure that metrics and incentives for collaboration are aligned properly with the realities of the business environment. For instance, operations employees who are rewarded for speed of execution and on-time delivery or sales professionals who are motivated by sales volume may have more to lose if expected to invest time and resources in meeting collaboration goals.

Leverage Technologies That Promote Collaboration and Connection

Learning leaders can't create community on their own, but they can invest in and leverage the technology needed to enable it. Millennials, in particular, expect to have access to the best tools for collaboration and execution. Before investing in the latest social networking platforms, however, it's important to develop a strategy outlining the why and how of collaboration in your unique environment. The technology needs to support the strategy. Before rolling out a comprehensive social learning strategy, Hilton Worldwide University conducted extensive research on how it could leverage existing social media initiatives, such as Twitter, Facebook, and custom social portals for idea sharing and crowdsourcing, within the organization. Social media was then used as the main communication platform for unveiling the new social learning strategy within Hilton Worldwide (Harris 2015c). Strategic use of social collaboration and digital talent management tools has the potential to drive business outcomes, transform the value of learning and talent management service delivery, and increase engagement levels. Supporting technologies include:

- **Social recruiting tools.** The ultimate goal of a collaborative culture is to attract, engage, and retain talent. Social recruiting tools used on LinkedIn, Facebook, and Twitter help increase candidate outreach and position organizations as an employer of choice in a competitive talent market. Learning leaders can add value here by providing creative videos or content that promotes the company's culture as a distinguishing "brand" for potential hires. For example, Ericsson's talent acquisition team built a foundation of brand communications using digital media platforms, a careers website, blogs, videos, and other social networks to bolster its talent acquisition profile. While the design and implementation of the strategy took years to establish, results include increased site traffic and social media engagement.

- **High-impact, on-demand videos.** Videos can be used to communicate important organizational messages, reinforce learning strategies, or articulate business priorities. They allow a two-way dialogue with employees and managers by creating an online collaborative forum to post comments, ask questions, and provide feedback. They can also be used to capture subject matter expert knowledge on topics of interest, without incurring the production costs of formal learning management system course content.

- **Live meeting platforms.** Meeting platforms such as Adobe Connect or WebEx are often used share knowledge and user-generated content.

- **Company-sponsored social platforms.** Many best-practice learning organizations foster connections and improve collaboration with company sponsored social platforms. Mindtree, a global technology firm with more than 200 clients in 14 countries, has 54 online communities of practice where employees learn, share, and create free content. Konnect, a social networking and knowledge-sharing platform, consists of blogs, document repositories, discussion forums, podcasts, and videos that employees can use, rate, or recommend. Formal learning programs, such as the company's technical certification programs, are fully aligned with Konnect. The certifications are delivered through a blended learning approach in which participants create communities of practice, coaching relationships, conferences, and contests. Cost savings through the use of technology has been an important efficiency measure for the global learning organization, along with increased reach and improved effectiveness in terms of developing critical capabilities (Salopek 2015a).

Model Collaboration

Learning leaders play a key role in promoting organization-wide collaboration and enabling connections. However, it's not possible to be a credible facilitator or collaborative business partner without modeling the way. Modeling a collaborative spirit also involves providing greater transparency to employees regarding compensation, rewards, and career decisions. Learning leaders who cannot successfully collaborate across all organizational levels cannot build and sustain a mature learning organization. Improving capabilities in collaboration is a critical challenge for today's fast-paced organizations and one in which learning leaders have great opportunities to add sustainable value (Figure 8-3).

Figure 8-3. Addressing Collaboration Challenges

Challenges

Effective collaboration is needed by managers and employees to:
- Promote innovation.
- Drive knowledge sharing across boundaries.
- Improve engagement.
- Increase competitive advantage.
- Increase organizational flexibility and agility.
- Improve performance.
- Build connection to a shared purpose.

Opportunities

Learning leaders can help managers and employees meet collaboration challenges by:
- teaching collaboration
- ensuring that talent management processes enable connections
- breaking down silos
- engaging senior leaders
- defining success measures
- leveraging technologies that support collaboration and connection
- modeling collaborative behaviors.

Outcomes

Ability to help solve critical collaboration challenges results in enhanced:
- innovation from improved knowledge sharing
- employee engagement
- productivity and performance
- customer experience and market advantage
- decision making
- support for a culture of continuous learning as a source of value creation.

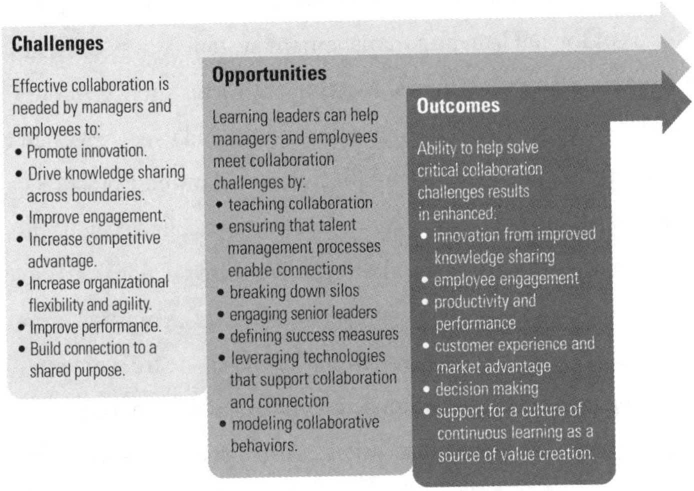

Chapter Summary

In today's connected economy the future of leadership is increasingly collective and collaborative. A truly collaborative environment is infused in workplace culture, identity, and daily operations. Connection enables knowledge sharing and encourages innovation across boundaries. This goes beyond social learning tools and technologies to how well connection is tied into the overall social fabric of an organization and the trustworthiness of its leaders. To help organizations create a collaborative and connected community, and to make their learning organization more relevant to modern workforce needs, learning leaders can add sustainable value by:

- growing collaborative capabilities across all levels
- creating mechanisms for boundary-free information sharing and continuous learning
- engaging senior leaders in modeling collaborative values and practices
- reaching and engaging employees through social networks
- building purpose-driven communities.

Use the chapter 8 self-assessment in appendix 2 to gauge how well your learning organization fosters collaboration, connection, and community, and to identify potential opportunities for improvement.

Figure 8-4. Key Actions

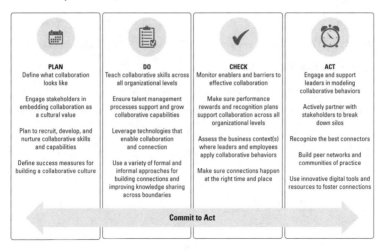

PLAN	DO	CHECK	ACT
Define what collaboration looks like	Teach collaborative skills across all organizational levels	Monitor enablers and barriers to effective collaboration	Engage and support leaders in modeling collaborative behaviors
Engage stakeholders in embedding collaboration as a cultural value	Ensure talent management processes support and grow collaborative capabilities	Make sure performance rewards and recognition plans support collaboration across all organizational levels	Actively partner with stakeholders to break down silos
Plan to recruit, develop, and nurture collaborative skills and capabilities	Leverage technologies that enable collaboration and connection	Assess the business context(s) where leaders and employees apply collaborative behaviors	Recognize the best connectors
Define success measures for building a collaborative culture	Use a variety of formal and informal approaches for building connections and improving knowledge sharing across boundaries	Make sure connections happen at the right time and place	Build peer networks and communities of practice
			Use innovative digital tools and resources to foster connections

Commit to Act

Chapter Highlights

A highly collaborative and connected workplace fosters engagement, increases productivity, lowers stress, and is a key source of competitive advantage.

When organizations consistently apply collaborative approaches to improve cross-functional connections and break down silos, even in a limited manner, they can achieve many sustained benefits, including a fully engaged workforce, improved organizational agility and flexibility, a competitive advantage in attracting and retaining top talent, improved performance and profitability, and increased innovation. Collaboration occurs when the organization accomplishes more than its individual elements could separately. Operational efficiencies are gained because knowledge, information, expertise, services, products, and technology are shared and leveraged across boundaries.

Learning leaders play a vital role in building and sustaining a collaborative work culture.

When collaboration is focused solely on teams or a single level of an organization, it is extremely difficult to sustain and benefits are fleeting. Learning leaders must help executives move beyond narrow definitions to redefine collaboration and connectivity as cultural values, and core capabilities, that should be woven into the organization's social fabric. Learning leaders play a critical role in terms of building collaborative capabilities and creating mechanisms that support collaboration, foster social connections, and promote a sense of community. This includes integrating collaboration and networking skills with talent management strategies and processes, including leadership development. Sustainable learning organizations effectively leverage social networks for employee recruitment, engagement, and development. Many best-practice learning organizations are also seizing opportunities to create collaborative, network-centric approaches in other areas, such as onboarding for new employees, knowledge retention, staffing, and succession planning.

A learning organization that does not intentionally practice and model collaboration cannot be sustained.

It is not possible to enable collaboration, build connections, or be a credible business partner without consistently modeling collaborative behaviors. Learning is about generating new knowledge and skills and sharing them across the organization. Moving ideas across boundaries—from one leader, one layer, or one division to another—can be accomplished through technology, social networks, communities of practice, and relationship building. But while technology may be a means, the social aspects of trust and relationship building are the end. Building collaboration and connection are intentional "inside-out" exercises that must be practiced consistently and rigorously.

Case in Point

The following Case in Point shows how a resilient group of learning leaders created a collaborative, purpose-driven community to build and sustain a viable learning organization following the devastating aftermath of Hurricane Katrina. The University of Southern Mississippi's (USM's) Cyndi Gaudet, chair of the College of Science and Technology, and Heather Annulis, professor of human capital development, volunteered to share their story about the power of collaboration, connection, and community in their journey toward sustainability.

HUMAN CAPITAL DEVELOPMENT GROWTH AT THE UNIVERSITY OF SOUTHERN MISSISSIPPI

Launched in 2006, the department of human capital development (HCD) doctoral program at USM Gulf Coast provides advanced study and research of human capital development.

The development of human capital will increasingly be the defining characteristic that determines the extent to which an economy can develop and exploit new technologies and compete in the global marketplace. HCD, in the context of the program, consists of three elements—technology, economic, and workforce development—that are interdependent and have important interactive effects. For example, technology development can catalyze and alter the U.S. workforce by enhancing the health and longevity of the population or by providing incentives for individuals to remain in the workforce or leave as job skill requirements evolve. In turn, the skills of the workforce can shape the future course of technology development through the applied use of high-end science and engineering knowledge or through the ability to adapt to changing technologies in the workplace.

Recognition Stage

In recognition of escalating market demands for a skilled workforce that could adapt to changing technologies, global competition, and shifting product demands, USM developed the doctoral program in HCD. Market analysis conducted with regional industrial, government, and educational institutions confirmed that human capital solutions were needed to help organizations meet the challenges of rapidly evolving labor trends. No other degree program existed to provide advanced study and research of HCD in high-growth, high-technology industries. The program's mission, then, is to prepare scholar-practitioners who can apply evidence-based knowledge and skills to improve organizational growth and performance, particularly within high-growth, high-technology industries. According to Gaudet, "The Gulf Coast represents a robust business community to support the things we teach in human capital development."

To meet diverse learning and business needs of students from such diverse industries as the military, business, education, and government, the HCD doctoral program developed an innovative executive delivery format, including distance learning, project-based courses, and weekend class sessions, specifically designed to expand instructional opportunities beyond the traditional boundaries of on-campus class delivery and to meet the demanding lifestyles of working professionals. The emphasis is on creating a meaningful learning experience with a balance of case analysis, discussion boards, email prompts, collaborative group projects, and various experiential techniques. Building business acumen is an integral part of the program, where real-world organizational issues are integrated with academic studies, action learning, and research for immediate application and value.

The Disruptive Force of Hurricane Katrina

In July 2005, the HCD program proposal was submitted and approved by the State College Board for fall 2006 implementation. Then, in August 2005, Hurricane Katrina hit the Gulf Coast, resulting in near-total devastation. One of the costliest natural disasters in U.S. history, Katrina decimated every mile of Mississippi's inland coastline. Hundreds were killed, tens of thousands were left homeless, and more than 1 million were affected by the storm in Mississippi. Almost six months later, the extent of the devastation in Mississippi was still described as staggering by multiple news reports.

A significant natural disaster not only devastates the landscape, but also causes substantial losses to needed infrastructure and dramatically alters the availability of human resources. Employees may face considerable difficulties with housing, transportation, childcare, medical care, and other basic necessities. In addition, workers may discover new opportunities and higher compensation in other organizations due to post-disaster workforce demands, particularly those for high-skilled employees. The disruption period that occurs immediately after a disaster may last anywhere from three months to several years. According to a 2011 study, "Man-made and natural disasters pose such a serious business threat that 40 percent of firms affected by a major [disaster] event never reopen" (Duncan et al. 2011).

"Implementing the new HCD doctoral program on schedule, post-Katrina, was difficult for any number of reasons," Gaudet says. "More than 50 percent of our faculty and staff were displaced from their homes. Either their homes were completely destroyed or they were unlivable at the time. We didn't have a campus, we didn't have the infrastructure."

To help students cope with the disaster, USM turned to assistance from partners on its advisory board as well as from our partners at ROI Institute and The Conference Board. "Students not only lost their homes but their workplaces. So one of the ways [our partners] helped was to connect our master's student alumni with jobs so they could get back on their feet. They also gave funding support for current students to attend class in Jackson, Mississippi, 150 miles away," Gaudet says. For out of state students, being able to travel to Jackson was key to continuity, because getting to the Gulf Coast was problematic after the hurricane.

With the destruction of infrastructure, and livelihoods in the balance, knowing how and when to rebuild was a big question mark. But according to Gaudet and Annulis, within two weeks of the hurricane, the USM president assured faculty and staff that their employment and programs were secure. This announcement was welcome news; Gaudet and Annulis had heard stories of universities in New Orleans whose fates were not as certain.

Remarkably, the university opened within six weeks of the hurricane with a temporary campus adjacent to Gulfport Memorial Hospital, about five miles from the main one. "We called it the hospital campus for a long time. Five people were crowded in a single office with no windows and one phone line. Our cell phones had no service because it used to be an x-ray area. Our department opted not to spend a lot of time there. It was a very depressing work environment and we were already depressed enough," Annulis says.

Instead, the department worked daily out of Gaudet's house. "We needed a sense of normalcy. We needed to get up every day and get dressed and go somewhere," she says. Her loft was turned into an office space, but no phone service was available. Hurricane Katrina hit on August 29, 2005, and it wasn't until late October that Internet service was up and running. Relief and rebuilding efforts initially focused on restoring power and clearing communities of debris up to eight feet in depth. With no wireless connectivity, the team had to go to another home to get phone service, to connect to a dial-up AOL account to receive or send email. "Imagine that. We only had AOL. It would be a lot different with the technology we enjoy today," Gaudet says.

When faced with a disaster, be it a hurricane or some organizational shakeup, survival depends largely on the type of actions taken by leadership immediately afterward. Modeling effective leadership during a crisis builds trust and improves individual and institutional resiliency. Annulis credits Gaudet's leadership skills with the department's ability to persevere through the uncertainty, stress, and complexity of the period following Katrina. "Cyndi was in a leadership position in our department, even if she didn't have the title of chair then," Annulis says. "She really rallied us to say 'Hey, you know, we're going to make this work. We're going to make it work in a way that is meaningful with a real student focus the entire time.'" It was here that Gaudet and her team put one of the collaboration building blocks to the test: shared purpose. "One of our key success factors was a shared purpose in putting students first," Annulis says. The department staff would ask themselves, "What do we need to do to help [the students] have a sense of normalcy and routine as well?"

This consistent, shared purpose helped guide the team through the early months after the disaster. "Those first two months were about securing food, clothing, household goods, and shelter for those 50 percent of the people in our university campus community that didn't have those things," Annulis says. "None of the people in our department had suffered that kind of loss. Charitable groups were bringing in resources as well, but their immediate focus was serving the homeless who were trying to get into FEMA trailers." In addition, the team wanted to make sure students could stay on track with their degree program. "For many people that continuity was extremely important. Needless to say, there wasn't a lot of intellectual capital being developed within those first couple of months after Katrina," Annulis adds.

Proving Value

As the College of Science and Technology gradually moved out of survival mode, it started to re-establish basic operating capacity. By the fall semester following Katrina, the university's master's program was still in place, and the department went about the business of reigniting energy and enthusiasm for the HCD doctoral program as a business-critical learning organization. Because material, people, money, and emotional reserves were still small in the hurricane's aftermath, continuous education and advocacy was needed to ensure continued resource investment in the learning organization. Gaudet and Annulis say they both spent a lot of time discussing the department's value with various administrators and managers within their department. This, according to them, contrasts with a more-traditional department, such as biology, where faculty and staff wouldn't need to spend as much time persuading stakeholders of its significance and worth.

ENABLING STRATEGIES

1. **Put people first.** "One of our biggest priorities as leaders during crisis and early development was to put students' needs and welfare at the center of all decisions. Helping our students take care of basic, fundamental needs helped them trust us to take care of their education and employment needs," says Gaudet.
2. **Provide direction and a clarity of focus.** "Communicating a message of hope and a commitment to recover gave us all a sense of shared purpose and stability. It also inspired the collective spirit of everyone to move forward with the vision of developing a human capital enterprise to support the economic growth of our community," says Gaudet.
3. **Build community.** "A sense of belonging and community was important. Faculty, staff, students needed something to hang on to, to believe in when everything seemed lost and we knew we could count on each other to persevere and be resilient in the tough times," says Gaudet.

Resistance Stage

Educating others about the program's value was especially important in early stages of development. The program initially resided in the department of economic and workforce development, where its worth was often challenged by other department members who may have lacked full knowledge and support of the HCD program as an investment worthy of resource allocations. In addition, the engineering technology and economic development departments are traditionally male-dominated, so "playing in that space and having an academic program that is not mainstream academia has been tough," Gaudet says. "Pushback or resistance is mostly about scarce resources. People sitting around the table are more likely to speak up for their own program than yours. If you're not at the table to sponsor your own efforts, your programs can be closed during restructuring or changes in presidents and provosts. Those things were realities. Had we not been of the mindset that we had to be strong and our voice needed to be heard, then our programs could have been those that nobody spoke up for and we would have gone away."

Influencing the department chair was an especially critical part of moving beyond early pockets of resistance and entirely new disruptions brought about by staff attrition and organizational restructuring. While university presidents set the general workplace tone, the sponsorship role with the most day-to-day impact on an initiative's resource support, design, development, and overall sustainability is the department chair. Gaudet and Annulis admit that it's been both a challenge and an opportunity to advocate to leadership on behalf of their department and program. Gaudet did not hold the chairwoman role in early stages of development, which was characterized by attrition and turmoil. For instance, the university went through three presidents, two interim presidents, and five provosts.

On its path to sustainability, this learning organization faced several development challenges such as limited sponsorship, resource constraints, competing priorities, misconceptions, and frequent disruptions related to business reorganizations and leadership attrition.

ENABLING STRATEGIES

1. **Be a visible advocate.** "We continued to be a visible participant in university and business committees. We continually advocated for the HCD program in terms of its economic and social value to the college as well as the Gulf Coast community," says Annulis.

2. **Educate and communicate.** "Ongoing education helped us disseminate the story of our degree program to leaders and those who could influence its future. Having a clear and consistent message about our value was important because human capital development is not always easily understood, especially by those in a college of science and technology. Continuous education and face-to-face communication was critical as various leaders and department members came and went," says Annulis.

3. **Educate and communicate.** "Ongoing education helped us disseminate the story of our degree program to leaders and those who could influence its future. Having a clear and consistent message about our value was important because human capital development is not always easily understood, especially by those in a college of science and technology. Continuous education and face-to-face communication was critical as various leaders and department members came and went," says Annulis.

4. **Have a plan and work the plan.** "We had a plan and a business model that kept our time and resources focused on achieving the promise of our value proposition. This was especially important given the limited number of faculty members available in the department. Our learning

organization had to do more than just survive tough times. We had to keep our program alive, with manageable performance targets and timelines, so we could deliver on our promise to the community," says Gaudet.

5. **Be flexible.** "Change is going to happen every day. One unexpected event or one person in leadership can disrupt even the best-laid strategic plans and cause any number of cascading effects. So being flexible is a big part of our adaptability and continued success," says Gaudet.

Renewal Stage

The HCD learning organization had a laser focus on creating sustainable value from the start, which was key to their success in renewing shared commitment and executive support for the program during tough times. "We were thinking long term from the start," Gaudet says. "Part of that sustainability plan was the acquisition of federal research dollars. High-growth, high-technology industries, in particular, have been our focus. When you're in a hundred-million-dollar research enterprise, we learned very quickly that becoming part of that enterprise was the best way to prove our value and preserve our program. Other departments or department heads might not always understand what we were doing, but they did understand the value of more money. And so the pursuit of externally funded research dollars was very deliberate. We had a plan and we had a business model. This is the model that works: You research what you teach and you teach what you research and you close that loop."

For example, Gaudet and Annulis conducted research sponsored by NASA and the Department of Labor that brought in $5 million, along with numerous workforce development research awards. "We developed the geospatial technology competency model, and we teach competency model development in our graduate program," Gaudet says.

ENABLING STRATEGIES

1. **Strengthen connections.** "We recently met with one of our associate deans who is managing a National Institutes of Health grant, during which time he had an epiphany of how a human capital development component was needed in that grant. So there is this growing sense among our colleagues of pure scientists that we bring something of value to them

> in being able to fund and implement their own grants. There's more collaboration and knowledge sharing, which cascades to our students," says Gaudet.
> 2. **Demonstrate how you add value.** "We use an accountability framework, based on the Phillips ROI Methodology, as the foundation for all our research grants. It's added to our credibility as evidence-based researchers and helped us gain more respect from our internal community of scientists in the College of Science and Technology. It's also a hallmark, and distinguishing characteristic, of the HCD curriculum, since more human capital professionals are being challenged to show how their work contributes to measures that matter to the business," says Gaudet.

Refinement Stage

Despite natural disasters, business disruptions, and politically charged challenges, the HCD learning organization has been able to thrive in difficult times. Gaudet now serves as the department chair. The current dean of the department is an engineer who "not only understands but embraces human capital development," Annulis says. "It goes back to having the right leaders in place. He does a really good job of creating a climate where people talk to each other, where people are encouraged to collaborate."

"With all of those changes in presidents, provosts, structures, and so on, there was a long period of time when we felt we were always playing defense," Gaudet adds. "Now we're no longer in a survival mode. Once we became our own department, we've had more opportunities to drive the bus."

The HCD learning organization has continued to strengthen its partnerships internally and externally, fostering a community for its students. "For example, we were recently able to help a colleague establish relationships with local industry so she could connect her chemistry students with internship opportunities and better satisfy prospective grant requirements," Annulis says. "Since we've spent a lot of time reaching out to nurture those industry partnerships, the business community has been an invaluable sponsor of student projects and research, both in and out of the HCD department. A big part of our value proposition is that we translate our research back to the workplace. Research that sits on a shelf or rests in a lab doesn't add value to the institution and doesn't help sustain a research enterprise."

The department has also experienced renewal due to the HCD research conducted by its doctoral students and alumni. "A bigger part of the plan to increase the capacity of our research enterprise was to have students publish, present, and disseminate their own research," Annulis says. Research topics included ROI, STEM education, student success, succession planning, social capital, welfare to work, employee volunteerism, employability skills, culture of innovation, leadership, emotional intelligence, online communities of practice, strategic human resource management, technology transfer, shared mental models, and workforce engagement. HCD doctoral students have been recognized for research excellence through international dissertation awards from the International Society for Performance Improvement in 2011 and the Association for Talent Development in 2014.

But the HCD learning organization still faces some sustainability challenges:

- **Resources.** Gaudet and Annulis both said they still need more faculty given the labor-intensive challenge of maintaining a reasonable faculty-to-student ratio for doctoral students while also maintaining active participation in doctoral committees.
- **Enrollment trends.** National trends suggest that there will be fewer 18-year-olds entering college over the next few years, which leads to greater competition and new priorities for the university. "So, we're trying to increase enrollment and student retention of undergraduates. We're also trying to leverage opportunities for helping people and employers rescale and retool skills in a shifting labor market."
- **Publications and preservation.** Like any college, the department's preservation is largely determined by its number of refereed and nonrefereed publications, the number of presentations to the professional community regionally and nationally, and its track record with research grants.

From the Sustainability Cycle perspective, the HCD department as a learning organization has not only progressively restored its facilities, infrastructure, operating capacity, and human resources to a state of alignment, but also is now reportedly functioning at optimal levels. The department's significant contribution to the college's mission-critical research enterprise has positioned it as a value creator and an engine for economic development in the Gulf Coast community. "We're focused on balancing the current and future needs of the institution to remain viable and economically sustainable," Annulis says. The addition of faculty provides further evidence of the program's growth and perceived value to the college. The Gulf Coast campus now has four full-time faculty members dedicated to HCD.

ENABLING STRATEGIES

1. **Lead with culture.** "The culture of our department is one that promotes mutual trust and respect for our colleagues, staff members, and students alike," Gaudet says. "We really care about each other and when people believe that others care about you, it is easier to attract support and succeed. It's something that we hear from other departments and, I think, one of the key success factors for sustaining what we're doing."

2. **Keep the long view.** "We were thinking long term from the start," Gaudet says. "Part of that sustainability plan was the acquisition of federal research dollars."
3. **Use evidence-based outcomes for value creation.** Gaudet and Annulis emphasize that evidence-based measures of learning, program, and research outcomes have helped to not only add organizational value, but also create it. For instance, they report that outcome measures have been used to improve:
   - institutional priorities and strategic plans
   - institutional decision making
   - student engagement and employment success
   - inter-institutional collaboration
   - learning assessment practices so that they are more multidimensional, integrated, and performance-based
   - community and industry representation and financial support.

Case Review

Research shows that there are three possible outcomes related to a natural disaster such as Hurricane Katrina. One is increased organizational change capacity, the second is maintenance of the status quo, and the third is organizational incapacitation (Phillips, Annulis, and McDonald 2013). The course that an organization takes is largely dependent upon the actions of its leaders during and after a crisis. This example shows how an organization's learning leaders helped pave the way from a disaster into an era of sustainable growth and change capacity. Here, leaders provided hope and clarity of direction during times of crisis and uncertainty. By creating a purpose-driven sense of collaboration and a culture of community among students and stakeholders, they were able to improve the capacity of their learning organization to deal constructively with business disruptions and sustain momentum for continuous growth and improvement.

Table 8-1 shows the characteristics of an adaptive, sustainable learning organization that enabled these accomplishments.

Table 8-1. Characteristics of a Sustainable Learning Organization

Characteristic	Examples	
C-Level Sponsorship	• Consistent sponsorship support from department chair despite times of reorganization, resource constraints, and competing priorities • The learning leader elevated to department chair role, indicating credibility and executive support of the HCD learning organization	✓
Efficiency	• An accountability framework (ROI) was used to continually assess efficiency measures associated with specific targets around enrollment, curriculum design, delivery, and access, among others	✓
Effectiveness	• An accountability framework (ROI) was used to provide a variety of qualitative and quantitative measures to continually assess academic quality and learning, program, and research outcomes, especially with regard to their institutional and economic impact	✓
Utility	• Sponsors and stakeholders (students, instructors, industry partners) across all locations regularly use HCD data to inform academic or business strategy	✓
Investment	• Investments in the HCD learning organization have steadily increased • Continued investments are viewed as mission critical by the university	✓
Credibility	• HCD learning organization is seen as a credible source of economic growth by sponsors and stakeholders (students, instructors, industry partners) • HCD team is perceived as credible business partners • Academic and research institutions have recognized the HCD program as award winning, credible, and evidence based	✓
Demand	• Sponsors and stakeholders (students, instructors, industry partners) regularly request HCD data for informed decision making and continuous improvement	✓
Governance	• Cross-functional governance committee engaged as academic governance group	✓
Continuous Improvement	• Lessons learned from benchmarking, HCD research, industry partnerships, academic reviews, and student feedback are regularly used to develop new or better learning solutions and to meet evolving business needs	✓
Resilience	• HCD leaders have built connections and community to weather natural disasters and other disruptive forces • Increased capacity of the program's research enterprise shows its ability to withstand and buffer changes in the internal and external environment	✓

Practice 7: Embrace the Art of Innovation

"We say that innovation is a lot like learning—it works best when you do a little bit every day."
—Kerry Hearns-Smith, Vice President of Learning Strategy and Delivery,
Xerox (Probst 2015)

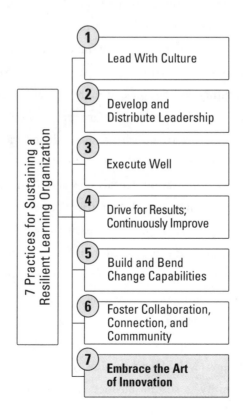

What's in This Chapter

- how innovation enables sustainable learning solutions
- how innovation adds sustainable value to the learning enterprise
- how times of crisis can breed unexpected times of opportunity
- how a sustainable learning organization can help encourage innovation across the organization.

TECHNOLOGY IS MOVING FASTER THAN EVER, and it's changing the way employees learn. Training in the digital age requires different demands. How significant are those demands? In an interview with McKinsey & Company (Kirkland 2016), Cisco's executive chairman, John Chambers, said the world has now entered a digital era that will be the "biggest technology transition ever." Customers demand more, faster. Products are more complex. Risk and compliance requirements have increased. Employees must know more and learn faster than ever before. Attention spans are shorter. No wonder the modern worker is overwhelmed, distracted by constant interruption, and, by some estimates, has only 1 percent of a typical workweek to focus on training and development (Tauber and Johnson 2014). These 21st-century realities make it more critical for learning leaders to design and deliver innovative, flexible solutions that can keep up with the accelerating information and performance demands of a digital era like no other.

Innovation can be described as the pursuit of the new and the ability to adapt (Gutsche 2009). Innovation can also be described as a new solution (product, process, or business model) that drives differentiation and measurable business value. Innovation used to be measured by the number of patents a company filed, but today it is measured more by how much and how fast a company changes business models, products, and strategy in keeping with how consumers do business, such as renting movies (Netflix), buying music (iTunes), finding transportation (Uber), arranging lodging (Airbnb), or shopping (Groupon). These companies understand that they must innovate to stay relevant and create new levels of market value. At its core, innovation increases an organization's ability to sustain business by continually fine-tuning and transforming models and processes in response to emerging needs. The same is true for a learning organization. For sustained business value, it must innovate and continually transform its models and processes to meet the changing needs of learning consumers and stakeholders.

Leveraging Technology to Drive Learning Innovation

The growing demand for technology-based, just-in-time information continues to highlight areas where the learning function can become more relevant and create new levels of value in development, delivery, and learner consumption. Accessible, technology-rich approaches have been shown to sustain high levels of learner engagement and peer collaboration, which contribute to innovation, compared with less technology-focused activities. Yet learning leaders have been slow to adapt existing learning or business models to these trends, despite their best intentions.

Take mobile technology as one example. Devices such as smartphones and tablets enable innovation by helping learners gain access to digital content and personalized assessment. These devices are essential tools for improved learning in a post-industrial world—especially when nearly two-thirds of Americans own personal smartphones to access online information (Smith 2015), and more than half of all employers will require employees to bring their own device to work by 2017 (Gartner 2013). Learning leaders need to be fast to adopt or adapt these tools to promote new ideas or develop new capabilities.

However, barely a third of learning organizations make learning content accessible on mobile devices, and less than 20 percent of those who shop for a learning management system (LMS) make mobile a "must-have" requirement (ATD and i4cp 2015). Learning organizations slow to adopt mobile or other technology-rich approaches cite a lack of strategy as more of a concern than a lack of tech resources. Developing a learning strategy that leverages technology as a source of innovation and value begins by understanding what types of technology-enabled approaches are available and what they can do.

Consider these common trends and approaches in innovative learning technology.

Social Learning

Social learning is characterized by less structured learning that employees own themselves. It can increase learning efficiency and effectiveness and reduce the time needed to find workplace knowledge. Social learning is also a cost-effective learning strategy because it complements traditional classroom training and relies heavily upon the use of peers as content resources. To support the launch of a global processing system, property insurance firm FM Global's learning organization used Skype and Yammer to facilitate social learning, collaboration, and communication among cohorts of peer coaches. These social learning tools were integrated with a comprehensive, blended learning strategy of online modules, virtual sessions, short videos, simulations, quick reference guides, and instructor-led training.

Mobile Learning

Also called m-learning, this approach uses personal electronic devices with multiple contexts, instantaneous sharing, collaboration, and feedback to facilitate learning. If implemented properly, mobile learning can replace the need for learners to carry around or consult books and binders while on the job. Mobile learning is undeniably changing the landscape of current and future education. For instance, employees are no longer dependent on the learning function to "push" content. A mobile device allows learners to continually "pull" content and drive their own learning without the restrictions of time and space, or the requirement of sitting in a classroom or in front of a computer for a specified amount of time. It facilitates learning on the go, maximizing flexibility and accessibility. It also dramatically changes the role of the learning leader from the chief owner of learning to a primary enabler of learning.

Gamification

Gamification involves using game-based mechanics, aesthetics, and game thinking to engage learners, promote learning, motivate action, and enable problem solving. Game play has been shown to increase high-level literacy skills, promote a multitask mentality, and improve focus for long-range planning (Marquis 2013). NTT DATA Corporation, one of the world's largest IT companies, used gamification to create a personalized, collaborative online leadership development experience. The voluntary tool, Ignite Leadership, was customized to each user's leadership style and incorporated game-based mechanics like leadership boards, rewards, report cards, game play, and social exercises. Peers shared game achievements, which were also tracked by managers to identify leadership potential (Siuty 2014). Other examples of how gamification can be used to increase development potential and engagement will be discussed later in the chapter.

Flipped Learning

Flipped learning is a form of blended learning in which learners watch video lectures out of class online, and then complete assignments in class with the guidance of in-person instructors. This approach has not only gained popularity in adult learning, but is currently a leading source of innovation in the K-12 space.

Massive Open Online Courses (MOOCs)

MOOCs are a "disruptive" innovation in distant education, in which classes are taught online to large numbers of students with minimal faculty involvement. A lone professor can potentially support a class with hundreds of thousands of participants. Typically, students watch short video lectures and complete assignments that are graded either by machines or other students. Most MOOCs follow a traditional course model that spans a quarter or a semester, although shorter options are available. Many learning organizations partner with MOOC providers to offer more flexible development opportunities for their internal talent, particularly executives and senior leaders.

Learning leaders who can harness forms of technology in their learning strategy and deploy them to boost learning outcomes will be better prepared to meet the needs of future learners and leverage innovations for greater organizational performance. Beyond a lack of strategy, most learning leaders still face common readiness barriers. These include a lack of supporting infrastructure and technology, a lack of skills by learning staff, an inadequate learning budget, and little senior leadership support. Figure 9-1 outlines some other struggles. These must all be addressed if learning organizations and their learning leaders are to meet the varying needs of future learners, such as wanting learning to be interactive, just-in-time, and on-demand; wanting access to mentors and coaches; and seeking out technology to enable learning.

Figure 9-1: Fast Facts

6%	5%	29%	59%
L&D professionals who rate themselves as very good at providing mobile learning	L&D professionals who rate themselves excellent at using advanced media such as video, audio simulations, or other new kinds of learning content	L&D professionals who say their learning function is a leader in using new learning techniques and technologies to help achieve L&D goals	L&D professionals who say learning will take place in ways we can't imagine today

Source: Deloitte (2015); ATD and i4cp (2015).

In the future, less and less learning will take place in the classroom, partly due to employees' increasing use of social and mobile technologies. Blended learning, technology-based learning, experiential learning, and microlearning will also greatly influence traditional learning methods. Given the prominence of microlearning as an emerging trend, let's look more closely at how learning leaders can use it to enhance innovation and provide sustainable value.

Microlearning

Best-in-class, sustainable learning organizations continually innovate their processes and practices to increase participation, engagement, impact, and value. One of the hottest topics in innovative learning design and delivery is microlearning, which is a way of delivering learning content in bite-size, easily digestible chunks. Microlearning content features "push" and "pull" content that is accessible everywhere, at any time, which is different from a traditional e-learning approach. Twitter is one microlearning tool that can be used to support learning and performance and help keep employees on track with industry trends or topics.

Some organizations use tools such as Skype for Business (formerly Lync), an online collaboration tool, and Yammer, a private social network, to supplement course work. Outsourcing firm ACS used Yammer to enable the approximately 25,000 global employees enrolled in an online leadership development course to share information with one another (Hartley 2010). The company also expanded its learning content to provide more context around how to apply specific leadership topics, such as coaching, within unique roles or regions. For instance, coaching in a call center environment is usually quite different from coaching in a consultative skills environment, coaching face-to-face is quite different from coaching virtually, and coaching in the Far East is quite different from coaching in North America.

In another example, Google has used enterprise microlearning to provide practical chunks of knowledge to employees during periods when they may otherwise be unoccupied. Julie Clow, former manager of learning and organizational development at Google and author of *The Work Revolution* (2012), has described how the company placed one-pagers on relevant topics in restrooms or engineering buildings.

To realize microlearning's true value as an enabler of learning and performance, learning leaders should leverage bite-sized learning in tandem with key elements of standard learning research (Figure 9-2).

Spaced Repetition ("Space It Out")

Also known as distributed practice or interval reinforcement, spaced repetition involves the repetition of four to five bites or chunks of information, presented in a different format or context for each repetition. However, the key is to spread the repetition out over an extended period, with "macro spacings" of a few days or weeks between each learning event. "Rather than focusing on long periods of learning, we learn better when our brain cells are switched on and off, or with short periods of learning and breaks in between," wrote Steven Boller, marketing director at Bottom-Line Performance, in a 2012 blog post. "The key to long-term memory formation is not the amount of time spent learning, but the amount of time between learning." In fact, spaced repetition can increase long-term memory by up to 90 percent compared with traditional learning and study techniques (Leaman 2016).

Figure 9-2: Leveraging Learning Research to Innovate and Improve Learning

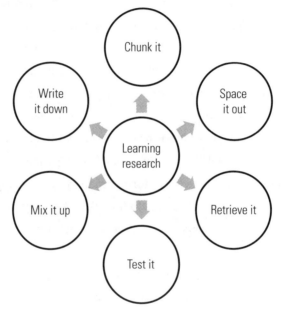

Adapted from Pichee (2016).

Retrieval Practice ("Retrieve It")

Retrieval is the process of recalling information stored in your memory, as you would during a test, for example. Here, the terms *recall* and *retrieval* refer to the same process. Retrieval practice refers to the fact that learners should practice their retrieval skills before the test for better recall and knowledge retention. In microlearning, this means designing motivating feedback loops in a learning solution. Most feedback only tells learners what they got wrong; it doesn't allow them to immediately go back and retry. The suggested practice is to give feedback immediately and have learners return to the question they missed and answer it correctly to advance. As Will Thalheimer (2008), founder of Work-Learning Research, notes, "the best preparation for later retrieval" of information is "a successful current retrieval."

Confidence-Based Assessments ("Test It")

Sometimes referred to as information reference tests, confidence-based assessments are an assessment and a learning methodology that accomplishes two critical goals. First, they extract the individual's response to a query; second, and most critically, they identify the confidence level associated with that response to generate a true knowledge profile. The true knowledge profile helps identify the learner's certainty of information along with any areas of misinformation. Test results are used to evaluate both the confidence learners have in the information and the correctness of their answer (Bruno 1995).

Engagement Methods ("Mix It Up")

Microlearning is also based on leveraging the latest engagement methods. For example, gamification can be used to engage learners, motivate action, promote learning, and solve problems. It involves using a combination of game-based mechanics (leaderboards, rewards, report cards) to drive high participation and recall. Game mechanics and game play work to get the brain focused and in a "flow" state before learners progress to the learning chunk that comes next. Mixing up learning content with gaming can significantly increase voluntary participation in microlearning. It can also lead to improved business results. For example, Walmart provided a daily three-minute gamification learning experience for 75,000 employees in 120 distribution centers and reported a 54 percent reduction in safety accidents. Toyota dealer representatives who consistently participated in gamification learning approaches reportedly sold two more cars a month than those who did not use the program or tools regularly. Bloomingdale's reported that gamification approaches increased their voluntary learning participation by more than 85 percent and contributed to a reduction in safety incidents by more than 22 percent (Leaman 2016).

Other organizations have experimented with the use of video and stationary messaging tools to mix up the flow and visually reinforce a concept on online social channels. Think of giving a learner a thumbs-up on a successful safety session, for instance. Beacons are another form of technology that allow learning leaders to create content that pops up on a learner's tablet or smartphone when it's nearby and in range. The pop-up can then prompt the learner to take a quiz, read an assignment, coach a peer, or write in a journal. Keeping up-to-date with new technology that can improve learning engagement, retention, and application is one of the best ways for learning leaders to provide sustainable value.

Memory Tactics ("Write It Down")

Retention increases when learners are asked to write a summary, in their own words, about what they learned. While taking notes on laptops rather than by hand is increasingly common, laptop note-taking is often less effective for learning (Mueller and Oppenheimer 2014). For instance, students who took notes on laptops performed worse on conceptual questions than students who took notes by hand. Laptop note-takers tend to transcribe content verbatim rather than processing information and reframing it in their own words, even when advised in advance to take notes in their own words. This results in shallower processing, which is detrimental to learning. In contrast, taking notes by hand means you have to process information as well as write it down, which leads to long-term retention.

In general, microlearning is about providing little chunks or bursts of "need-to-know" information, consistently, faster, and more effectively than traditional e-learning. Bite-sized learning enables cost-effective, peer-to-peer knowledge sharing across the enterprise and helps position the learning organization as a facilitator of organizational innovation. According to author Julie Clow (2012), the key to its success is to weave it into employees' regular workday and make the learning content accessible from any device.

Microlearning pieces help engage the organization by being easy to create and quick to distribute, which ultimately helps beef up a learning strategy. A learning organization that combines innovative microlearning bursts with such reinforcements as spaced repetition, retrieval practice, confidence testing, engagement methods, and memory tactics will improve the short- and long-term learning outcomes critical to sustaining an organization's competitive advantage (Figure 9-3). In short, microlearning is about more than just abbreviated content; it's about driving continuous learning and innovative behavior change in the digital age.

Figure 9-3. What Learning Innovation Looks Like

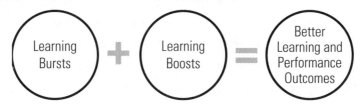

Adapted from Brubaker (2016).

Innovation as a Core Capability

Learning leaders play a key role in leveraging innovation to drive organizational performance. For example, high-performing organizations are up to three times more likely to implement learning and people practices that drive innovation (Deloitte 2015).

Here are some examples of how organizations are working to accelerate their pace of innovation and weave it into the fabric of their workplace. At the federal government level, the U.S. Department of Health and Human Services has hired an "entrepreneur in chief," while the U.S. Department of State has an Office of Innovation that reports directly to the secretary. At the state level, Maryland has a chief innovation officer, who reports directly to the governor, ensuring the state government keeps pace with technology and citizen needs while using innovative tools to manage government programs and services effectively. In the private sector, Walt Disney pledges a commitment to creativity, technology, and innovation as a driver for long-term shareholder value. And at Qualcomm, a wireless communications company, Tamar Elkeles, former vice president of L&D, has said that the learning organization gets credit for the company's success because, from a business perspective, creating new technologies is only possible when people are learning, generating, and selling ideas—and ideas, like any other asset, need to be nurtured and developed (Sosbe 2003).

Executives in the public and private sectors are pushing learning leaders to build progressive performance solutions that will grow employees' ability to innovate and propel the organization forward. Driving the pressure for increased innovation is the need to increase employee engagement, create a culture of innovation, and decrease the cost of doing business. While most executives and leaders agree about the importance of innovation, it is often difficult to comprehend what it means, how it relates to everyday work, or how it looks in action. Best-practice learning organizations drive and institutionalize organizational innovation by treating it as a core capability and a learnable skill. Key behaviors associated with innovative leaders include the ability to inspire curiosity, challenge current perspectives, create freedom, and drive execution discipline. Although many leaders believe they exhibit such innovative characteristics, employee perceptions of their supervisors are generally much less favorable. Learning leaders can use leadership and frontline management development, action learning, coaching, stretch assignments, and mentoring opportunities to help leaders gain awareness of their innovation skills and to close skill gaps.

As an organizational capability, innovation occurs when all employees are actively and continuously contributing toward the generation and implementation of new ideas of all types, from small to transformational. While creativity involves thinking out of the box to generate new ideas, innovation puts creativity into action.

Here are some of the most effective learning and people practices at organizations known for putting innovation into action (Jue 2013).

Leverage Technology for Knowledge Sharing

As chapter 8 discussed, collaboration drives creativity and innovation, and social learning approaches can help bring people together (or virtually together) for collaboration and idea generation. By encouraging continuous collaboration to improve on existing products and services, companies such as UPS and IBM have seen innovation capabilities grow.

Foster Innovative Values and Mindsets

Part of building an innovative culture is having leaders who value, model, and inspire curiosity. Embedding these values into daily behaviors and mindsets requires a broader focus on organization culture, structure, and business strategy. With an astonishing employee retention rate of 97 percent, Dream-Works is known for fostering an innovative culture in which employees are encouraged to take risks in the pursuit of creativity and innovation (Henneman 2012). Executives make time for spontaneous and regular discussions with staff members to explore how new ideas can support strategic goals. Fostering an innovative culture is a common theme among companies renowned for innovative practices.

Make Innovation a Core Competency

Innovation is a key competency required for all organizations that expect to thrive and stay relevant in changing times. It starts with attracting the best people, developing and building the innovative capability of those people, and then connecting those capabilities to the other systems, functions, and business goals.

Approach Innovation as a Learnable Skill

Creative thinking skills can be developed and nurtured. The most innovative companies grow innovative skills and mindsets through various learning initiatives. To help managers strengthen innovation capabilities of their team members, Adobe developed a managerial essentials program that builds managers' ability to lead innovation and help employees think and act in more innovative ways. In part, training involves teaching people how to define and solve ambiguous and complex problems by shedding old mindsets, generating new ideas, and then implementing a solution. Challenging the definition of a problem is a key component when training to improve skills in innovation (Parker 2013).

Hire for Innovation and Creativity

Core competencies that are critical to sustained business success, such as innovation, must be properly integrated with holistic workforce planning and talent management strategies to gain traction, just like the change management capabilities discussed in chapter 7. At IBM, for example, hiring focuses on attracting people with diverse backgrounds who can drive creative design and out-of-the-box thinking.

Link Compensation to Innovation

Linking incentives to creative solutions and innovative behaviors helps signal that innovation is an important cultural value. While there's some debate about the association between financial rewards and increased innovation, in general, tying individual bonuses and salary increases to innovation can help drive more of it in the workplace. Financial rewards become more relevant when the process of bringing an idea to market or rolling it out globally throughout the organization is taken into account.

Reward Innovation With Engaging Work

Organizations can reinforce and enhance creative abilities by providing relevant projects, inside or outside the organization, for creative employees to tackle. Google, the oft-praised employer of choice, encourages its engineers to take 20 percent of their work time to focus on something company-related that interests them personally. Employees self-manage their schedule and regular deadlines and take the "20 percent time" whenever the creative spirit strikes. It's been estimated that 50 percent of Google's innovative products have come from this 20 percent time (Azulay 2012).

Create Systems That Support Innovation

Even the best ideas need help taking shape. Innovative companies build systems and processes for refining, developing, and identifying the ideas with the most potential business value. This may include a formal review process, an "idea-finding" program, or a funding program for further development of strategic ideas. A lot of companies flounder because they don't have the necessary support and infrastructure in place to reinforce the right behaviors.

Innovative companies and progressive organizations consistently apply, to some degree, each of these practices. They are a good place for learning leaders to focus when examining how and where to start embracing the art of innovation to add more sustainable value (Figure 9-4).

Figure 9-4. Embrace the Art of Innovation

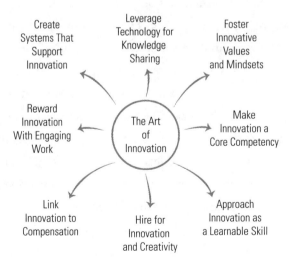

Innovation as a Mindset

For the learning leader, embracing the art of innovation means more than just adopting new techniques or technologies. It's also about adopting new ways of thinking, leading, managing, learning, and working, which comprise an innovative mindset (Table 9-1).

Table 9-1. Conventional Mindset vs. Innovative Mindset

Conventional Mindset	Innovative Mindset
Defining the right answer	Defining the right question
Avoiding uncertainties	Embracing uncertainties
Black and white perspective	Shades of gray
Fixed assumptions	Challenged assumptions
One best way	Multiple alternatives
Get it done	Get it right
Either/or	Both/and
Linear thinking	Fluid thinking
Eliminating risk and failure	Acknowledging risk and failure as part of the process

Adapted from Legrand (2007).

Innovative learning leaders not only embrace an innovative mindset to adapt to the changing world of work, but they also change how L&D itself works. At Samsung, innovation starts with a learning culture that nurtures, welcomes, and fosters an environment where employees can succeed in a highly competitive tech industry. For example, its yearlong Super Rookies onboarding program places new hires in a "cozy and supportive technology incubation environment that fosters a culture of creativity, collaboration, and exchange." The program provides experiential learning around various topics, including leadership skills, that are blended with elements of competition and reward. New hires then work toward a personally chosen developmental project, such as a process innovation or new business concept. The program contributed more than 300 product concepts during its roll-out year. Generating innovative ideas from employees before they are exposed to the "fixed frame" of existing processes has been an equally important payoff from promoting and rewarding innovative thinking with Samsung's new hires from day one. To succeed in its industry, Samsung needs its learning organization to continue to deliver innovative approaches to talent development (Harris 2015b).

Figure 9-5. Key Actions

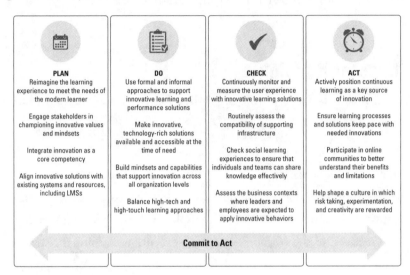

Chapter Summary

Innovation is needed at every turn in a world of constant disruption, and high-performing organizations consider it very important to their success. CEOs are pushing learning leaders and talent management professionals to accelerate the pace of organizational innovation for increased competitive advantage. These pressures, combined with the 21st-century realities of the modern learner and workplace, make it more critical than ever for learning leaders to continually transform learning and performance models and methods to stay relevant amid changing needs. Finally, it's important to remember that innovation is about more than just adopting new techniques or technologies. The art of innovation means embracing new ways of thinking, leading, managing, and learning. In short, innovative learning leaders must not only adapt to the changing world of work, but also buffer change while simultaneously reinventing how L&D works. The capacity to do so is the hallmark of a resilient, sustainable learning organization. Use the chapter 9 self-assessment in appendix 2 to identify patterns and possibilities for improving the art of innovation within your own learning organization.

Chapter Highlights

Innovation is an essential capability for the modern workplace and worker.

Best-practice learning organizations, such as Adobe or Samsung, drive and institutionalize organizational innovation by approaching it as a core capability and learnable skill. Key behaviors associated with innovative leaders include the ability to inspire curiosity, challenge current perspectives, create freedom, and drive execution discipline. Learning leaders can use leadership and frontline management development, action learning, coaching, stretch assignments, and mentoring opportunities, in combination with innovative learning technologies and content, to help grow innovative skills and close innovation skill gaps.

Sustainable learning organizations drive organizational innovation with innovative learning strategies and approaches.

The goal of everyday innovation is to have everyone participating in and contributing to innovation. Learning leaders who can harness new forms of learning technology in their learning strategy and deploy them to boost just-in-time, on-demand knowledge sharing and collaboration will be better prepared to help organizations grow the capabilities needed to drive innovation. After all, a learning organization cannot expect to drive innovation across the organization with stagnant and obsolete learning approaches.

Innovative learning leaders must not only embrace and adapt to the changing world of work, but also get more innovative about the way L&D works.

In the future, less learning will take place in the classroom, partly due to employees' increasing use of social and mobile technologies where content is "pulled" rather than "pushed." Learning leaders have been slow to adapt existing learning or business models to growing demands for technology-based, user-generated, on-demand information sharing. To become more relevant and meet modern learner needs, L&D professionals must continually innovate their processes and practices to increase participation, engagement, and impact. This also means shifting from being a learning provider to a learning enabler. An intentional focus on innovation will help your learning organization gain a competitive advantage, optimize performance growth, and avoid obsolescence by adding sustainable value.

Case in Point

This Case in Point describes how Blue Shield of California's performance and learning (P&L) team embarked on an evolutionary journey toward a more adaptive and innovative learning culture. This shift spanned more than four years of grassroots pioneering efforts. The driver for this transformation was a major overhaul of Blue Shield of California's core legacy claims processing systems, which led to the P&L team shifting its learning strategies from a fully instructor-led classroom model to more modern, blended, and innovative learning approaches like microlearning. According to Erika Steponic, senior instructional designer of performance and learning, "Our organic learning revolution encountered end-to-end challenges, successes, pitfalls, roadblocks, and epiphanies." Aspects of the team's journey mirror phases of the Sustainability Cycle.

Overall, their story illustrates how one group of learning leaders embraced the art of innovation to deliver flexible, scalable learning approaches that helped build a more adaptive and entrepreneurial culture, within the learning and performance organization and the organization at large.

ORGANIC LEARNING INNOVATION AT BLUE SHIELD OF CALIFORNIA

Established in 1939, Blue Shield of California is a not-for-profit health plan in California with a corporate giving foundation. Blue Shield is guided by its mission, "to ensure all Californians have access to high-quality healthcare at an affordable price," and its values, which encourage innovation. Its corporate offices are in San Francisco, a "technology nursery" where cutting-edge ideas and solutions are born. Blue Shield of California is 5,800 strong with a mix of staffed employees and contractors, with offices up and down the state, as well as business partners nationally and globally including India, the Philippines, and Costa Rica.

Within Blue Shield of California, P&L provides innovative solutions, facilitated learning, and performance coaching to support strategic goals focused on driving a world-class, integrated customer experience. As the company's customer experience learning organization, its main function is to provide frontline employees with the skills needed to further the company brand as a trusted adviser and deliver customer service from the operations side of the business that is "worthy of our friends and family." "Our main talent management challenges deal with developing strategies to shift the transactional workers of today into the knowledge workers of tomorrow," says Lisa Nunes, senior director of P&L. "We're now looking at a multiyear 'build versus buy' upskilling strategy focused on the customer experience, which has unique geographic implications and challenges."

P&L consists of five departments within the customer experience organization, the largest operational organization within Blue Shield of California. Customer experience supports the customer care, claims, and installation and billing business units. The five P&L departments and their functions include:

- **Instructional design.** Analyze, design, and develop learning solutions for customer experience, its vendors, and Shield Advance (the initiative to replace legacy software systems).
- **Learning delivery.** Deliver technical training solutions to customer experience new hires, current employees, and vendors for sustainable learning and development.
- **Center of excellence for call center quality.** Create and drive strategy, tools, and quality evaluations to achieve a high-quality customer experience.

- **Technical publications.** Provide enterprise-wide content management solutions and support.
- **Management trainee program.** Conduct a 12-month rotation and development program that is a combination of formal training, leadership development, and challenging job assignments with the goal of placing these resources in key positions throughout customer experience.

A Complete Technology Modernization

"When Blue Shield of California embarked on a comprehensive, A-Z technology replacement of its membership, provider, network utilization, and coordination of care systems—a long-term modernization project known as Shield Advance—we knew it would impact every single business unit and every team . . . in different, yet significant, ways," Erika Steponic says.

Shield Advance represented one of the largest, most complex initiatives that Blue Shield of California had undertaken since its inception in the 1930s. "We were moving from decades of administrative operations under disparate legacy systems, each containing a vital piece of our end-to-end business processes, to a modern, integrated system that supports our enterprise business needs," Nunes says. "Many of our competitors are in the same boat. We're in the process of making very deliberate plans to transform, rather than to simply change, our customers' experience from cradle to grave. In order for that to happen, we really have to engage them in how we provide services. So we're in the midst of a long-term plan based on a purposeful transformation of our service delivery model."

For Blue Shield of California, the key objectives in moving to a single source system were to:

- Deliver stellar, seamless customer care to members.
- Streamline a technology infrastructure for an enterprise-wide workforce.
- Contain the ever-rising cost of healthcare through modern efficiencies.

The overarching Shield Advance implementation plan included controlled, phased data migrations to the new system, spanning multiple years, with tandem instructor-led training in support of each phase. It was paramount to minimize disruption to members and the workforce, while simultaneously achieving business goals. To meet project objectives, Shield Advance required company-wide training on the new data platform, Facets by TriZetto. Training challenges included initial user training of thousands of employees, followed by ongoing makeup and fresher training, post-training performance support (manuals, job aids, P&L staff resources), and new hire learning solutions.

The initial training strategy focused on providing end users with customized, role-based instructor-led training solutions that would support every phased data migration and every business unit affected by the change. The preliminary target audience was the sales organization. Up until 2010, employees were comfortable with instructor-led training and the standard P&L practice. In contrast, blended and e-learning technical skill-building solutions were new territory for Blue Shield of California, and often viewed as less effective and even intimidating. Leadership and learners alike preferred live hands-on instruction, because they thought they learned best by doing. The preliminary learning and performance strategy, then, was to design and deliver scalable, replicable live instruction that would emphasize experiential, hands-on exercises in a training environment that matched or mirrored specific job scenarios.

The desired outcomes for the training strategy were to:

- Drive user adoption of learning and performance platforms.
- Demonstrated knowledge transfer and recall through measurable Level 2 assessment data.
- Increased confidence in using the new healthcare administration platform on the job.
- Convert 80 percent of instructor-led training to e-learning by year three (82 percent by year four).

To develop and deliver training to all business teams affected by Facets, Blue Shield of California formed a Shield Advance project team. In P&L alone, roles included Shield Advance instructional designers, data analysts, training coordinators, environment and security profile coordinators, project managers, and classroom trainers. On a broad scale, each affected business unit assigned subject matter experts (SMEs) to assist P&L Shield Advance instructional designers. The SMEs attended briefings, worked with the instructional designers to validate learning content, and participated in subsequent reviews for ongoing assessment of project scope and impact.

Most important, resource allocation had to remain true to the company's culture of affordability. "Training had to get the job done without breaking the bank," Steponic says. To that end, the project team deployed its P&L strategy with a "no frills" toolkit consisting of WebEx, Captivate, PowerPoint, Snagit, and Jive, in addition to "a lot of passion, inspiration, drive, commitment, skills, and willingness."

Given the scale, scope, and criticality of the Shield Advance initiative, project planning included an early risk assessment. The project team identified three risk categories:

- **Brand and market share risks.** During the modernization effort, the project team needed to preserve the long-standing and trusted Blue Shield brand and business identity, which is shared by franchised Blue Cross and Blue Shield Association health plans nationwide.
- **Data integrity risks.** During the migration of data systems, the project team needed to maintain adherence to strict state and federal regulations governing the integrity of member and provider information. It also needed to maintain continuity of care during the transition process and avoid disrupting member benefits.
- **Broad geography impact.** With offices throughout California, a high percentage of full-time telecommuters, and business partners located nationally and globally, the project team needed considerable coordination

and planning to successfully deploy a learning strategy that relied heavily on instructor-led training.

Recognition Stage: Assess, Design, and Deliver

Early on (2012-2014), executives and learning leaders recognized the need to transform, rather than simply change, the customer experience through modernized legacy systems. Technical training was vital to building employees' capabilities with new system requirements and ensuring business continuity during this comprehensive, complex initiative. From a Sustainability Cycle and value proposition perspective, the Shield Advance project team was not really being challenged to "prove their value" as a function, per the recognition stage in the Sustainability Cycle. In this case, executives already viewed P&L as an important strategic lever in helping the company achieve its business strategies. "Our leaders firmly believe that we can only reach our goals through our people and our culture, including our learning culture," Nunes says.

However, P&L was positioned to prove that it had the business acumen to create learning and performance solutions that support critical business needs and deliver on the promise of their perceived value. To that end, a team of seven statewide Shield Advance instructional designers was tasked with the rapid development of this complex, enterprise-wide technical training initiative, one that needed to be customized to various corporate audiences. For example, a sales assistant might need access to group plan demographics, benefits, and commissions, whereas an underwriter might require visibility into member claims figures, network utilization, and payment history.

In preparation for each planned phase of Facets data migration, Shield Advance instructional designers interviewed department SMEs statewide to capture current and desired performance states, along with "day in the life" legacy data as seen by individual business units and user groups. Specifically, the instructional design team documented how members of each business unit were currently using the legacy data stored in current systems to identify and prioritize the performance requirements for capturing and using the same data in the emerging Facets system. Front-end analysis activities included reaching out to senior management to assess the upstream and downstream business impact of moving member and provider data to a new single system. It also included documenting specific job processes and performance capabilities that would be required to support the emerging Facets system. Over time, the instructional designers streamlined the needs assessment process to a standard template, boosting efficiency and accuracy.

In addition, the instructional design team asked SMEs and their managers to acknowledge a service-level agreement so that they fully understood the knowledge and time commitment needed to support the process. This was vital in ensuring proper resource support throughout each phase of implementation—and in leveling expectations of the project team. Without dedicated commitment of organizational resources and visible management support across all business units, the Shield Advance team could not have succeeded.

Following the preliminary training needs assessment, the Shield Advance project team presented a proposed project plan and curriculum blueprint to senior management and SMEs. Early success measures focused on satisfaction questionnaires to determine content relevance and platform ease of use, along with open-book, multiple-choice learning assessments that required a passing score of 80 percent or higher. Learners who did not achieve a passing score were allowed to retake the assessment. For learners who were unable to pass after three attempts, their managers determined next steps regarding training.

The team also presented optimal delivery methods, customized to various user group and business unit needs. For instance, a finance team might train for two-and-a-half days in the classroom lab, while a new hire group of customer service representatives might train for three weeks. "Close coordination between the instructional designers and the business SMEs was critical as changes to business process occurred sometimes as often as daily and these changes had to be reflected in the courseware to ensure the learners were receiving accurate learning," says Jeff Hopp, P&L senior manager and Shield Advance project team member. The project team allowed stakeholders to request more detail in specific areas, add or remove content, and generally weigh in on the plan's proposed schedule, scope, and resource requirements. Follow-up surveys were sent to targeted users 60 days post-training to assess how learners were applying skills, although responses were lower than expected.

ENABLING STRATEGIES

1. **Enlist executive support.** The commitment of executive and business unit leaders paved the way for learners to get engaged early on. Executive leaders, particularly the C-suite, kept Shield Advance as a number one priority and in the forefront of all corporate communication channels, including internal social media articles, videos, blog posts, and town hall meetings. Substantial funds and resources were allocated to the project so that Blue Shield could sustain its competitive advantage in the California healthcare market. Service-level agreements were key to documenting expectations and helping leaders hold managers accountable for providing learning support.

2. **Anticipate risks.** Scope creep was a real risk in a project of such magnitude and complexity. The curriculum outline sign-off and design approach between P&L and business unit management was key to preventing scope creep. Another

unexpected risk arose with a security breach issue. This caused the IT department to temporarily revoke social media platform access for all Blue Shield contingent workers, which meant members of the instructional design team and learning audiences could not access the e-learning library. P&L factored brand, market share, data integrity, and geographic impact risks into solution design and implementation planning.

3. **Define roles and responsibilities.** Clarifying roles and responsibilities, along with defining selection criteria for key resources such as SMEs, was important in early project planning. For example, some business units assigned SMEs to the project who were not in the best position to assist the effort because they had only been on the job for six months or were already heavily over-allocated. By identifying roles up front, P&L ensured that all involved were best utilized.

4. **Openly address fears and concerns.** Becoming adept and agile in the new healthcare administration platform required employees' ongoing commitment and practice. Addressing the psychology and fear of change in the midst of a monumental technology facelift was critical to moving forward. "We gave employees a no-holds-barred voice in the process. We were purposely authentic and 'all ears' with our audience so that we could fully assess pain points and address them," Steponic says.

Resistance Stage: Early Challenges

As expected with the implementation of any new technology, many Facets learners who had previously mastered legacy systems were resistant to change. In addition, the target audience consisted of more than 80 fast-paced, dynamic sales team members who had real pressures to be in the field contributing to the bottom line. They had little time for training, especially classroom training that impeded project schedules. The new performance requirements, which demanded proficiency in new business processes and work habits, led to learning anxiety and resentment from some user groups.

Change management was a real issue during early iterations. "We had to not only develop the learning concept and build the initial course materials, but we realized that we also had to sell the solution to the managers and learning audiences. The transformation effort was completely organic and a monumental undertaking," said Brian Erickson, senior instructional designer.

ENABLING STRATEGIES

1. **Proactively manage change.** Use a variety of
   communication channels, such as team meetings, corporate
   town halls, executive social media videos, blogs, and articles,
   to send out consistent change messages. Communicate, early
   and often, across all levels. Establish supportive relationships
   with management and learners so they understand what's
   coming and when. Keep emphasizing the "why" of what's
   happening to help focus on the bigger picture.
2. **Design learner-centered solutions that alleviate pain
   points.** Designing solutions that addressed identified pain
   points was critical to removing barriers. "We provided resources
   and showed how they could help resolve key issues or real-time
   business concerns. It was also important to remind learners and
   project team members that it's natural to have growing pains
   and stumble along the way to something new," Steponic says.
3. **Remember audiences can be very different.** By defining
   learning and performance needs and preferences up front
   and considering cultural and generational challenges, the
   team worked to provide learning options and alternative
   delivery methods that fit learners' unique needs and
   "crunch demands."
4. **Build and use partnerships.** The team put stock into setting
   expectations for learners to be partners in the process so
   that they can contribute to designing solutions that have the
   most relevance to them and their daily work. It also involved
   leadership and sponsors as partners in defining expectations
   of learners and their managers and holding them accountable.
   If senior management is not fully behind the learning
   evolution, direct reports may often resist it.

To help managers and learning audiences navigate the change, Shield Advance instructional designers and frontline Facets trainers focused on making sure that employees had the right performance support available when they needed it. For example, the project team worked with business units to ensure that learning content was relevant and job-specific. To address concerns about time constraints, the team developed bite-sized learning modules to be completed in three-week intervals, prompting learners weekly by email. They engaged learners through live webinars and introduced them to an e-learning library of training resources.

They also focused on making sure that end users knew how system changes would provide them with more job support, once they were fully integrated. Given the extent of change issues that unfolded during the legacy transformation, the project team began to think of themselves as learning "sherpas," or seasoned guides, on the enterprise's trek toward peak performance.

Renewal Stage: Shift From Traditional to Modern Modalities

By the start of year three in this multiyear, multidisciplinary effort, all Shield Advance Facets training had been delivered in the classroom, apart from some basic navigation videos. To meet evolving training needs, the project team added more interactive group exercises to existing modules, delivered more job aids, and started recording live Facets demos that could be used for future refresher, makeup, and new hire training.

Then, as Steponic says, everything unraveled. On the evening that a key user group was expected to submit quiz results confirming their completion of a series of required e-courses, the team received a blizzard of panicked and agitated emails. Most members of this sales group had not completed any of their assignments, despite repeated prompts and reminders from the project team. The team then had to extend the training period and quickly determine how to respond to this speed bump. The team initially considered flying to the location to train the sales group. But it was not a cost-effective solution and, ultimately, the dilemma led to creative problem solving. The user group was given the choice of receiving Facets training through a full-day, instructor-led classroom experience or a through a half-day virtual webinar. Citing deadline pressures with "no good time for training," the group opted for the online, live webinar. According to Steponic, concerns about the time needed for training were a real issue among managers and employees. Training hours diverted time from important revenue-generating activities such as sales calls, which affected individual and business unit performance goals.

The drive to meet just-in-time user demands led to the project team's pioneering shift from an instructor-led training focus to a no-barrier microlearning approach. Here, the project team worked quickly to develop an interactive system demo, which was divided into two 90-minute sessions with corresponding job aids. The team tailored the demo content to respective job roles and recorded the content using WebEx. This approach was well received, as shown by sample user group comments:

- "I learned everything I needed to know to do my job in Facets without having to travel to another location—no logistics!"
- "I liked that this necessary training did not impact my current critical project schedule or deliverables."
- "Having the training recording will refresh my memory down the line and is going to be invaluable."
- "Viewing the system demo on my own monitor, and not projected on a wall, was much easier to see, to follow along, and to understand."

After averting this crisis, the team took a hard look at misguided assumptions around their learning strategy. Team members realized that they had erred on the side of too much autonomy and not enough guidance, direction, and coaching. Because targeted employee groups were, by and large, self-directed high performers, the team had assumed that simply providing the tools and technology to enable learning would be enough to facilitate user-group adoption and job application. They realized that if they replicated the same "high-touch, high-tech" just-in-time learning model used for the errant sales group, they could significantly optimize the user experience for all employee groups during the remaining phases of Facets training (Figure 9-6). An added bonus was that this approach would significantly alleviate pressure on the design and delivery staff responsible for providing the training. This reflection and review process led to serious efforts to revamp existing project plans and curriculum designs.

Figure 9-6. High-Touch, High-Tech Learning Model

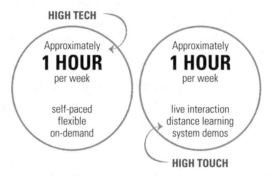

Adapted from Blue Shield of California. Used with permission.

"We began to see repetition among all the live training recordings and thought we could create a bank of recorded webinars that addressed common denominators in all the Facets modules," Steponic says. These common denominators covered such basics as user navigation and member, group, and provider search and demographics.

The goal was to create webinars short enough that users could learn what they needed in less than 10 minutes. "We wanted [instructional designers] to be able to snap them together like LEGOs in a clean, concise learning syllabus for specific audiences," Steponic says. Thus, the NanoModule was born.

NanoModules are precise, targeted online demos or tutorials, with an average length of five to 10 minutes. Developed to cover day-to-day tasks in nuggets, NanoModules ideally support immediate, on-demand help and eliminate the need for paper manuals. To enable rapid, uniform development, a standard NanoModule "sandwich" was developed and housed in a PowerPoint shell. Each instructional designer imported the sandwich into existing Captivate Facets e-courses for a consistent look and feel.

Over the next few months, the Shield Advance team converted all recorded webinars to Captivate with NeoSpeech text-to-speech software. By the end of the third year, the eLibrary contained more than 20 NanoModules in more than 10 categories. The courses were viewed enterprise-wide by the thousands.

Enhancing the User Experience

After the Shield Advance project team developed the eLibrary of recorded webinars on Facets Basics, the focus revolved around adding value by enhancing the user experience. The project team needed a centralized repository where learners statewide could access material around the clock. Initially, an LMS option was discussed, but the login process presented a barrier. So instead, the team turned to the company's social media platform, powered by Jive, which would enable on-demand, instant job performance support. Time was spent considering the user experience and the graphic user interface of the eLibrary landing page. Rather than listing webinar text links, the team designed colorful, iconic category buttons, which linked to all NanoModules.

The NanoModule tagline became "Rapid and effective learning in less than 10 minutes." The team's interface button design was very purposeful. From a functionality perspective, it was meant to promote learners' ability to quickly digest a Facets course category, title, synopsis, and duration within a quick glance. "We found ourselves inspired by the volume of data well organized in a standard title block of an architect's blueprint, separated by clean hairlines," Steponic says. "It became the model for our button design" (Figure 9-7).

Figure 9-7. Sample Button Designs

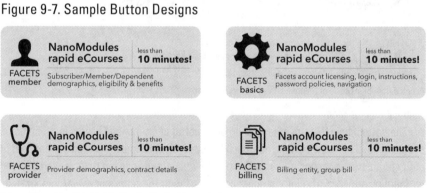

Adapted from Blue Shield of California. Used with permission.

This first collection of NanoModules eliminated many paper-based instruction materials and provided immediate web-based help to users on the job at the time of need. Previous resistance levels dissipated due to the easy access of training support and the realized promise of learning in less than 10 minutes. Suddenly, employees were saying, "All training at Blue Shield should be like this!" and "Thank you for listening to our pain points and addressing each and every one with a custom learning program!"

An innovative learning-centered response model emerged from design iterations and lessons learned. Employees on the fringe of Shield Advance began to explore the public NanoModules out of curiosity. Hits to the social media eLibrary climbed daily. By the end of year four, the eLibrary grew to offer more than 60 NanoModules with more than 12,000 views.

A complete success from a business value standpoint, the eLibrary of NanoModules supported the Facets migrations and became more fully integrated in employees' daily job performance. The robust library of generic NanoModules and a master hyperlinked syllabus (Figure 9-8) allowed instructional designers and trainers to maintain, customize, and leverage material repeatedly. Some trainers used the NanoModules as pre-work or supplemental instruction to their Facets classroom training. Others began to blend them effectively with job aids and a live Facets webinar demo and question and answer session, as a completely virtual program. Accessible e-learning shorts provided instant online help for user groups. Collecting and cataloging e-learning also eliminated paper manuals, which quickly become obsolete.

Figure 9-8. Abbreviated Master Course Syllabus

Facets Category Button	Facets eCourse Modules Within the Category	Minutes	Total
FACETS basics NanoModules rapid eCourses	• Navigation Basics • Training Environment & Password Overview • Live Production Environment & Password Overview • Account Request & Password Policies	• 5 • 5 • 6 • 4	20
FACETS member NanoModules rapid eCourses	• Subscriber Look Up • Subscriber/Family Basic Sections • Subscriber/Family Eligibility Inquiry	• 4 • 7 • 8	19

Adapted from Blue Shield of California. Used with permission.

The bottom line: P&L spearheaded an open portal of on-demand Facets learning using a four-pronged blended learning approach (Figure 9-9). This innovation had a great deal of utility for instructional designers and employee work groups and led to increased demand for learning services. The internal buzz connected with the team's new learning strategy significantly increased the credibility of P&L as a value-added business partner among senior leaders.

Figure 9-9. Four-Pronged Blended Learning

Live Distance Learning	Online Self-Paced Learning
• Training period kickoff using live webinar with all participants • Live office hours: instructor and student review, demos, Q&A	• Learning paths customized by job role in a tailored syllabus • On-demand NanoModules presenting system tutorials and demonstrations

Social Learning	Discovery Learning
• Dedicated training portal on the corporate social networking platform • Centralized hub for training communications and resources	• Hands-on system experience in the training environment through exercises developed to simulate your job role

Adapted from Blue Shield of California. Used with permission.

Focusing on Continuous Improvement

By year five, P&L's primary focus was on adding value by continuously improving and updating material so that it remained current and relevant. When faced with update needs, the team realized it was time to shift from recorded webinars to Captivate videos with NeoSpeech text-to-speech capability. This allowed for quick updates, including system and process changes, to slides and narration when republishing the course. It enabled trainers to reuse common narration segments between multiple courses. It helped prevent having to rerecord a webinar from scratch. And it created the ability to provide add-on voices. But most important, it added cost-effectiveness, which helped justify the conversion to senior leaders.

Continuous improvement efforts also included enhancing measurement and evaluation, especially at the job application level (Level 3). For example, feedback from follow-up surveys helped identify barriers to on-the-job application of skills, including the finding that there was too much time between training completion and when trainees were able to apply new skills on the job. "We knew how critical it was for the learners to apply their new skills as quickly as possible after training," says Jeff Hopp, "but the Level 3 data reinforced the need to work with the business units to ensure the training was scheduled just in time instead of too far in advance."

In addition, as internal accountability for training compliance increased, and as the visibility of P&L efforts grew, managers started to focus more on helping members of their department use their new knowledge and skills.

Previous attempts to effectively determine how well employees were applying key concepts and tools had been partly deterred by limitations in the LMS. While employees' completion of knowledge checks were originally intended to trigger an automatic follow-up questionnaire within 30 days of course completion, it became apparent over time that the LMS couldn't support that level of automation.

Subsequently, early metrics were weak, especially given the team's charge to deliver "round-the-clock" migration training at breakneck speed. "We literally had no bandwidth to wrangle with effective metrics until last year," Steponic says.

"In 2015, we started exploring more robust measurement tools to assess the cost savings and effectiveness of learning retention with blended learning solutions as compared to one-and-done, traditional instructor-led training," Hopp says. "We learned a lot about how challenging it can be to get learners to provide feedback. We're now focusing on other ways to capture learning data and assess the impact of our programs on the success of our business partners."

Ultimately, the NanoModule four-pronged blended learning approach not only allowed quality training to be delivered faster and better, but also greatly reduced the time and effort to distribute content. Specific business benefits include:

- **increased flexibility in learning:** no time away from the office or from job tasks that influence performance goals
- **increased access to learning at the time of need:** 24 hours a day, seven days a week, 365 days a year
- **increased scalability:** no limit to the number of learners
- **improved cost efficiencies:** no travel or per diem expenses; all costs contained
- **improved sustainability:** relevant refresher, new hire, and makeup training content, plus online performance support, to meet on-demand learning and performance needs for multiple users over time.

Current Status and Sustainability Issues

The Shield Advance successfully phased out its lead role in the legacy overhaul project on December 31, 2015. Upon completion, the Shield Advance team began addressing sustainability concerns about the new legacy system and the e-learning infrastructure that evolved during P&L's overhaul of its own processes and practices. Specific questions included:

- Who will maintain this well-oiled machine when instructional designers move on to other teams?
- How will quality and consistency be preserved, if content is parsed out to various business units to own?

- Who will maintain the more than 60 on-demand NanoModules for the 6,000 users who rely on them?
- Who will regularly update the content and perform Jive and LMS maintenance?
- How will leadership support and demand for blended learning solutions be sustained as a viable, practical, and durable best practice?
- How will the momentum of the last four-plus years be maintained to forge forward and upward as a learning organization?

To address these issues and maintain business continuity, the Shield Advance data analyst established a detailed transition plan. Ownership of Facets courseware materials was progressively transferred over a 60-day period to the Blue Shield of California enterprise departments affected by Facets. The transition plan represented the final acceptance documents outlining the processes, tasks, schedules, and agreements for transferring ownership (Table 9-2).

Table 9-2. Transition Process Tasks: An Abbreviated Sample

Phase: Task	Who's Responsible?	When Is It Due?	Comments	Status
Schedule kickoff meeting				
Schedule working sessions				
Plan: Resource assignment				
Plan: Determine timeline and milestone tasks				
Analysis: Validate matrix spreadsheet				
Analysis: Assess status of existing materials				
Develop: Update courseware/training materials				
Implementation: Move documentation and materials to repository				

Critical success factors (such as learners' and managers' commitment to continued development) and potential risk areas were also documented in the plan. The plan served as formal notice that P&L would no longer provide resources or materials to support Shield Advance training efforts, and served as formal project completion. A dedicated P&L resource was allocated as the transition planning liaison and project lead to facilitate a collaborative, seamless, and sustainable transition process.

ENABLING STRATEGIES

1. **Provide "lifelines."** Rather than setting learners adrift in a vast sea of self-directed learning, Blue Shield of California gave them a road map, milestones, and appropriate lifelines. It broke learning content into manageable chunks to support any level of granularity needed. And it ensured that learners and managers have centralized, intuitive, no barriers access to e-learning solutions.

2. **Look for common denominators.** The Shield Advance project team didn't design eCourses specific to any particular department; it avoided referencing business unit jargon. This ensured that the courses were accessible and applicable to multiple audiences and the maximum number of learners in the organization. The team used standard templates, with the learner experience at the core, to consistently and rapidly develop high-quality e-learning.

3. **Experiment, innovate.** Faced with a crisis in how learning and performance solutions were being used, the team subsequently went back to the drawing board to design learner-centered approaches that would provide more ease of use and drive increased demand.

4. **Stay the course.** Throughout the multiyear project, the Shield Advance project team grew weary of the long hours and stressful deadlines, as is common with most critical, long-term corporate shifts. Leadership helped the team stay the course, shared accolades, and visibly celebrated successes and milestones along the way.

Beyond documenting transition roles and responsibilities to help sustain progress with the legacy transformation, P&L is continuing to explore how to incorporate lessons learned from this effort into daily learning operations. The end goals are to drive continued business innovation through relevant, accessible, on-demand learning and to grow mature, adaptive learning processes (especially around measurement) that will add and create value for multiple stakeholders consistently over time.

Implications for Learning Leaders

Sustainable learning organizations have a formal process that signifies the definitive ending of a major change project, particularly one such as Shield Advance, which represented a significant investment of time, money, and resources. A closing process helps to show stakeholders that:

- The value of the project was realized.
- Deliverables were met.
- Lessons learned were captured for continuous improvement and action planning.

While closing out a project represents the typical end point in a project management cycle, it also signifies a new beginning. Many project management methods have formal systems, templates, or approaches for not only closing out a project, but also transitioning it to its new beginning. By some accounts, the transition plan is the most important addendum of the project close. The purpose of a major transformation project, such as the one described here, is to introduce and drive change. But it's the change process and its ultimate impact that present the real value proposition to the organization. A transition plan acknowledges that change impact, and the business value it can add, does not occur overnight. Instead, achieving impact represents an ongoing process of institutionalizing new practices and building internal capacity for their use. This requires transition planning and follow-up time and attention from learning leaders, change agents, and sponsors.

Lessons Learned

Throughout any project, there are a great number of lessons that are learned collectively among project team members, stakeholders, and sponsors alike. It is important to gather insights from all these various stakeholders, because they are a major source of value and can help pave the way for continuous improvement. Here are some lessons learned from Steponic's experience with this high-profile transformation:

- **Add high tech and high touch to blended learning options.** Blending self-directed, learner-centered content with instructor-led solutions fit in more readily with the business environment and learners' needs, schedules, and demands for deliverables. "One of our most important lessons when we transitioned to e-learning alternatives is that we went out too 'high-tech' and overlooked a higher-touch engagement model," says Steponic.
- **Be creative and innovative with existing tools and resources.** P&L learned that it did not need to buy expensive "whiz-bang" tools, e-learning programs, or consulting services; instead, the solution existed in house and simply needed to be refashioned or repurposed.
- **Manage change.** P&L learned the importance of having a change plan to garner buy-in before implementing learning and performance solutions. The team embraced the role of change practitioner in defining what the change means to daily jobs and building tools to help people be successful in the change.
- **Define success measures early on.** Early measures of success focused on driving user adoption. Simplifying the learning process and enabling widespread content sharing paid off in faster user adoption, although adoption targets and

progress indicators were not as well defined or tracked as they could have been, given how quickly the project progressed.

- **Prepare for the future at the beginning.** The team could have prepared earlier for maintenance and update issues, as well as the sustainability piece of the puzzle.

Case Review

This example shows how a resourceful learning organization, P&L, embarked on an evolutionary journey that led to not only more innovative ways of working and learning, but also a more adaptive and innovative learning culture. In the process of overhauling Blue Shield of California's corporate IT infrastructure, P&L shifted its learning strategy from a fully instructor-led classroom model to modern, blended learning modalities. This strategy emerged in response to demands for:

- more innovative, relevant learning solutions with a business critical, enterprise-wide culture change
- the learning organization to embrace continued innovation of its processes and practices to add immediate and sustainable value amid change.

Table 9-3 shows the characteristics of an adaptable, sustainable learning organization that enabled these accomplishments.

Table 9-3. Characteristics of a Sustainable Learning Organization

Characteristic	Examples	
C-Level Sponsorship	• Senior leaders actively engaged in linking the Shield Advance project and P&L transformational efforts to critical business needs • Participated actively in town halls and social media channels • Senior leaders actively committed to leadership validation processes used to document resource allocations for P&L learning strategy	✓
Efficiency	• Partial monitoring of time and usage indicators (some automation challenges) • In-house, centralized repository increased efficiencies in learning management and enabled on-demand performance support • Four-pronged learning strategy improved cost efficiencies by reducing travel and employees' time away from the office for training (also reduced learning scrap and rework)	✓

Characteristic	Examples	
Effectiveness	• Effectiveness measures being refined, particularly around effectiveness of learning solutions upon job performance • Other effectiveness measures in progress and in development	In Progress
Utility	• Stakeholders, user groups across all locations, and P&L regularly utilize e-learning data to stay current with customer and regulatory requirements • High utility of new e-learning design and delivery processes for instructional designers	✓
Investment	• Significant investment of dedicated P&L resources to design and deliver a multiyear, phased rollout of the new legacy system • Investment of dedicated P&L resources to manage transition planning to ensure business continuity and sustained progress	✓
Credibility	• Sponsors and stakeholders perceived learning approaches and P&L team designers, facilitators as credible business partners • Strategic partnerships with business units and select SMEs increased credibility of learning design and delivery	✓
Demand	• Flexible, scalable curriculum development (NanoModules) provides relevant and accessible learning on demand • Ease of access and innovative, just-in-time pull content creates and sustains user demand for eLibrary resources	✓
Governance	• Partial governance of resource allocations through documented service-level agreements	✓
Continuous Improvement	• High-touch, high-tech, "four-pronged" learning strategy emerged as an improvement opportunity to better meet learner and business needs • Lessons learned formally were captured and documented, with the P&L team acting upon improvement opportunities for measuring learning effectiveness and on-the-job application	✓
Resilience	• P&L team developed validation and sign-off processes to mitigate potential risks with resource constraints or scope creep • Flexible, scalable curriculum development (NanoModules) utilized to withstand the pressures of potential work disruption • Implementation plans included change management approaches to identify and mitigate "pain points" in the transition	✓

Because the following characteristic remains in progress and is not yet fully integrated or operationalized, this learning organization has not reached the refinement stage of maturity.

- **Effectiveness.** P&L continues to evolve its measurement practice and is working closely with business units to extend beyond satisfaction (Level 1) and learning (Level 2) measures of effectiveness.

The team has acknowledged the need to develop more robust and quantitative measures of on-the-job application and business impact. Barriers included challenges with the pace of implementation, some limitations with automation, and some difficulties collecting timely feedback from learners and managers.

Final Thoughts

"If you wait until all the lights are green before you leave home,
you'll never get started on your trip."

—Zig Ziglar

What If?

IMAGINE YOU AND YOUR TEAM ARE RECEIVING A PRESTIGIOUS AWARD that recognizes your achievements in building a best-in-class learning organization. Imagine your excitement when you see your name among the elite list of winning teams and organizations.

Picture the type of innovative best practices that demonstrate how well learning has been embedded into the culture and fabric of your organization.

Imagine the various ways you and your team seized opportunities to serve as a learning leader, strategic business partner, talent builder, and change agent as you developed these best practices and worked with others to have them take hold.

Picture the impact of your team's exemplary performance upon the performance goals of your organization. Imagine the standards, metrics, and tools you've used to show how learning has contributed to strategic business objectives. Imagine how executives in your organization would describe the critical value of your learning organization in a press release about the award.

Reflect on those images for a moment. Absorb how it feels to be considered an extraordinary learning leader in an extraordinary learning organization, to have been part of building a learning legacy.

What Now?

Now picture your learning organization as it is today. How close is your current reality to your winning vision? How well do you, as a learning leader:

- Shape culture?
- Influence business strategy?
- Execute strategy?
- Drive talent attraction, retention, and development?
- Monitor and measure learning's contribution to the business?
- Leverage learning to foster innovation?
- Grow change capabilities across all organizational levels?

No matter where you and your learning organization are in relation to your vision, there's likely room for improvement. As illustrated throughout this book, a learning organization, like any organization, will go through natural growth cycles in its journey toward best-in-class excellence. The Sustainability Cycle illustrates various touch points along a learning organization's evolution as it progresses toward higher levels of process excellence and innovation. Knowing where you are in the cycle helps you take advantage of your position and focus your actions in areas where they will have the most impact. Many learning leaders have shared their stories here about what sustainable impact means to their function and their organization and how they've leveraged learning to achieve it. All agree that achieving sustainable impact goes beyond temporary gains in individual learning and performance to creating lasting, meaningful improvements in organizational learning as a core capability.

Some may argue that a sustainability focus is not a practical or even desirable goal for today's learning enterprise, given the ambiguities and uncertainties of accelerating change. Yet, as shown by our many examples, sustainability does not mean clinging blindly to archaic practices that no longer serve you or your stakeholders. Sustainability is a responsible business practice emphasizing stewardship of resources and process excellence. How many times have you had to reinvent the wheel to realize that it's not an efficient or effective use of resources? A sustainability focus is really a way of working smarter to ensure that our programs, processes, and practices survive and thrive longer. A sustainable learning enterprise benefits everyone because it is inextricably tied to issues of engagement, innovation, high performance, leadership strength, and durable commitments to personal and organizational change.

Despite its benefits and rewards, it's a tall order for most learning organizations to keep core processes intact and manage the basics, much less focus on future-proofing their function during these complex, turbulent times. Even the most motivated and capable learning leaders can get burned out by excessive demands, moving targets, and diminishing resources. The good news is that we've seen how diverse, determined learning leaders, each with great vision and aspiration, have drawn upon their resilience to stretch themselves and their function to progressively higher levels of accomplishment, capability, and value creation to make their vision a reality.

General guidelines and consistent themes from contributors include:

CONTRIBUTORS' THEMES

1. Lead through a business lens, not through a learning lens—think like a CEO.
2. Continuously grow your brand and credibility.
3. Remember to take advantage of data.
4. Integrate learning with day-to-day work—link learning and performance.
5. Develop talent by leveraging learning capability across the entire organization.
6. Avoid urgent trivialities, and focus on what matters most—cut the clutter and dump practices that have outlived their usefulness.
7. Create systems and structures that strengthen connections.
8. Stay connected but get out of the way so others can connect.
9. Build resilience like you'd build a muscle. Draw upon it to buffer setbacks.
10. Be willing to innovate. Explore, experiment, and take risks.

As the future rushes toward us at dizzying speed, we need more resilient learning leaders and more mature, resilient learning organizations. Resiliency is at the heart of sustainability. In short, a sustainable focus is about redefining and transforming how learning and development is done and perceived in an organization so that it can deliver on its promise of value.

The tips, tools, and lessons learned throughout this book highlight examples of how some inspiring learning leaders have applied the seven practices to transform how learning is performed and perceived in their organizations. Here are some suggestions for making the most of the tips, tools, and resources provided.

10 Characteristics of a Sustainable Learning Organization

1. Review the 10 characteristics of a sustainable learning organization from chapter 2. See if your views about those characteristics have shifted since learning more about sustainability in action.

2. Review the corresponding self-assessments in appendix 2. This can be used to routinely assess your progress toward a mature, sustainable learning organization.

Seven Practices of a Sustainable Learning Organization

Practice-Specific Self-Assessments

1. Complete the chapter-specific self-assessments in appendix 2 to identify strengths and prioritize areas for continuous improvement and action planning.

2. Invite members of your team or your stakeholders to assess your learning organization's proficiency in each practice area. Use findings from your combined assessment to identify priority areas for immediate or future action. Make sure these are aligned with business needs.

3. Implement and monitor your action plan. Get support and feedback from peers, colleagues, or co-workers as you move

forward. Monitor your progress toward goal completion regularly and establish new goals on a quarterly or annual basis.

"Plan, Do, Check, Act" Job Aid

1. Review the seven practices for sustaining a resilient learning organization from chapter 1. Next, fill out the "Plan, Do, Check, Act" job aid in appendix 2, which incorporates key actions identified for each of the seven practices covered in chapters 3 through 9. Take this assessment to identify priority areas for immediate or future action.

2. When prioritizing, consider the opportunities that may be coming in the next one to three years that you can prepare yourself for today. Identify resources available to assist you in achieving your goals.

3. Share your action plan with a peer, a coach, a mentor, or a friend to help with accountability. Then implement your plan and self-coach as you move forward. Monitor your progress toward goal completion regularly and establish new goals on a quarterly or annual basis.

Enabling Strategies

1. Use the Case Profile job aid in appendix 1 to review the enabling strategies from case study examples in chapters 3 to 9.

2. Highlight the case example or strategies that mean the most to you and commit to share, maintain, or replicate them.

3. Consider sharing your own enabling strategies through a blog post, article, or professional presentation.

Remember that growth is continual. No matter how effective you or your learning organization may be, keep stretching yourself to greater levels of capability. Work the practices and the practices will work for you!

What Next? A Call to Action

Learning and development matters now more than ever as executives around the world struggle to attract and engage talent, close leadership skills gaps, and accelerate the idea generation needed to fuel innovation and remain competitive in a global, digital marketplace. Learning and development is the engine that drives these strategic capabilities.

Ultimately, learning leaders aren't the only ones responsible for building capabilities that last. If we want continuous, organizational learning to matter, spread, and endure, then the organizations where learning leaders do their work must make sustainability a priority.

But we don't have to wait for permission from senior leaders to prepare the soil and plant the seeds for sustainable learning to take root. More than anything, reshaping the immediate and long-term value of our learning organization begins with a proactive, intentional mindset. After all, the best way to prepare for the future is to help create it.

The future of learning and development is ours to create. The need for transformation is here; the time for action is now. It's our job to make sure that the value we add can go the distance. As human performance expert Bob Mager used to say, "You gotta wanna." What lasting value do you "wanna" create as a learning leader?

Use these tips, tools, insights, and practices, along with your own learning networks, to prepare for the long run and make it happen.

Case Profiles

	Enabling Strategies			
Case in Point	Recognition	Resistance	Renewal	Refinement
Tennessee Department of Human Resources	• Assess where you are • Define where you're heading • Follow the rules of engagement • Adapt strategies to needs • Engage executive support	• Link learning to business objectives • Use a planned change process • Build capability • Create meaningful experiences	• Keep it flexible • Foster connections • Increase accountability • Focus on continuous improvement	• Focus on benchmarking and improving measurement practices
Horizon House	• Begin with the end in mind • Integrate learning priorities with 10-year strategic plan • Provide tools and resources to support continuous learning	• Model "servant leadership" • Demonstrate commitment to continuous learning and leadership • Customize learning	• Initiate succession planning • Build responsive, collaborative infrastructure • Link efficiency measures of learning to financial indicators	• Strengthen succession planning • Maintain fiscal strength and stability • Enhance data collection and reporting • "Sharpen the saw"
Community Healthcare Association of the Dakotas	• Define business and performance objectives • Establish a shared purpose • Adopt a disciplined, data-driven approach to strategy execution	• Openly address change issues • Approach strategic change as a collaborative process • Cascade major process changes to ease the transition	• Manage potential risks • Reinforce shared accountabilities for results • Establish processes to review lessons learned	• Continue establishing links and infrastructures for full integration • Increase organizational resilience to setbacks

	Enabling Strategies			
Case in Point	Recognition	Resistance	Renewal	Refinement
FlightSafety International	• Get sponsors on board • Link strategies to business measures • Use data to inform strategies • Include risk assessment in project planning	• Be prepared for challenges • Conduct ongoing evaluation • Use a transition plan	• Speak the language of the business • Be flexible	• Talk to your customers
The U.S. Army Warrant Office Career College	• Develop a learning strategy • Engage sponsors • Encourage risk	• Provide support, educate, and build capability • Keep the end in mind • Solve real-world, real-time problems	• Maintain the long view • Focus on continuous improvement	• Focus on benchmarking and improving measurement practices
University of Southern Mississippi	• Put people first • Provide direction and focus • Build community	• Be a visible advocate • Educate and communicate • Have a plan and work it • Be flexible	• Strengthen connections • Demonstrate how you add value	• Lead with culture • Keep the long view
Blue Shield of California	• Enlist executive support • Anticipate risks • Define roles and responsibilities • Openly address fears and concerns	• Manage change • Design learner-centered solutions to alleviate pain points • Customize and contextualize learning • Build and leverage partnerships	• Provide lifelines for learners and leaders • Look for common denominators • Experiment and innovate • Stay the course and foster resiliency	• Focus on improving measurement practices that show learning's contribution to the business

Characteristics of a Sustainable Learning Organization

Sustainability Cycle: Chapter 2 Self-Assessment

Instructions: Use this assessment tool to rate the maturity of your learning organization, based on the characteristics of sustainability listed below. Consider each item carefully in terms of your learning organization as a whole and its patterns of practice. You might also want to have individual team members or stakeholders complete the assessment to compare notes, identify areas of strength, and prioritize areas where improvement opportunities may exist.

1 = Strongly Disagree   4 = Agree

2 = Disagree   5 = Strongly Agree

3 = Neither Agree nor Disagree

Characteristic	Description	Rating 1-5
C-Level Engagement	Senior leaders are engaged as visible business partners and learning advocates. Executives can clearly describe how performance-based learning capabilities contribute to organizational mission, values, and effectiveness.	
Efficiency	We provide easy access to employee-centered, flexible learning content and routinely monitor time, usage, and cost indicators. A large portion of resources go toward the efficient use of automated and nontraining performance solutions.	
Effectiveness	We use a variety of qualitative and quantitative methods to evaluate the organizational impact of organizational learning strategies and overall progress toward key outcomes. We regularly assess how services and practices are aligned with, and contributing to, critical talent development and capability needs across the organization.	

Characteristic	Description	Rating 1-5
Investment	A percentage of the total HR, L&D, or talent development budget is regularly applied toward organizational learning, including staffing resources and systems for effectively collecting, analyzing, and displaying results data. This also includes investment in continuing education around learning best practices for the enhanced capabilities of learning staff and key business partners.	
Utility	We facilitate learning anytime, anywhere at the time of need. Learning and performance scorecards are routinely used by our senior leaders, managers, and business units to monitor results and track business outcomes (including negative outcomes) of learning, talent development, or performance improvement initiatives.	
Demand	Stakeholders across all organizational levels regularly request learning and performance results data for continuous process improvement and improved decision making. Learning, talent development, and performance improvement strategies, processes, and practices are adapted to meet evolving user needs and business demands.	
Credibility	Results data generated from our learning and talent management processes are consistently perceived as timely, trustworthy, and relevant to multiple stakeholder needs. Learning and performance staff members are considered credible experts and organizational leaders in learning, talent development, and performance improvement.	
Governance	Operating policies, procedures, and standards are in place for governing learning, talent development, and performance improvement practices in our organization. A cross-functional governance committee ensures that standards are applied in a consistent manner and that processes and practices remain relevant and trustworthy over time.	
Continuous Improvement	We use a variety of innovative approaches to identify, share, and apply results and lessons learned from our strategic initiatives. We use outcome data to develop new or better solutions that meet evolving business needs and performance requirements.	
Resilience	We have the capacity to successfully adapt or alter direction in the face of continuous change or unexpected risks. We use a variety of change or risk management approaches to buffer disturbances and still keep core learning functions intact during times of disruption or adversity.	

Lead With Culture: Chapter 3 Self-Assessment

Instructions: The following practice areas have been shown to promote, develop, and sustain a learning culture in which continuous learning is viewed as a strategic asset and competitive advantage. Consider each item carefully in terms of your learning organization as a whole and its patterns of practice. Use this assessment to identify possibilities for adding more sustainable value to your own learning culture. You may also want to consider how your sponsors, business partners, and stakeholders would respond. Use the findings to identify strengths and prioritize areas for continuous improvement and action planning.

1 = Strongly Disagree

2 = Disagree

3 = Neutral

4 = Agree

5 = Strongly Agree

1 = Not a Priority

2 = Low Priority

3 = Moderate Priority

4 = High Priority

5 = One of Our Highest Priorities

Practice Areas	Agreement 1-5	Priority 1-5
We engage stakeholders in defining continuous learning as a key component of company culture.		
We use strategic business objectives to determine learning priorities.		
We continuously review and refresh our learning and performance strategies to ensure alignment with business objectives.		
We are viewed as credible business partners during culture change efforts.		
We actively model a commitment to personal and professional development to support continuous learning across all organizational levels.		
Learning agility and risk taking are valued capabilities in our organization.		
We function more as learning consultants and facilitators than gatekeepers of learning.		
We lead with culture by continually upskilling, retooling, refreshing, and elevating the role of the learning organization as a key source of competitive advantage.		
We continually grow our cultural literacy and sensitivity as learning leaders and change agents.		

Practice Areas	Agreement 1-5	Priority 1-5
We create a continuous learning environment where learning is built into everyday work activities rather than episodic events.		
We provide tools, resources, and social and collaboration platforms that enable employees to have control over their own development.		
Our learning organization is viewed as a value-added function across all levels of the enterprise.		

Areas of Strength: _____

_____

_____

Opportunities for Improvement: _____

_____

_____

Priority Areas for Continuous Improvement: _____

_____

_____

Planned Actions (for ideas, see chapter 3): _____

_____

_____

By When: _____

_____

_____

Develop and Distribute Leadership: Chapter 4 Self-Assessment

Instructions: The following practice areas have been shown to promote, develop, and sustain leadership support for a learning organization. Consider each item carefully in terms of your learning organization as a whole and its patterns of practice. Use this assessment to identify possibilities for adding more sustainable value to current leadership development processes and practices. You may also want to consider how your sponsors, business partners, and stakeholders would respond. Use the findings to identify strengths and prioritize areas for continuous improvement and action planning.

1 = Strongly Disagree   1 = Not a Priority

2 = Disagree   2 = Low Priority

3 = Neutral   3 = Moderate Priority

4 = Agree   4 = High Priority

5 = Strongly Agree   5 = One of Our Highest Priorities

Practice Areas	Agreement 1-5	Priority 1-5
We actively engage senior leaders and stakeholders in promoting a growth mindset in support of continuous learning.		
We routinely assess the leadership capabilities needed for immediate and future organizational growth.		
We continuously improve leadership development programs and processes to meet evolving business and capability needs across all management levels.		
We regularly provide the proper blend of formal learning, learning from others, and experiential learning to create relevant development experiences for leaders.		
We actively engage senior leaders as facilitators of leadership development programs and processes.		
We regularly assess the context in which leaders across all levels will be using leadership skills and behaviors.		
We use a variety of formal and informal approaches for distributing leadership skills across all parts of the organization.		
We provide essential, accessible performance management tools and resources to managers across all levels at the time of need.		

Practice Areas	Agreement 1-5	Priority 1-5
We use data-driven qualitative and quantitative approaches for measuring the effectiveness of our leadership development programs and practices.		
We have credibility as both business leaders and learning leaders. Our learning organization is seen as a center of process excellence and a source of competitive advantage.		

Areas of Strength: _____

_____

_____

Opportunities for Improvement: _____

_____

_____

Priority Areas for Continuous Improvement: _____

_____

_____

Planned Actions (for ideas, see chapter 4): _____

_____

_____

By When: _____

_____

_____

Execute Well: Chapter 5 Self-Assessment

Instructions: The following practice areas have been shown to promote, develop, and sustain a learning organization that is able to successfully align learning strategy and execution. Consider each item carefully in terms of your learning organization as a whole and its patterns of practice. Use this assessment to identify possibilities for adding more sustainable value to the execution of your learning and performance or talent development strategies and solutions. You may also want to consider how your project sponsors, business partners, and stakeholders would respond. Use the findings to identify strengths and prioritize areas for continuous improvement and action planning.

1 = Strongly Disagree	1 = Not a Priority
2 = Disagree	2 = Low Priority
3 = Neutral	3 = Moderate Priority
4 = Agree	4 = High Priority
5 = Strongly Agree	5 = One of Our Highest Priorities

Practice Areas	Agreement 1-5	Priority 1-5
We actively support stakeholders in aligning business strategy and execution to desired results.		
We use disciplined, data-driven plans and practices to coordinate the execution of learning and performance solutions with stakeholders.		
We have accountability mechanisms in place to ensure consistent and reliable execution of learning strategies.		
We actively build mindsets and capabilities that support effective execution of business strategies across all organizational levels.		
We continuously improve leadership development programs and processes to drive execution of results across all management levels.		
We consciously manage potential risks and barriers that might hinder successful execution of learning and performance solutions.		
We are adept at modifying tactics or adjusting approaches to learning execution as business changes or conditions demand.		

Practice Areas	Agreement 1-5	Priority 1-5
We continuously improve our approaches to learning execution by formally capturing and reflecting upon lessons learned.		
We have governance processes in place to monitor the effectiveness of our learning and performance practices.		
We have credibility for doing what we say and saying what we do. Executives seek our expertise about aligning and executing business strategies.		

Areas of Strength: _____

_____

_____

Opportunities for Improvement: _____

_____

_____

Priority Areas for Continuous Improvement: _____

_____

_____

Planned Actions (for ideas, see chapter 5): _____

_____

_____

By When: _____

_____

_____

Drive for Results; Continuously Improve: Chapter 6 Self-Assessment

Instructions: The following practice areas have been shown to promote, develop, and sustain a learning organization that is able to successfully drive for results and apply those results for continuous improvement purposes. Consider each item carefully in terms of your learning organization as a whole and its patterns of practice. Use this assessment to identify possibilities for adding more sustainable value to the results orientation within your own learning organization. You may also want to consider how your sponsors, business partners, and stakeholders would respond. Use the findings to identify strengths and prioritize areas for continuous improvement and action planning.

1 = Strongly Disagree

2 = Disagree

3 = Neutral

4 = Agree

5 = Strongly Agree

1 = Not a Priority

2 = Low Priority

3 = Moderate Priority

4 = High Priority

5 = One of Our Highest Priorities

Practice Areas	Agreement 1-5	Priority 1-5
We actively engage stakeholders in defining the business objectives of learning and performance strategies.		
We actively communicate stories and examples of how the learning organization has helped solve critical business issues.		
We work with stakeholders to design and develop multiple performance solutions, beyond learning and development.		
We continually look for ways to strengthen the alignment of learning and performance processes and practices to strategic priorities.		
We regularly work with stakeholders to strengthen enablers and remove barriers to performance.		
We routinely provide follow-up mechanisms and performance support tools to reinforce the application of learned skills.		
We use disciplined, data-driven processes and tools—including technology—to collect, analyze, and report performance data.		

Practice Areas	Agreement 1-5	Priority 1-5
We use a variety of qualitative and quantitative approaches to measure the impact of learning and performance strategies.		
We ensure that performance data are available and accessible to multiple users at the time of need.		
We have credibility as results-based learning leaders. Executives and business units regularly seek learning and performance results for improved decision making.		

Areas of Strength: _____

_____

_____

Opportunities for Improvement: _____

_____

_____

Priority Areas for Continuous Improvement: _____

_____

_____

Planned Actions (for ideas, see chapter 6): _____

_____

_____

By When: _____

_____

_____

Build and Bend Change Capabilities: Chapter 7 Self-Assessment

Instructions: The following practice areas have been shown to develop change capable leaders, teams, and organizations. Consider each item carefully in terms of your learning organization as a whole and its patterns of practice. Use this assessment to identify possibilities for adding more sustainable value to your role as a strategic change agent. You may also want to consider how your change sponsors, business partners, and stakeholders would respond. Use the findings to identify strengths and prioritize areas for continuous improvement and action planning.

1 = Strongly Disagree

2 = Disagree

3 = Neutral

4 = Agree

5 = Strongly Agree

1 = Not a Priority

2 = Low Priority

3 = Moderate Priority

4 = High Priority

5 = One of Our Highest Priorities

Practice Areas	Agreement 1-5	Priority 1-5
We regularly analyze the business environment for current and future change demands, threats, and opportunities.		
We routinely assess our talent pool for change capability needs and gaps.		
We align change capability needs with a holistic talent management strategy.		
We engage stakeholders in defining the context in which change capabilities will be used by leaders (frontline, midlevel, and senior management).		
We continuously improve leadership development programs and processes so that leaders and managers have relevant tools and resources for driving strategic change across the enterprise.		
We use a variety of formal and informal approaches (action learning, change networks, e-learning) to build change capability across all management levels.		
We use a common language and a consistent, planned change methodology for initiating and implementing significant change efforts.		

Practice Areas	Agreement 1-5	Priority 1-5
We routinely monitor post-change performance to assess the impact of change initiatives upon strategic objectives.		
We help leaders anticipate and manage risks associated with successful change implementation, including the risk of change fatigue.		
We partner with stakeholders in defining change capacity as a strategic readiness issue.		
We consistently follow up and follow through with refresher training or performance support at later stages of a change effort.		
We have credibility as a strategic change agent. Leaders seek our expertise about the nature of change and best practices in change leadership and management.		

Areas of Strength: _____

_____

_____

Opportunities for Improvement: _____

_____

_____

Priority Areas for Continuous Improvement: _____

_____

_____

Planned Actions (for ideas, see chapter 7): _____

_____

_____

By When: _____

_____

_____

Foster Collaboration, Connection, and Community: Chapter 8 Self-Assessment

Instructions: The following practice areas have been shown to foster collaboration, connection, and community among leaders, teams, and organizations. Consider each item carefully in terms of your learning organization as a whole and its patterns of practice. Use this assessment to identify possibilities for adding more sustainable value to your collaborative initiatives and strategic partnerships. You may also want to consider how your sponsors, business partners, and stakeholders would respond. Use the findings to identify strengths and prioritize areas for continuous improvement and action planning.

1 = Strongly Disagree

2 = Disagree

3 = Neutral

4 = Agree

5 = Strongly Agree

1 = Not a Priority

2 = Low Priority

3 = Moderate Priority

4 = High Priority

5 = One of Our Highest Priorities

Practice Areas	Agreement 1-5	Priority 1-5
We engage senior leaders in promoting and modeling collaborative behaviors across all organizational levels.		
We integrate collaborative skill sets and capabilities within our suite of talent management processes, including recruiting, onboarding, performance management, leadership development, and succession planning.		
We actively partner with senior leaders in breaking down silos and removing barriers to effective collaboration and connection.		
We engage stakeholders in defining the context where collaborative behaviors and connections can be applied.		
We continuously improve learning and talent development programs and processes to drive collaboration and connection across all management levels.		
We use a variety of formal and informal approaches for building connections and improving knowledge sharing across boundaries.		
We leverage technology to build and sustain social networks and communities of practice.		

Practice Areas	Agreement 1-5	Priority 1-5
We partner with senior leaders in defining success measures for effective collaboration and connection.		
We routinely monitor learning tools and resources to make sure that collaboration and connection are happening with the right people, at the right time, and at the right place.		
We have credibility as collaborative business partners. Leaders seek our expertise about how to promote collaboration and grow connections across business units throughout the organization.		

Areas of Strength: _____

_____

Opportunities for Improvement: _____

_____

Priority Areas for Continuous Improvement: _____

_____

Planned Actions (for ideas, see chapter 8): _____

_____

By When: _____

_____

Embrace the Art of Innovation: Chapter 9 Self-Assessment

Instructions: The following practice areas have been shown to promote, develop, and sustain an innovative learning organization. Consider each item carefully in terms of your learning organization as a whole and its patterns of practice. Use this assessment to identify possibilities for adding more sustainable value and innovation to your learning and talent development processes and practices. You may also want to consider how your sponsors, business partners, and stakeholders would respond. Use the findings to identify strengths and prioritize areas for continuous improvement and action planning.

1 = Strongly Disagree	1 = Not a Priority
2 = Disagree	2 = Low Priority
3 = Neutral	3 = Moderate Priority
4 = Agree	4 = High Priority
5 = Strongly Agree	5 = One of Our Highest Priorities

Practice Areas	Agreement 1-5	Priority 1-5
We engage stakeholders in developing innovative, employee-generated learning strategies and content.		
We have talent management strategies and reward and recognition systems that enable innovative learning and performance.		
We make flexible, innovative learning and performance content available and accessible at the time of need so that employees have more choice and personal responsibility for their own development.		
We actively build mindsets and capabilities that support innovation across all organizational levels.		
We continuously improve leadership development programs and processes to drive innovation across all management levels.		
We consciously manage learning processes, practices, and metrics to support the kind of innovation that will lead to organizational growth.		
We have actively positioned continuous learning as a key source of innovation within our organization.		

Practice Areas	Agreement 1-5	Priority 1-5
We routinely experiment with high-tech and high-touch learning and performance solutions to achieve better balance, engagement, and outcomes.		
We are active participants in a number of online communities so we can better understand their benefits and limitations.		
We help manage and support social learning experiences to help individuals and teams share knowledge effectively.		
We encourage risk taking, experimentation, and learning from failure in the pursuit of learning innovation.		
We have credibility as innovative learning leaders. Executives seek our expertise about new or innovative best practices in learning and performance.		

Areas of Strength: _____

_____

_____

Opportunities for Improvement: _____

_____

_____

Priority Areas for Continuous Improvement: _____

_____

_____

Planned Actions (for ideas, see chapter 9): _____

_____

_____

By When: _____

_____

_____

Plan, Do, Check, Act Job Aid

Building a sustainable learning organization typically represents a significant culture change and transformation effort. Although there is no best way to manage the process, one place to start is by assessing areas of strengths and opportunities for improvement in current practices.

This job aid reflects the key Plan, Do, Check, Act actions identified for each of the seven practices in chapters 3 through 9. Use it in combination with the chapter-specific self-assessments as a framework for assessing your learning organization's current orientation toward sustainability.

Consider each item carefully in terms of your learning organization as a whole and its patterns of practice. You might also want to have individual team members complete the assessment to compare notes and identify areas of strength and areas with potential improvement opportunities. Identify high-priority areas that might require immediate action planning. When prioritizing, consider the opportunities or challenges that may be coming in the next one to three years that may require preparation today.

Rating Scale

1 = Not Able to Put Into Practice

2 = Need More Guidance or Experience to Put Into Practice

3 = Able to Put Into Practice but Need More Experience to be Fully Proficient

4 = Able to Put Into Practice and Perform Tasks at Fully Proficient Level

5 = Able to Put Into Practice and Perform Tasks at Expert Level of Proficiency

NA = Not Applicable to Job Tasks

Practice 1: Lead With Culture

PLAN	Position learning as a chief enabler to a high-performance, high-engagement culture	1	2	3	4	5	NA
	Engage leaders as continuous learning champions and role models	1	2	3	4	5	NA
	Establish alignment between learning and business strategies	1	2	3	4	5	NA
	Establish mechanisms to reward and reinforce behaviors that support culture transformation	1	2	3	4	5	NA
DO	Build policies, practices, and programs that drive the learning and performance agenda	1	2	3	4	5	NA
	Create a continuous learning environment that enables engagement and high performance	1	2	3	4	5	NA
	Build adaptive structures and processes to enable cultural shifts	1	2	3	4	5	NA
	Consistently demonstrate the impact and business value of a learning culture	1	2	3	4	5	NA
CHECK	Continuously review and refresh learning and performance strategies to ensure alignment with business priorities	1	2	3	4	5	NA
	Assess the business contexts where leaders and employees are expected to demonstrate behaviors in line with desired culture	1	2	3	4	5	NA
	Continually assess potential risks and barriers to building and sustaining a learning culture	1	2	3	4	5	NA
ACT	Approach culture change, on both an organizational and functional level, as an inside-out process	1	2	3	4	5	NA
	Build your cultural literacy and intelligence	1	2	3	4	5	NA
	Build mindsets and capabilities that support learning across all organization levels	1	2	3	4	5	NA
	Actively manage, upskill, and elevate your learning culture to sustain its value and relevance	1	2	3	4	5	NA

Practice 2: Develop and Distribute Leadership

PLAN	Routinely assess the leadership capabilities for immediate and future organizational growth	1	2	3	4	5	NA
	Align development needs with strategic priorities	1	2	3	4	5	NA
	Actively engage stakeholders in promoting a growth mindset	1	2	3	4	5	NA
	Take the long view (plan for sustainability)	1	2	3	4	5	NA
DO	Build credibility as a strategic business leader	1	2	3	4	5	NA
	Grow and distribute leadership capabilities across all levels	1	2	3	4	5	NA
	Use a variety of formal and informal development approaches to enhance leaders' learning experience	1	2	3	4	5	NA
	Demonstrate the impact of leadership development through the use data-driven qualitative and quantitative approaches for measuring effectiveness	1	2	3	4	5	NA
CHECK	Continuously improve leadership development processes	1	2	3	4	5	NA
	Ensure learning processes and solutions are meeting immediate and future business needs	1	2	3	4	5	NA
	Regularly assess the context in which leadership skills will be used	1	2	3	4	5	NA
	Continually assess the compatibility of infrastructures, such as workforce planning, performance management, and succession planning	1	2	3	4	5	NA
ACT	Be the leader you expect to influence	1	2	3	4	5	NA
	Improve performance management systems	1	2	3	4	5	NA
	Develop learning champions across all levels	1	2	3	4	5	NA
	Demonstrate how learning is adding value as a capability builder and talent developer	1	2	3	4	5	NA

Practice 3: Execute Well

PLAN	Align execution plans with strategic priorities	1	2	3	4	5	NA
	Adopt disciplined, data-driven processes to coordinate the execution of learning and performance or business solutions with stakeholders	1	2	3	4	5	NA
	Plan for internal or external factors that can help or hinder success	1	2	3	4	5	NA
DO	Guide execution from the top, but drive from the middle	1	2	3	4	5	NA
	Maintain consistency of purpose	1	2	3	4	5	NA
	Leverage expertise from all organizational levels	1	2	3	4	5	NA
	Honor commitments	1	2	3	4	5	NA
CHECK	Use accountability mechanisms to ensure consistent and reliable execution of learning strategies	1	2	3	4	5	NA
	Take time to reflect and learn from what worked and what didn't	1	2	3	4	5	NA
	Actively use governance mechanisms as a quality check	1	2	3	4	5	NA
ACT	Modify tactics or adjust approaches to learning execution as conditions demand	1	2	3	4	5	NA
	Practice risk and change management	1	2	3	4	5	NA
	Regularly reward progress toward goals and achievement of milestones	1	2	3	4	5	NA
	Actively capture, reflect, and act on lessons learned for continuous improvement	1	2	3	4	5	NA

Practice 4: Drive for Results; Continuously Improve

PLAN	Engage stakeholders in defining what success looks like for each initiative (clarify business objectives of learning and performance strategies)	1	2	3	4	5	NA
	Work with stakeholders to design and develop multiple performance solutions beyond learning and development	1	2	3	4	5	NA
	Continually strengthen alignment of learning and business strategies for sustained value	1	2	3	4	5	NA
	Analyze and address all environmental factors (employee motivation or readiness, management support, performance consequences, feedback loops, necessary tools, information, and resources) that may help or hinder results	1	2	3	4	5	NA
DO	Provide necessary performance support and remove barriers	1	2	3	4	5	NA
	Make performance data available and accessible at the time of need	1	2	3	4	5	NA
	Standardize data-driven measurement processes for improved consistency and credibility	1	2	3	4	5	NA
	Leverage technology for collecting, analyzing, and reporting performance data (qualitative and quantitative)	1	2	3	4	5	NA
CHECK	Continuously monitor and measure results on a micro and macro level	1	2	3	4	5	NA
	Regularly confirm the credibility of performance data	1	2	3	4	5	NA
	Routinely assess and remove barriers to desired results	1	2	3	4	5	NA
	Provide a variety of formal and informal follow-up mechanisms to reinforce application of skills	1	2	3	4	5	NA
	Monitor attitudes, beliefs, and fears about performance expectations	1	2	3	4	5	NA

Practice 4: Drive for Results; Continuously Improve (cont.)

ACT	Position measurement as a compelling piece of organizational strategy	1	2	3	4	5	NA
	Use dashboards (scorecards) to communicate results for action planning and continuous improvement	1	2	3	4	5	NA
	Build evaluation capability (including learning analytics skills) across all organization levels to promote shared ownership for results	1	2	3	4	5	NA
	Shape a culture of accountability and evidence-based decision making	1	2	3	4	5	NA

Practice 5: Build and Bend Change Capabilities

PLAN	Define change capable competencies and characteristics needed across all organizational levels and functions	1	2	3	4	5	NA
	Routinely assess the talent pool for change capability needs and gaps	1	2	3	4	5	NA
	Align change capabilities with talent attraction, retention, and development priorities	1	2	3	4	5	NA
	Partner with stakeholders in defining success measures for significant change initiatives	1	2	3	4	5	NA
DO	Customize and contextualize leadership development programs and processes to build change capability across all management levels (senior, midlevel, frontline)	1	2	3	4	5	NA
	Engage stakeholders in defining the context in which change capabilities will be used by leaders (senior, midlevel, frontline)	1	2	3	4	5	NA
	Use a consistent, disciplined, planned change process for initiating and implementing significant change efforts	1	2	3	4	5	NA
	Cascade multiple, overlapping change efforts to minimize change fatigue and performance dips	1	2	3	4	5	NA
	Follow up and follow through with significant change efforts to capture lessons for continuous improvement and action planning purposes	1	2	3	4	5	NA
CHECK	Continuously monitor risks to change efforts, especially the risk of change fatigue	1	2	3	4	5	NA
	Monitor and measure the impact of major change efforts to determine if they've met strategic objectives	1	2	3	4	5	NA
	Routinely analyze the business environment for current and future change demands, threats, and opportunities	1	2	3	4	5	NA
	Monitor your own bias and aversion to change	1	2	3	4	5	NA

Practice 5: Build and Bend Change Capabilities (cont.)

ACT	Embrace your role as a strategic change agent	1	2	3	4	5	NA
	Leverage individual and collective change capabilities to foster change readiness and commitment	1	2	3	4	5	NA
	Provide immediate and readily accessible performance support during and after change initiatives	1	2	3	4	5	NA
	Partner with senior leaders in defining change capacity as a strategic readiness issue	1	2	3	4	5	NA

Practice 6: Foster Collaboration, Connection, and Community

PLAN	Define what collaboration looks like	1	2	3	4	5	NA
	Engage stakeholders in embedding collaboration as a cultural value	1	2	3	4	5	NA
	Plan to recruit, develop, and nurture collaborative skills and capabilities	1	2	3	4	5	NA
	Define success measures for building a collaborative culture	1	2	3	4	5	NA
DO	Teach collaboration skills across all organizational levels	1	2	3	4	5	NA
	Ensure that talent management processes (performance management, succession planning, career development) support and grow collaborative skills and capabilities	1	2	3	4	5	NA
	Leverage technologies that enable collaboration and connection	1	2	3	4	5	NA
	Use a variety of formal and informal approaches for building connections and improving knowledge sharing across boundaries	1	2	3	4	5	NA
CHECK	Monitor enablers and barriers to effective collaboration	1	2	3	4	5	NA
	Ensure that performance rewards and recognition plans support collaboration across all organizational levels	1	2	3	4	5	NA
	Assess the business contexts in which leaders and employees are expected to apply collaborative behaviors	1	2	3	4	5	NA
	Routinely monitor learning tools and resources to make sure that collaboration and connection are happening with the right people, at the right time, at the right place	1	2	3	4	5	NA

Practice 6: Foster Collaboration, Connection, and Community (cont.)

ACT	Engage and support leaders in modeling collaborative behaviors	1	2	3	4	5	NA
	Actively partner with senior leaders in breaking down silos and removing barriers to effective collaboration and connection	1	2	3	4	5	NA
	Recognize and reward the best connectors	1	2	3	4	5	NA
	Use innovative digital tools, technologies, and resources to build peer networks and communities of practice	1	2	3	4	5	NA

Practice 7: Embrace the Art of Innovation

PLAN	Reimagine the learning experience to meet the needs of the modern learner	1	2	3	4	5	NA
	Engage stakeholders in championing innovative values, behaviors, and mindsets	1	2	3	4	5	NA
	Integrate innovation as a core competency	1	2	3	4	5	NA
	Align innovative solutions with existing systems and resources, including LMSs	1	2	3	4	5	NA
DO	Use formal and informal approaches to support innovative learning and performance solutions	1	2	3	4	5	NA
	Make innovative, technology-rich solutions available and accessible at the time of need	1	2	3	4	5	NA
	Build mindsets and capabilities that support innovation across all organization levels	1	2	3	4	5	NA
	Balance high-tech and high-touch learning and performance approaches	1	2	3	4	5	NA
CHECK	Continuously monitor and measure the user experience with innovative learning solutions	1	2	3	4	5	NA
	Routinely assess the compatibility of supporting infrastructure	1	2	3	4	5	NA
	Assess and manage social learning experiences to ensure that individuals and teams can share knowledge effectively	1	2	3	4	5	NA
	Assess the business context(s) in which leaders and employees are expected to apply innovative behaviors for integration with leadership development	1	2	3	4	5	NA
ACT	Actively position continuous learning as a key source of innovation	1	2	3	4	5	NA
	Ensure that learning processes and solutions keep pace with needed business innovations	1	2	3	4	5	NA
	Participate in online communities to better understand their benefits and limitations	1	2	3	4	5	NA
	Help shape a culture where risk taking, experimentation, and creativity are rewarded	1	2	3	4	5	NA

References

Aguirre, D., R. von Post, and M. Alpern. 2013. *Culture's Role in Enabling Organizational Change.* Booz & Company, November 14. www.strategyand.pwc.com/reports /cultures-role-organizational-change.

American Management Association (AMA). 2006. *Agility and Resilience in the Face of Continuous Change.* New York: AMA. www.amanet.org/images/hri-agility06.pdf.

American Management Association (AMA) and the Institute for Corporate Productivity (i4cp). 2007. *How to Build a High-Performance Organization.* New York: American Management Association. www.amajapan.co.jp/j/pdf/HRI _HIGH-PERFORMANCE_Organization.pdf.

——. 2015. *Developing Global-Minded Leaders to Drive High-Performance.* www .amajapan.co.jp/j/pdf/i4cp_Developing_Global_Minded_Leaders_to_Drive_High _Performance_E.pdf.

American Society for Training & Development (ASTD). 2011. *Learning to Innovate: Exploring Learning's Critical Role in Fostering Innovation.* Alexandria, VA: ASTD Press.

American Society for Training & Development (ASTD) and the Institute for Corporate Productivity (i4cp). 2014a. *Change Agents: The Role of Organizational Learning in Change Management.* Alexandria, VA: ASTD Press.

——. 2014b. *The Value of Learning: Gauging the Business Impact of Organizational Learning Programs.* Alexandria, VA: ASTD Press.

American Society for Training & Development (ASTD) and the University of Pennsylvania. 2006. *Chief Learning Officer Profile Research Report.* Alexandria, VA: ASTD Press.

Andersen, E.S., and S.A. Jessen. 2003. "Project Maturity in Organisations." *International Journal of Project Management* 21(6): 457-461.

Anderson, C. 2014. "Bad Measurement Affects Training Impact." *Chief Learning Officer,* April 23. www.clomedia.com/2014/04/23/bad-measurement-affects -training-impact.

Anderson, C. 2015. "Stagnant Outlook for Training Measurement." *Chief Learning Officer,* May 4. www.clomedia.com/2015/05/04/stagnant-outlook-for-learning -measurement.

Armenakis, A.A., S.G. Harris, and K.W. Mossholder. 1993. "Creating Readiness for Organizational Change." *Human Relations* 46(6): 681-703.

Asghar, R. 2014. "What Millennials Want in the Workplace (and Why You Should Start Giving It to Them)." *Forbes*, January 13. www.forbes.com/sites /robasghar/2014/01/13/what-millennials-want-in-the-workplace-and-why-you -should-start-giving-it-to-them/#75267452fdfb.

Ashkenas, R. 2015. "There's a Difference Between Cooperation and Collaboration." *Harvard Business Review*, April 20. https://hbr.org/2015/04/theres-a-difference -between-cooperation-and-collaboration.

Association for Talent Development (ATD). 2015a. *Aligning for Success: Connecting Learning to Business Performance.* Alexandria, VA: ATD Press.

———. 2015b. *Global Trends in Talent Development.* Alexandria, VA: ATD Press.

———. 2015c. *State of the Industry.* Alexandria, VA: ATD Press.

———. 2016a. *Building a Culture of Learning.* Alexandria, VA: ATD Press.

———. 2016b. *Evaluating Learning: Getting to Measures That Matter.* Alexandria, VA: ATD Press.

Association for Talent Development (ATD) and the Institute for Corporate Productivity (i4cp). 2015. *Learners of the Future.* Alexandria, VA: ATD Press.

ATD Staff (Association for Talent Development). 2015a. "Building Talent: The Very BEST of 2015." *TD* 69(11). www.td.org/Publications/Magazines/TD /TD-Archive/2015/11/BEST-Intro.

———. 2015b. "Haworth Inc." *TD* 69(11). Alexandria, VA: ATD Press. www.td.org /Publications/Magazines/TD/TD-Archive/2015/11/BEST-Haworth.

———. 2016. "Talent Development at EY." *CTDO*, June 15. www.td.org/Publications /Magazines/CTDO/Archives/2016/Summer/Talent-Development-at-EY.

Azulay, H. 2012. *Employee Development on a Shoestring.* Alexandria, VA: ASTD Press.

Beatty, R.W., and C.E. Schneier. 1997. "New Human Resource Roles to Impact Organizational Performance: From 'Partners' to 'Players.'" In *Tomorrow's HR Management*, edited by D. Ulrich, M.R. Losey, and G. Lake. Boston: Harvard Business School Press.

Bell, R. 2015. "A Legacy of Learning." *Chief Learning Officer*, June.

Benko, C., U. Bohdal-Spiegelhoff, J. Geller, and H. Walkinshaw. 2014. "The Reskilled HR Team: Transform HR Professionals Into Skilled Business Consultants." Deloitte University Press, March 7. http://dupress.com/articles/hc-trends-2014 -reskilled-hr-team.

Benson-Armer, R., S.-S. Otto, G. Webster, C. Benkert, and T. Koch. 2015. "Building capabilities for Performance." *McKinsey & Company*, January. www.mckinsey .com/business-functions/organization/our-insights/building-capabilities-for -performance.

Bersin, J. 2014. "Spending on Corporate Training Soars: Employee Capabilities Now a Priority." *Forbes*, February 4. www.forbes.com/sites/joshbersin/2014/02/04/the-recovery-arrives-corporate-training-spend-skyrockets/#4877babf4ab7.

Bill & Melinda Gates Foundation. 2016. *How We Work.* www.gatesfoundation.org/How-We-Work.

Bingham, T., and M. Conner. 2015. *The New Social Learning: Connect. Collaborate. Work.* Alexandria, VA: ATD Press.

Boller, S. 2012. "Spaced Learning and Repetition: Why They Work." Bottom-Line Performance Lessons on Learning Blog, October 16. www.bottomlineperformance.com/spaced-learning-and-repetition-why-they-work.

Bossidy, L., and R. Charan. 2002. *Execution: The Discipline of Getting Things Done.* New York: Crown Business.

Bowley, J. 2015. "Collaboration Catalysts." *Talent Management*, August 18. www.talentmgt.com/2015/08/18/collaboration-catalysts.

Brinkerhoff, R.O. 2003. *The Success Case Method.* San Francisco: Berrett-Koehler.

Brubaker, K. 2016. "BizLibrary Introduces Reinforcement Boosters to Improve Learning Retention." BizLibrary, May 23. www.bizlibrary.com/press-releases/bizlibrary-reinforcement-boosters-improve-learning-retention....

Bruno, J. 1995. *Information Reference Testing (IRT) in Corporate and Technical Training Programs.* UCLA.

Burjek, A. 2016. "Vanguard Devotes Year to Learning Innovation." *Chief Learning Officer*, May 16. www.clomedia.com/2016/05/16/vanguard-devotes-year-to-learning-innovation.

Burkett, H. 2008. "Measuring ROI in a Career Development Initiative." In *Measurement and Evaluation Series Casebook*, edited by P. Phillips and J.J. Phillips. San Francisco: Pfeiffer.

———. 2011. "Case Study: Community Healthcare Association of the Dakotas." In *Fundamentals of Performance Improvement*, 3rd edition, edited by J. Dessinger, J. Moseley, and D. Van Tiem. San Francisco: Wiley.

———. 2013. "Sustainable Performance: The New Agenda for Adding Value." *Performance Improvement*, 52(4): 6-10.

———. 2015a. "Talent Managers as Change Agents." In *ATD Talent Management Handbook*, edited by T. Bickham. Alexandria, VA: ATD Press.

———. 2015b. "The Case for Change Capability: How HR Can Step Up and Stand Out as a Strategic Change Leader," in *The Rise of HR: Wisdom From 73 HR Thought Leaders*, edited by D. Ulrich. Alexandria, VA: HR Certification Institute.

Chambers, B., M. Foulon, H. Handfield-Jones, S.M. Hankin, and E.G. Michaels III. 1998. "The War for Talent." *McKinsey Quarterly*.

Cherry, K. 2015. "10 Ways to Become More Resilient." *Very Well*, May 10. http://psychology.about.com/od/crisiscounseling/tp/become-more-resilient.htm.

Christensen, C.M. 2013. *The Innovator's Dilemma: When New Technologies Cause Great Firms to Fail*. Cambridge, MA: HBR Press.

Clow, J. 2012. *The Work Revolution*. New York: Wiley.

———. 2015. "Organizational Culture as a Foundation for Retention." In *ATD Talent Management Handbook*, edited by T. Bickham, 107-121. Alexandria, VA: ATD Press.

Coffin, J. 2016. "Why I Chose Workday, and Why It Was the Best Decision I Ever Made." LinkedIn Pulse, June 24. www.linkedin.com/pulse/why-i-chose-workday -best-decision-ever-made-josh-coffin.

Collins, J. 2009. *How the Mighty Fall*. New York: HarperCollins.

Coutu, D. 2002. "How Resilience Works." *Harvard Business Review*, May. https://hbr .org/2002/05/how-resilience-works.

Curtis, B., W.E. Hefley, and S. A. Miller. 2001. *The People CMM: A Framework for Human Capital Management*. Boston: Addison-Wesley Professional.

DDI. 2015. *15 Metrics That Matter About Your Mid-Level*. DDI. www.ddiworld.com /DDI/media/trend-research/15-metrics-that-matter-mid-level_tr_ddi.pdf?ext =.pdf.

de Geus, A. 2002. *The Living Company*. Boston: MA: Harvard Business Review Press.

De Grip, A., and J. van Loo. 2002. "The Economics of Skills Obsolescence: A Review." In *The Economics of Skills Obsolescence*, edited by A. de Grip, J. van Loo, and K. Mayhew. Vol. 21, Research in Labor Economics, edited by S. Polachek and K. Tatsiramos. Bingley, UK: Emerald Group Publishing. www.emeraldinsight.com /doi/book/10.1016/S0147-9121(2002)21.

Dearborn, J. 2015. "Why Your Company Needs a Learning Culture." *Chief Learning Officer*, June 3. www.clomedia.com/2015/06/03/why-your-company-needs-a -learning-culture.

Deloitte. 2015. *Global Human Capital Trends 2015*. Deloitte University Press. www2.deloitte.com/content/dam/Deloitte/at/Documents/human-capital /hc-trends-2015.pdf.

DeTunq, T.H., and L. Schmidt, L. 2013. *Integrated Talent Management Scorecards*. Alexandria, VA: ASTD Press.

Dinwoodie, D.L., L. Quinn, and J.B. McGuire. 2014. *Bridging the Strategy/Performance Gap*. Center for Creative Leadership. www.ccl.org/leadership/pdf/research /bridgingthestrategy.pdf.

Dixon, L. 2015. "Foot Locker Inc.: Predictable Hiring Approved." Talent Management, December 4. www.talentmgt.com/2015/12/04/foot-locker-inc-predictable-hiring -approved.

———. 2016a. "How Ericsson Revived Its Employer Brand." *Talent Management,* February 5. www.talentmgt.com/2016/02/05/how-ericsson-revived-its-employer -brand.

———. 2016b. "How Radio Flyer Improved Its First-Year Turnover." *Talent Management,* March 4. www.talentmgt.com/2016/03/04/how-radio-flyer-improved-its-first -year-turnover.

Duncan, R.D. 2014. "How Campbell's Soup's Former CEO Turned the Company Around." *Fast Company,* September 18. www.fastcompany.com/3035830 /hit-the-ground-running/how-campbells-soups-former-ceo-turned-the -company-around.

Duncan, W.J., V.A. Yeager, A.C. Rucks, and P.M. Ginter. 2011. "Surviving Organizational Disasters." *Business Horizons* 54(2): 135-142.

Elance-oDesk and Millennial Branding. 2015. "The 2015 Millennial Majority Workforce Study." www.slideshare.net/oDesk/2015-millennial-majority -workforce.

Feser, C., F. Mayol, and R. Srinivasan. 2015. "Decoding Leadership: What Really Matters." *McKinsey Quarterly,* January. www.mckinsey.com/global-themes /leadership/decoding-leadership-what-really-matters.

Fierce. 2011. "New Study: 86 Percent of Employees Cite Lack of Collaboration for Workplace Failures." *Fierce,* May 23. www.fierceinc.com/about-fierce /press-room/press-releases/new-study-86-percent-of-employees-cite-lack-of -collaboration-for-workplace-failures.

Filigree Consulting. 2012. *Instructional Technology and Collaborative Learning Best Practices.* Filligree Consulting and SMART Technologies, July. http://vault .smarttech.com/assessment/education_whitepapers_web.pdf?WT.ac=edresearch.

Filipkowski, J. 2015. *2015 Talent Pulse: Empowering the HR and Business Partnership.* Human Capital Institute, March 9. www.hci.org/hr-research/2015-talent-pulse -empowering-hr-and-business-partnership.

Filippone, T., D. Youden, K. Pennington, and P. Fersht. 2012. *Human Resources Transformation: Is It Driving Business Performance?* HfS Research, May. www.pwc .com/us/en/people-management/publications/assets/pwc-hfs-hr-transform.pdf.

Gale, S.F. 2016. "Speak Your CEO's Language." *Chief Learning Officer,* January 27. www.clomedia.com/2016/01/27/speak-your-ceos-language.

Gallup. 2006. "Gallup Study: Engaged Employees Inspire Company Innovation." *Gallup Management Journal,* October. http://missionfacilitators.com /wp-content/uploads/2013/03/Engaged-Employees-Drive-Organizations-Forward .pdf.

———. 2013. *State of the American Workplace.* Gallup, June. http://employeeengagement.com/wp-content/uploads/2013/06/Gallup-2013 -State-of-the-American-Workplace-Report.pdf.

Gartner. 2013. "Gartner Predicts by 2017, Half of Employers Will Require Employees to Supply Their Own Device for Work Purposes." Gartner, May 1. www.gartner.com/newsroom/id/2466615.

Gerstner, L. 2003. *Who Says Elephants Can't Dance?* New York: Harper Business.

Gilbert, F. 2015. "Interview With Dr. Jac Fitz Enz—the Father of HR Metrics." Franz HR, December 4. http://franzgilbert.com/interview-with-dr-jac-fitz-enz-the-father-of-hr-metrics.

Gossage, W.G., Y. Silverstone, and A. Leach. 2010. "The Change-Capable Organization." *Outlook*, October. www.accenture.com/us-en/~/media/Accenture/Conversion-Assets/DotCom/Documents/Global/PDF/Industries_16/Accenture-Outlook-Change-Capable-Organization.pdf.

Graber, J. 2016. "UL's Unique Look at Development." *Chief Learning Officer*, April 8. www.clomedia.com/2016/04/08/uls-unique-look-at-development.

Gurdjian, P., T. Halbeisen, and K. Lane. 2014. "Why Leadership Development Programs Fail." *McKinsey Quarterly*, January. www.mckinsey.com/insights/leading_in_the_21st_century/why_leadership-development_programs_fail.

Gutsche, J. 2009. *Exploiting Chaos: 150 Ways to Spark Innovation During Times of Change.* New York: Gotham.

Happiness Research Institute, Krifa, and TNS Gallup. 2015. *Job Satisfaction Index 2015.* Happiness Research Institute. www.happinessresearchinstitute.com/publications/4579836749.

Harris, P. 2015a. "Brewing Up a New Tradition." *TD* 69(11). www.td.org/Publications/Magazines/TD/TD-Archive/2015/11/BEST-Millercoors.

———. 2015b. "Don't Just Train Them, Nurture Them." *TD* 69(11). www.td.org/Publications/Magazines/TD/TD-Archive/2015/11/BEST-Samsung.

———. 2015c. "Serving Up Innovation." *TD* 69(11). www.td.org/Publications/Magazines/TD/TD-Archive/2015/11/BEST-Hilton

———. 2015d. "Impact and Alignment." *CTDO*, December 15. www.td.org/Publications/Magazines/CTDO/Archives/2015/Winter/Impact-and-Alignment.

Hart, J. 2015. *Modern Workplace Learning: A Resource Book for L&D.* Centre for Learning & Performance Technologies.

Hartley, D. 2010. "Is There Macro Value in Microlearning?" *Chief Learning Officer*, June 27. www.clomedia.com/2010/06/27/is-there-macro-value-in-microlearning.

Harvard Business Review. 2014a. *Frontline Managers: Are They Given the Leadership Tools to Succeed?* Cambridge, MA: Harvard Business School Publishing. https://hbr.org/resources/pdfs/tools/Halogen_Report_June2014.pdf.

———. 2014b. "How Companies Can Profit from a 'Growth Mindset.'" *Harvard Business Review*, November. https://hbr.org/2014/11/how-companies-can-profit-from-a -growth-mindset.

———. 2015. *The Changing Role of the CHRO.* Cambridge, MA: Harvard Business School Publishing. https://hbr.org/resources/pdfs/comm/visier/Changing_Role_of_the _CHRO_April_2015.pdf.

Heathfield, S.M. 2016. "20 Ways Zappos Reinforces Its Company Culture." The Balance, June 28. www.thebalance.com/zappos-company-culture-1918813.

Helgesen, S. 2015. "Frances Hesselbein's Merit Badge in Leadership". *Strategy + Business*, May 11. www.strategy-business.com/article/00332?gko=afedc.

Henneman, T. 2012. "DreamWorks Animation Cultivates a Culture of Creativity." *Workforce*, August 4. www.workforce.com/2012/08/04/dreamworks-animation-cultivates-a-culture-of-creativity.

Herold, D., and D. Fedor. 2008. *Change the Way You Lead Change.* Stanford, CA: Stanford Business Books.

Hesselbein, F. 2013. *Hesselbein on Leadership.* San Francisco, CA: Jossey-Bass.

High, P. 2016. "Forbes CIO Innovation Award: Intel's CIO Drives $1 Billion of Value Through Analytics." *Forbes*, March 22. www.forbes.com/sites /peterhigh/2016/03/22/forbes-cio-innovation-award-intels-cio-drives-1-billion-of -value-through-analytics/print.

Holliday, T. 2015. "Success(ion) Planning: Preparing Leaders for the Workforce of the Future." In Talent Management Webinar Series. www.slideshare.net /humancapitalmedia/062315-tm-silkroadsuccessionplanningfinal.

Howard, L. 2015. "Powered by Women." *Sacramento Magazine*, October 12. www .sacmag.com/Sacramento-Magazine/October-2015/Powered-by-Women.

Hughes, R.L., K. Colarelli Beatty, and D. Dinwoodie. 2011. *Becoming a Strategic Leader*, 2nd edition. San Francisco: John Wiley & Sons.

Hunt, S. 2014. Commonsense Talent Management. San Francisco: Pfeiffer.

IBM. 2010. *Working Beyond Borders.* Somers, NY: IBM. www-01.ibm.com/common /ssi/cgi-bin/ssialias?infotype=PM&subtype=XB&appname=GBSE_GB_TI _USEN&htmlfid=GBE03353USEN&attachment=GBE03353USEN.PDF.

Institute for Corporate Productivity (i4cp). 2014. *The Top 10 Critical Human Capital Issues: Enabling Sustained Growth through Talent Transparency.* Seattle: i4cp.

Izzo, J. 2015. "Consistency Drives Success at Telus." *Strategy+Business*, August 31. www .strategy-business.com/article/00360?gko=32975.

Jones, K. 2011. *Pillars for Performance: Integrating Learning and Talent Management.* Bersin & Associates Research Bulletin 6(52): 1-9. Oakland, CA: Bersin & Associates.

Jue, N. 2013. "i4cp Research: Human Capital Practices Drive Organizational Innovation." Institute for Corporate Productivity (i4cp), April 1. www.i4cp.com /productivity-blog/2013/04/02/i4cp-research-human-capital-practices-drive -organizational-innovation.

Kahn, J. 2013. "New York Life: Ensuring Permanence and Legacy." *Chief Learning Officer*, June 17. www.clomedia.com/articles/new-york-life-ensuring -permanence-and-legacy.

Kalman, F. 2015. "Chicago Cubs: The Cubs Way." *Talent Management*, October 2. www .talentmgt.com/2015/10/02/chicago-cubs-the-cubs-way.

Kanter, R.M. 2009. "The Secret to Getting Your Message Across." *Harvard Business Review*, February 4. https://hbr.org/2009/02/the-secret-to-getting-your-mes.html.

Kearns Goodwin, D. 2006. *Team of Rivals*. New York: Simon & Schuster.

Kellerman, B. 2012. *The End of Leadership*. New York: HarperCollins.

Kelly, K., and G. Pease. 2015. *Driving Talent Management With Data*. Chapel Hill, NC: UNC Executive Development. www.kenan-flagler.unc.edu/~/media /Files/documents/executive-development/unc-white-paper-driving-talent -development-with-data.pdf.

Kirkland, R. 2016. "Cisco's John Chambers on the Digital Era." *McKinsey & Company*, March. www.mckinsey.com/industries/high-tech/our-insights/ciscos-john -chambers-on-the-digital-era.

Knowledge@Wharton. 2012. "Why Companies Can No Longer Afford to Ignore Their Social Responsibilities." *Time*, May 28. http://business.time.com/2012/05/28 /why-companies-can-no-longer-afford-to-ignore-their-social-responsibilities.

Korn Ferry. 2014. "Korn Ferry Executive Survey: Companies Struggle to Align Culture With Business Strategy." Korn Ferry, September 8. www.kornferry.com /press/15195.

Korn Ferry Institute. 2015. *Real World Leadership: Develop Leaders Who Can Drive Real Change*. Korn Ferry Institute, October 12. www.kornferry.com/institute/real -world-leadership-part-one-develop-leaders-who-can-drive-real-change.

Kouzes, J.M., and B.Z. Posner. 2016. *Learning Leadership: The Five Fundamentals of Becoming an Exemplary Leader*. Hoboken, NJ: Wiley.

Kropp, B. 2013. "Is the Performance Management System Dead or Creating Zombies?" CEB Human Resources blog, November 15. www.cebglobal.com/blogs/is-the -performance-management-system-dead-or-creating-zombies.

Leaman, C. 2016. Microlearning in Action: Small Bites, Big Impact. Webinar. TrainingIndustry.com, May 17. www.trainingindustry.com/webinars /microlearning-in-action-small-bites-big-impact.aspx.

Legrand, C. 2007. *Does Our Brain Operating System Need an Upgrade?* Ideaction. www.ideaction.net/images/documents/White-Paper-Does-our-Brain-Operating -System-Need-an-Upgrade2.pdf.

Locwin, B. 2016. "Peeling Back the Veil on Biogen's Top-Class Learning Program." *TD* 70(7). www.td.org/Publications/Magazines/TD/TD-Archive/2016/07/Peeling -Back-the-Veil-on-Biogens-Top-Class-Learning-Program.

Mankins, M.C., and R. Steele. 2005. "Turning Great Strategy into Great Performance." *Harvard Business Review*, July-August. https://hbr.org/2005/07/turning-great -strategy-into-great-performance.

Marquardt, M.J. 2011. *Building the Learning Organization.* 3rd ed. Boston: Nicholas Brealey America.

Marquis, J. 2013. "Gamification and Education: Value Added or Lost?" Online Universities, April 4. www.onlineuniversities.com/blog/2013/04/gamification -and-education-value-added-or-lost.

Masie, E. 2011. "Challenge Your Leadership Rituals." *Chief Learning Officer*, July 7. www.clomedia.com/2011/07/07/challenge-your-leadership-rituals.

McCall, M.W. Jr. 1998. *High Flyers: Developing the Next Generation of Leaders.* Boston: Harvard Business Review Press.

McGraw, M. 2016. "Part Psychologist, Part Scientist." *Human Resource Executive*, May 13. www.hreonline.com/HRE/view/story.jhtml?id=534360599.

Mindrum, C. 2013. "Screening for Adaptability and Resiliency." *Talent Management*, September 13. www.talentmgt.com/2013/09/13/screening-for-adaptability-and -resiliency.

Mitchell, C., R. Ray, and B. van Ark. 2014. *The Conference Board CEO Challenge 2014.* New York: The Conference Board. www.conference-board.org/retrievefile .cfm?filename=TCB_R-1537-14-RR1.pdf&type=subsite.

———. 2015. *The Conference Board CEO Challenge 2015.* New York: The Conference Board. www.conference-board.org/retrievefile.cfm?filename=TCB_1570_15_RR _CEO_Challenge3.pdf&type=subsite.

Moore, E.F. 2015. "How Did the Blackhawks Become the Most Beloved Team in the NHL?" *Chicago Magazine*, May 15. www.chicagomag.com/city-life/May-2015 /Blackhawks.

Moran, L., and C. Blauth. 2008. *Creating a Change-Capable Workforce.* Tampa, FL: AchieveGlobal. www.bhcc.mass.edu/media/03-documents /CreatingAChangeCapableWorkforceReport.pdf.

Morrison, C. 2014. "How High-Performance Organizations Avoid the Crash-and-Burn of Change". Institute for Corporate Productivity, October 1. www.i4cp.com /trendwatchers/2014/10/01/how-high-performance-organizations-avoid-the -crash-and-burn-of-change.

Mueller, P.A., and D.M. Oppenheimer. 2014. "The Pen Is Mightier Than the Keyboard." *Psychological Science*, April 23. http://pss.sagepub.com/content/early /2014/04/22/0956797614524581.abstract.

Nabaum, A., L. Barry, S. Garr, and A. Liakopoulos. 2014. "Performance Management Is Broken." Deloitte University Press, March 4. http://dupress.com/articles /hc-trends-2014-performance-management.

Neilson, G.L., K.L. Martin, and E. Powers. 2008. "The Secrets to Successful Execution." *Harvard Business Review*, June. https://hbr.org/2008/06/the-secrets -to-successful-strategy-execution.

O'Leonard, K. 2010. "Talent Management: Benchmarks, Trends & Best Practices." Bersin & Associates, June. www.hreonline.com/pdfs /TalentMgmtBenchmarks06162010.pdf.

———. 2014. *The Corporate Learning Factbook 2014: Benchmarks, Trends, and Analysis of the U.S. Training Market*. Oakland, CA: Bersin by Deloitte. www.bersin.com /corporate-learning-factbook-2014.

Oakes, K., and P. Galagan. 2011. *The Executive Guide to Integrated Talent Management*. Alexandria, VA: ASTD Press.

Ovans, A. 2015. "What Resilience Means, and Why It Matters." *Harvard Business Review*, January 5. https://hbr.org/2015/01/what-resilience-means-and-why-it -matters.

Overton, L. 2016. "In-Focus: Preparing for the Future of Learning." *Towards Maturity*, May 9. www.towardsmaturity.org/article/2016/05/09/in-focus-preparing-future -learning-2016.

Owen, H. 1991. *Riding the Tiger: Doing Business in a Transforming World*. Potomac, MD: Abbott Publishing.

Parker, A. 2013. "Bright Ideas." *TD* 67(4). www.td.org/Publications/Magazines/TD /TD-Archive/2013/04/Bright-Ideas.

———. 2016. "Future Focused." *CTDO*, March 15. www.td.org/Publications/Magazines /CTDO/Archives/2016/Spring/Future-Focused.

Patel, S. 2015. "10 Examples of Companies With Fantastic Cultures." *Entrepreneur*, August 6. www.entrepreneur.com/article/249174.

Paulk, M.C., C.V. Weber, and M.B. Chrissis. 1999. *The Capability Maturity Model: A Summary*. Carnegie Mellon University Research Showcase. Institute for Software Research. http://repository.cmu.edu/cgi/viewcontent .cgi?article=1013&context=isr.

Pease, G., B. Beresford, and L. Walker. 2014. *Developing Human Capital*. Hoboken, NJ: Wiley.

Pew Research. 2014. "6 New Facts About Facebook." Factank, February 3. www .pewresearch.org/fact-tank/2014/02/03/6-new-facts-about-facebook.

Phillips, J. 2015. "10 Myths About Learning and Performance." *Chief Learning Officer,* November 30. www.clomedia.com/2015/11/30/10-myths-about-learning-and -performance.

Phillips, J.J., and P.P. Phillips. 2009. *Measuring for Success.* Alexandria, VA: ASTD Press.

Phillips, P., H. Annulis, and J. McDonald. 2013. "Best Practices for Developing Change Leadership in Turbulent Times." *Conference Board,* May. www.conference-board .org/topics/publicationdetail.cfm?publicationid=2501.

Pichee, D. 2016. "4 Scientifically Proven Ways to Improve Your Employee Training Program." BizLibrary, March 3. www.bizlibrary.com/article/4-scientifically -proven-ways-to-improve-your-employee-training-program.

Powers, S. 2015. "Blackhawks Built Winning Team by Changing Culture." Cross Checks blog, May 16. http://espn.go.com/blog/nhl/post/_/id/37294/blackhawks -built-winning-team-by-changing-culture.

PricewaterhouseCoopers (PwC). 2011. "Millennials at Work: Reshaping the Workplace." www.pwc.com/gx/en/managing-tomorrows-people/future-of-work /assets/reshaping-the-workplace.pdf.

———. 2014. "Strategy-Execution Survey." PwC, April 23. www.strategyand.pwc.com /media/file/Strategyand_Slide-Pack-Strategy-execution-survey.pdf.

———. 2015. "2015 Global Operations Survey." http://operationssurvey.pwc.com.

Probst, C. 2015. "Xerox and the New Learning Ecosystem." Degreed, October 23. http://blog.degreed.com/xerox-and-the-new-learning-ecosystem.

Prokopeak, M. 2013. "DAU. Keeping Above the Fiscal Fray." *Chief Learning Officer,* May 20. www.clomedia.com/2013/05/20/dau-keeping-above-the-fiscal-fray.

PwC Saratoga. 2010. *Managing People in a Changing World.* PricewaterhouseCoopers. www.pwc.be/en/hr-management/pdf/managing-people-changing-world.pdf.

Quinn, C. 2014. *Revolutionize Learning & Development.* Alexandria, VA: ASTD Press; San Francisco: Wiley.

Ramani, R. 2012. "What to Do With a Broken LMS." *Chief Learning Officer,* November 5. www.clomedia.com/2012/11/05/what-to-do-with-a-broken-lms.

Ray, R.L., and D. Learmond. 2013. *DNA of Leaders: Leadership Development Secrets.* New York: The Conference Board. www.conference-board.org/publications /publicationdetail.cfm?publicationid=2572.

Ray, R., D. Dye, P. Hyland, J. Kaplan, and A. Pressman. 2016. "How to Build a Culture of Engagement." In *ATD Talent Management Handbook,* edited by T. Bickham, 77-92. Alexandria, VA: ATD Press.

Ringen, J. 2015. "How Lego Became the Apple of Toys." *Fast Company,* January 8. www .fastcompany.com/3040223/when-it-clicks-it-clicks.

Robinson, D.G., J.C. Robinson, J.J. Phillips, P.P. Phillips, and D. Handshaw. 2015. *Performance Consulting: A Strategic Process to Improve, Measure, and Sustain Organizational Results.* Oakland, CA: Berrett-Koehler.

ROI Institute. 2015. "ROS Is the Fastest Growing Metric." ROI Institute, August. www.roiinstitute.net/roi-is-the-fastest-growing-metric.

Rouen, E. 2012. "When Leaders Are Scarce, Employees Look to Peers." *Fortune*, April 19. http://fortunecom/201/04/19/when-leaders-are-scarce-employees-look-to-peers.

Russell, L. 2016. *Project Management for Trainers.* 2nd edition. Alexandria, VA: ATD Press.

Salopek, J. 2015a. "Creating the Engineers of Tomorrow, Today." *TD* 69(11). www.td.org/Publications/Magazines/TD/TD-Archive/2015/11/BEST-Mindtree.

———. 2015b. "Sea Change in the Container Shipping Business." *TD*, November 8. www.td.org/Publications/Magazines/TD/TD-Archive/2015/11/BEST-Maerskline.

———. 2015c. "Training at the Crossroads of Tradition and Technology." *TD* 69(11). Alexandria, VA: ATD Press. www.td.org/Publications/Magazines/TD/TD-Archive/2015/11/BEST-BNSF.

Savitz, A.W. 2006. *The Triple Bottom Line.* San Francisco: Jossey-Bass.

Senge, P.M. 1990. *The Fifth Discipline.* New York: Doubleday.

Shlomo, B-H., B. Jaworski, and D. Gray. 2015. Aligning Corporate Learning With Strategy. *Harvard Business Review.*

SHRM Special Expertise Panels. 2014. "Future Insights." Society for Human Resource Management. www.shrm.org/hr-today/trends-and-forecasting/labor-market-and-economic-data/Documents/13-0724%202014%20Panel%20Trends%20Report%20v4.pdf.

Sinar, E., R.S. Wellins, R. Ray, A.L. Abel, and S. Neal. 2014. *Ready-Now Leaders.* Bridgeville, PA: Development Dimensions International; New York: The Conference Board. www.ddiworld.com/DDI/media/trend-research/global-leadership-forecast-2014-2015_tr_ddi.pdf?ext=.pdf.

Sinek, S. 2014. *Leaders Eat Last.* New York: Portfolio.

Sipek, S. 2015a. "Development: The Cure for Turnover at Vi." *Chief Learning Officer*, June 1. www.clomedia.com/2015/06/01/development-the-cure-for-turnover-at-vi.

———. 2015b. "Peer Review to the Rescue?" *Talent Management*, October 9. www.talentmgt.com/2015/10/09/peer-review-to-the-rescue.

Siuty, L. 2014. "Learning In Practice 2014: Business Impact Division 1 Winners." *Chief Learning Officer*, November 18. www.clomedia.com/2014/11/18/learning-in-practice-2014-business-impact-division-1-winners.

Smith, A. 2015. "U.S. Smartphone Use in 2015." Pew Research Center, April 1. www
.pewinternet.org/2015/04/01/us-smartphone-use-in-2015.

Society for Human Resource Management (SHRM) Research. 2014. *Future Insights: The Top Trends for 2014 According to SHRM's HR Subject Matter Expert Panels.* Alexandria, VA: SHRM. www.shrm.org/Research/Documents/13-0724%20 2014%20Panel%20Trends%20Report%20v3.pdf.

Sosbe, T. 2003. "Tamar Elkeles: Technology and Training at QUALCOMM." *Chief Learning Officer*, September 4. www.clomedia.com/2003/09/04/tamar-elkeles -technology-and-training-at-qualcomm.

Staff. 2012. "Bringing Performance Management to Life." *Talent Management*, June 27. www.talentmgt.com/2012/06/27/bringing-performance-management-to-life.

Stallard, M.L. 2015. *Connection Culture.* Alexandria, VA: ATD Press.

Statista. 2016a. "Number of Active Instagram Users From January 2013 to June 2016 (in Millions)." Statista. www.statista.com/statistics/253577/number-of-monthly -active-instagram-users.

———. 2016b. "Number of Active Twitters Users Worldwide From 1st Quarter 2010 to 2nd Quarter 2016 (in Millions)." Statista. www.statista.com/statistics/282087 /number-of-monthly-active-twitter-users.

———. 2016c. "Number of LinkedIn Members From 1st Quarter 2009 to 2nd Quarter 2016 (in Millions)." Statista. www.statista.com/statistics/274050/quarterly -numbers-of-linkedin-members.

Stoddard, A. 2007. *Gracious Living in a New World: Finding Joy in Changing Times.* New York: William Morrow.

Strategy&. 2016. "Research on the Strategy Execution Gap." PricewaterhouseCoopers. www.strategyand.pwc.com/global/home/what-we-think/cds_home/the_concept /research-strategy-execution-gap.

Sull, D., R. Homkes, and C. Sull. 2015. "Why Strategy Execution Unravels—and What to Do About It." *Harvard Business Review*, March. https://hbr.org/2015/03 /why-strategy-execution-unravelsand-what-to-do-about-it.

Tauber, T., and D. Johnson. 2014. "Meet the Modern Learner (Infographic)." Bersin by Deloitte, November 26. www.bersin.com/Practice/Detail.aspx?id=18071.

Thalheimer, W. 2008. *Providing Learners With Feedback—Part 1: Research-Based Recommendations for Training, Education, and E-Learning.* Somerville, MA: Work-Learning Research. http://willthalheimer.typepad.com/files/providing_learners _with_feedback_part1_may2008.pdf.

Thomas, M.J.W. 2003. "Operational Fidelity in Simulation-Based Training: The Use of Data From Threat and Error Management Analysis in Instructional Systems Design." *Proceedings of SimTecT2003: Simulation Conference*, 91-95.

Towards Maturity. 2012. *Bridging the Gap: Integrating Learning and Work.* Towards Maturity.

———. 2015. *Embracing Change: Improving Performance for Business, Individuals and the L&D Team.* Towards Maturity.

U.S. Army Training and Doctrine Command. 2011. *The U.S. Army Learning Concept for 2015.* Fort Eustis, VA. www.tradoc.army.mil/tpubs/pams/tp525-8-2.pdf.

U.S. Army. 2013. *Army Leadership Development Strategy 2013.* U.S. Army. http://usacac .army.mil/sites/default/files/documents/cal/ALDS5June%202013Record.pdf.

Ulrich, D. 1997. *Human Resource Champions.* Boston: Harvard Business School Press.

———. 1998. "A New Mandate for Human Resources." *Harvard Business Review,* January-February. https://hbr.org/1998/01/a-new-mandate-for-human-resources.

Ulrich, D., J. Allen, W. Brockbank, J. Younger, and M. Nyman. 2009. *HR Transformation: Building Human Resources From the Outside In.* New York: McGraw-Hill.

Van Adelsberg, D., and E.A. Trolley. 1999. *Running Training Like a Business.* San Francisco: Berrett-Koehler.

Vance, D. 2010. *The Business of Learning.* Poudre River Press.

Vector Learning. 2013. "Study: Companies With Strong Learning Cultures Are More Successful." RedVector, October 31. https://blog.redvector.com/2013/10/31/study -companies-with-strong-learning-cultures-are-more-successful.

Vi Living. 2015. Vi's Award-Winning Leadership and Training Programs Help Employees Work and Grow." Vi Living. www.viliving.com/news-and-awards /news/2015/leadership-and-training-program.

Welch, J. 2016. "Former GE CEO Jack Welch Says Leaders Have 5 Basic Traits—and Only 2 Can Be Taught." *Business Insider,* May 15. www.businessinsider.com /former-ge-ceo-jack-welch-says-leaders-have-5-basic-traits-and-only-2-can-be -taught-2016-5.

Whitney, K. 2015. "Melissa Daimler: How @Twitter Handles #Learning." *Chief Learning Officer,* September 10. www.clomedia.com/articles/6459-how-twitter -handles-learning.

Workday Staff. 2016. "Work Talk Episode 3: Why Performance Enablement Is Replacing Performance Management." *Work Talk,* June 23. http://blogs .workday.com/work-talk-episode-3-why-performance-enablement-is-replacing -performance.

World Commission on Environment and Development. 1987. *Our Common Future.* New York: United Nations.

Further Reading

Introduction

Kaufman, R. 2006. "Mega Planning and Thinking: Defining and Achieving Measurable Success." In *Handbook of Human Performance Technology*, 3rd edition, edited by J.A. Pershing. San Francisco: Pfieffer.

Marquardt, M.J. 2011. *Building the Learning Organization*. 3rd ed. Boston: Nicholas Brealey America.

Senge, P.M. 1990. *The Fifth Discipline*. New York: Doubleday.

Chapter 1

Carter, L., D. Ulrich, and M. Goldsmith. 2004. *Best Practices in Leadership Development and Organization Change*. San Francisco: Pfeiffer.

Phillips, P.P., and J.J. Phillips. 2007. *The Value of Learning*. San Francisco: Pfieffer.

Quinn, C. 2014. *Revolutionize Learning & Development*. Alexandria, VA: ASTD Press.

Ulrich, D., J. Allen, W. Brockbank, J. Younger, and M. Nyman. 2009. *HR Transformation: Building Human Resources From the Outside In*. New York: McGraw-Hill Education.

Chapter 2

Hodges, T.K. 2011. *Linking Learning and Performance*. New York: Routledge.

Kaufman, R., and I. Guerra-Lopez. 2013. *Needs Assessment for Organizational Success*. Alexandria, VA: ASTD Press.

Robinson, D.G., J.C. Robinson, J.J. Phillips, P.P. Phillips, and D. Handshaw. 2015. *Performance Consulting: A Strategic Process to Improve, Measure, and Sustain Organizational Results*. Oakland, CA: Berrett-Koehler.

Stone, R.D. 2008. *Aligning Training for Results*. San Francisco: Pfeiffer.

Chapter 3

Bock, L. 2015. *Work Rules! Insights From Inside Google That Will Transform How You Live and Lead*. New York: Twelve.

Clow, J. 2012. *The Work Revolution: Freedom and Excellence for All*. Hoboken, NJ: Wiley & Sons.

Sinek, S. 2009. *Start With Why: How Great Leaders Inspire Everyone to Take Action.* New York: Penguin Books.

Tindall, K. 2014. *Uncontainable: How Passion, Commitment, and Conscious Capitalism Build a Business Where Everyone Thrives.* New York: Grand Central Publishing.

Chapter 4

Duarte, N., and P. Sanchez. 2016. *Illuminate: Ignite Change Through Speeches, Stories, Ceremonies, and Symbols.* New York: Portfolio Press.

Goldsmith, M., and L. Lyons, eds. 2006. *Coaching for Leadership: The Practice of Leadership Coaching From the World's Greatest Coaches.* San Francisco: Pfeiffer.

Kouzes, J.M., and B.Z. Posner. 2016. *Learning Leadership: The Five Fundamentals of Becoming an Exemplary Leader.* Hoboken, NJ: Wiley.

Phillips, P.P., J.J. Phillips, and R. Ray. 2015. *Measuring the Success of Leadership Development.* Alexandria, VA: ATD Press.

Chapter 5

Collins, J. 2004. *Built to Last: Successful Habits of Visionary Companies.* New York: Harper Business Essentials.

Patterson, K., J. Grenny, R. McMillan, A. Switzler, and D. Maxfield. 2013. *Crucial Accountability: Tools for Resolving Violated Expectations, Broken Commitments, and Bad Behavior.* 2nd edition. New York: McGraw-Hill.

Russell, L. 2016. *Project Management for Trainers.* 2nd edition. Alexandria, VA: ATD Press.

Van Tiem, D., J.L. Moseley, and J.C. Dessinger. 2011. *Fundamentals of Performance Improvement.* 3rd edition. San Francisco: Wiley.

Chapter 6

Kirkpatrick, D.L., and J.D. Kirkpatick. 2006. *Evaluating Training Programs.* 3rd edition. San Francisco: Berrett-Koehler.

Pease, G., B. Boyce, and J. Fitz-enz. 2012. *Human Capital Analytics.* Hoboken, NJ: Wiley & Sons.

Phillips, P.P., ed. 2010. *ASTD Handbook of Measuring and Evaluating Training.* Alexandria, VA: ASTD Press.

Thalheimer, W. 2016. *Performance-Focused Smile Sheets: A Radical Rethinking of a Dangerous Art Form.* Work-Learning Press.

Chapter 7

Anderson, D., and L. Ackerman. 2010. *Beyond Change Management: How to Achieve Breakthrough Results Through Conscious Change Leadership.* 2nd edition. San Francisco: Pfeiffer.

Herold, D., and D. Fedor. 2008. *Change the Way You Lead Change.* Stanford, CA: Stanford Business Books.

Kotter, J.P., and D.S. Cohen. 2002. *The Heart of Change: Real-Life Stories of How People Change Their Organizations.* Boston: Harvard Business School Publishing.

Schmidt, L., and K. Nourse. 2016. *Shift Into Thrive: Six Strategies for Women to Unlock the Power of Resilience.* Washington, D.C.: Bobo Publishing.

Chapter 8

Blanchard, K., C. Olmstead, and M. Lawrence. 2013. *Trust Works! Four Keys to Building Lasting Relationships.* New York: William Morrow.

Conant, D., and M. Norgaard. 2011. *TouchPoints: Creating Powerful Leadership Connections in the Smallest of Moments.* San Francisco: Jossey-Bass.

Sinek, S. 2014. *Leaders Eat Last.* New York: Portfolio.

Stallard, M.L. 2015. *Connection Culture.* Alexandria, VA: ATD Press.

Chapter 9

Christensen, C.M. 2011. *The Innovator's Dilemma: The Revolutionary Book That Will Change the Way You Do Business.* New York: HarperBusiness.

Clark, R.C., and R.E. Mayer. 2008. *E-learning and the Science of Instruction.* 3rd edition. Hoboken, NJ: Wiley.

Grant, A. 2016. *Originals: How Non-Conformists Move the World.* New York: Viking.

Hart, J. 2015. *Modern Workplace Learning: A Resource Book for L&D.* Centre for Learning and Performance Technologies.

Acknowledgments

The more you read, the more things you will know. The more you
learn, the more places you'll go.
—Dr. Seuss

I'M HUGELY INDEBTED TO ALL THE WRITERS, teachers, mentors, coaches, clients, and practitioners over the years who have inspired me to read more, know more, learn more, and travel more to places in my mind and in my practice that I never would have dreamed possible. Special thanks to the many friends, colleagues, and family members who guided me through the inspiration and perspiration of this book by providing support, in-depth feedback, and a helping hand or a listening ear whenever needed. Your input and enthusiasm about this topic kept me going through thick and thin. Some of these incredibly helpful folks include Charlotte Chase, Sal Faletta, Kim Green, Dick Handshaw Jack Phillips, George Piskurich, Ernie Ricketts, Lynn Schmidt, and Ron Stone.

I'm grateful to all the talented learning and performance professionals who generously volunteered to share their time, expertise, and experience through extended interviews or lengthy conversations:

- Specific thanks to Bob Anderson, Dr. Heather Annulis, Deputy Commandant Rich Ayers, Dr. Cyndi Gaudet, Don Highley, Dr. Trish Holliday, Ron Morey, Chad Raney, and Erica Steponic for trusting me to convey your message and tell your story through case examples. Your stories illustrate how tough it is to transform a learning culture, how powerful purposeful actions and a spirit of resiliency can be, and how rewarding it is to create a learning legacy that adds sustainable value.

- Many thanks to all the learning leaders who lent their insights as a formal or informal "voice from the field." This renowned group includes David Atack, Ronnie Ashline, Kori Czasnojc, Jason Deleon, Kay Diamond, Mary Ellen Kassotokis, Steven Kelley, Donald Kirkey, Javiel Lopez, Carina Celesia Moore, Thomas Moore, Lisa Nunes, Dr. David Powe, Patrick Taggart, Kevin Sheridan, and Sarah Thompson.

Collectively, these individuals represent an impressive cross-section of practitioners, consultants, talent managers, change agents, researchers, and educators who have each made significant contributions to the field of learning and performance. I'm honored and privileged to shine a light on their accomplishments.

Many thanks, as well, to the progressive learning organizations and clients that have allowed their names and initiatives to be used for publication.

Finally, because *Learning for the Long Run* focuses on sustaining learning momentum for the long haul, this multiyear effort would not have been possible without the sustained support of ATD and Ann Parker, in particular. Thank you, Ann, for your encouragement and support of the publishing effort from the very beginning. Special thanks to Developmental Editor Jack Harlow for lending your considerable time, patience, and expertise to the editing process. Your contributions and steady hand helped make the book immeasurably better. Thanks, too, to Associate Editor Caroline Coppel and Senior Associate Editor Melissa Jones for their editing assistance, perpetual calm, and keen eye for detail during the final throes of bringing this publication to life.

And in closing, thank you! Thank you for reading this far. Thank you for your interest in pushing forward to transform the value of learning in your organization. I hope you'll put some of these ideas into practice. Share your lessons learned and success stories and please let me know how I can help.

About the Author

HOLLY BURKETT, PhD, is principal of Evaluation Works, a performance consultancy in Davis, California. For more than 20 years, she has helped global organizations improve the strategic impact of diverse talent management initiatives. She is passionate about developing resilient learning and performance capabilities that foster high engagement, drive operational excellence, and create sustainable value. Sample clients include a range of public and private sector entities, including the International Union Against Tuberculosis and Lung Disease, Chevron, Premera Blue Cross, the UC Davis Talent Management Center of Expertise, and the National Security Agency.

Formerly with Apple Computer, she led enterprise-wide learning and development, managed high potential leader development and succession planning, and designed performance measurement systems to evaluate the business impact of HRD initiatives. In previous roles, Holly built corporate universities, led organization development efforts, partnered with business leaders in guiding culture change, led diversity initiatives, created individual and organizational assessment tools to monitor employee development and engagement, and designed peer coaching and employee certification programs. The World Training and Development Congress recently recognized her contributions to learning and development with the 2017 Global Training and Development Leadership Award.

An accomplished Senior Professional in Human Resources, Holly has served as a volunteer item writer and reviewer for the Human Resource

Certification Institute for more than 10 years and was a select contributor to its landmark anthology, *The Rise of HR: Wisdom from 73 Thought Leaders* (2015), published in collaboration with HR luminaries David Ulrich and Libby Sartain. A certified ROI professional, Holly is a recognized evaluation expert with the Office of Performance Review, and an original member of the ASTD ROI Network Advisory Committee. An active member of the International Society for Performance Improvement (ISPI) and a certified performance technologist, Holly currently serves as an elected member of the association's Certification, Accreditation, and Governance Committee and formerly served as editor of ISPI's *Performance Improvement* journal for six years. She also designed the curriculum for human performance improvement studies with Drexel University's HRD Graduate Studies program, where she served as adjunct faculty. Finally, she regularly shares her expertise with grant managers and nonprofits and is an elected member of the board of governors for Nonprofit Organizations & Executives.

Holly is a sought-after speaker, an international workshop leader, and an award-winning author. Recent publications include a chapter in the *ATD Talent Management Handbook* (2015), along with multiple contributions to other books in the field. Holly holds a PhD in human capital development and master's degree in human resources and organization development. She can be reached through Twitter (@evalworks), email (burketth@earthlink.net), or LinkedIn.

Index

In this index, *f* denotes figure and *t* denotes table.